SHAKESPEARE AND THE ARTS

A Collection of Essays from the Ohio Shakespeare Conference, 1981 Wright State University, Dayton, Ohio

Selected and Edited by
Cecile Williamson Cary
and
Henry S. Limouze

UNIVERSITY
PRESS OF
AMERICA

Copyright © 1982 by

University Press of America, Inc.

P.O. Box 19101, Washington, D.C. 20036

All rights reserved

Printed in the United States of America

ISBN (Perfect): 0-8191-2820-1
ISBN   (Cloth): 0-8191-2819-8

Library of Congress Catalog Card Number: 82-17486

ACKNOWLEDGMENTS

The 1981 Ohio Shakespeare Conference, "Shakespeare and the Arts: Yesterday and Today," from which these papers were selected, was funded by a grant from the Ohio Program in the Humanities (OPH) and supported by the Wright State University Research Council, the Liberal Arts College, and the English Department. Monies for typing the manuscript were granted by the Wright State University Liberal Arts Research Committee.

The Editors wish to thank the Holding Committee of the Ohio Shakespeare Conference-1981 for their permission to publish the proceedings: Professors Sam Crowl, David Evett, Robert Fleissner, William Godshalk, Robert Johnson, Robert Jones, Alan Kimbrough, Michael Manheim, Robert P. Merrix and Robert Pierce; the Program Committee for help in selecting papers: Robert M. Correale, Patricia H. Olds and Susan Page; The Dean of the College of Liberal Arts, Eugene B. Cantelupe, for his participation and support; the Chairman of the English Department, Lawrence E. Hussman, for his support; Leanne Smith for typing the manuscript; and Susan Limouze and Norman Reed Cary for their encouragement.

TABLE OF CONTENTS

PREFACE vii

I. SHAKESPEARE AND THE ARTS OF HIS TIME

INTRODUCTION 1

"Pericles: Shakespeare's Divine Musical Comedy"
  by Patricia K. Meszaros 3

"The Visual and Symbolic in Shakespeare's Masques"
  by Catherine M. Shaw 21

"Venus, Lucrece, and Bess of Hardwick: Portraits
  to Please" by Elizabeth Truax 35

"Hamlet: Shakespeare's Mannerist Tragedy"
  by Lois Ziegelman 57

"The Iconography of Illusion and Truth in
  The Winter's Tale" by Clifford Davidson 73

II. SHAKESPEARE AND PERFORMANCE

INTRODUCTION 93

"Mannerism in Hamlet Scene Designs"
  by Peter B. Young 95

"Ophelia's Mad Scene and the Stage Tradition"
  by Ellen J. O'Brien 109

"Shakespeare and Television: The BBC-TV Hamlet"
  by H. R. Coursen 127

"The Set in Early Television: Maurice Evans'
  Shakespeare Productions" by Bernice W. Kliman . . 135

"Making All's Well: The Arts of Televised Drama
  at the BBC" by Susan Willis 155

"Shakespeare and Acting Theory in the English
  Renaissance" by Jane Donawerth 165

III. SHAKESPEARE AND ARTISTIC THEORY

INTRODUCTION 179

"Shakespeare's 'Living Art': A Live Issue from
  Love's Labour's Lost" by Mary E. Hazard 181

"Discovering a Dramaturgy of Human Relationships
  in Shakespearean Metadrama: Troilus and Cressida"
  by Richard Snyder 199

"Imitations and Creation in Measure for Measure"
  by J. S. Lawry 217

"Shakespeare's Apology for Poetic Wisdom"
  by Michael Platt 231

NOTES ON CONTRIBUTORS 245

PREFACE

The articles in this collection were selected from the papers presented at the fifth Ohio Shakespeare Conference, hosted by Wright State University. The theme of the 1981 conference was "Shakespeare and the Arts: Yesterday and Today." The papers chosen for this collection demonstrate the theme of the conference and communicate the excitement generated not only by the individual arguments, but also the connections between them.

The topics discussed fall into three groups: <u>Shakespeare and the Arts of His Time</u>, <u>Shakespeare and Performance</u>, and <u>Shakespeare and Artistic Theory</u>. Articles which could be placed in more than one category have been classified according to their central focus. Indeed, the categories themselves overlap. Thus insights gleaned from a consideration of iconography or artistic style may have practical implications for the director of a play or its set designer. Furthermore, an artist's developing conception of the nature and function of his art, or of Art itself, cannot but shape his creations.

What seems to develop most clearly from the collection taken as a whole is a widening of the conception of the "language" of a play. The understanding of "the text" is enriched by a knowledge of iconography, mannerism, speculative music, masques, and the stage tradition. We must look at the picture as well as listen to the words, and if the picture speaks, we must listen. Lorenzo directs us to "mark the music"; Lear directs us to look and asks if we see. If we cannot "see so much" as Lear, we might nonetheless "see better" than we do; if we shall never "live so long," yet we might better understand Shakespeare's "living art," the "imitations and creations" that make up his dramatic world.

Cecile Williamson Cary

Bartholomeus Spranger (Flemish, 1546-1611), "Fortune," c. 1570. The Dayton Art Institute, museum purchase 62.13, copyright 1962 DAI

PART ONE

SHAKESPEARE AND THE ARTS OF HIS TIME

All the authors in this section try to recapture the full scene, the speaking picture, the total language of Shakespeare's plays. This attempt involves other critical tools in addition to the necessary sensitivity to the words of the text.

Ever since the 1961 publication of John Hollander's <u>The Untuning of the Sky</u>, there has been some appreciation of the relevance of speculative music to visual and literary musical images. A close scrutiny of such references in a literary text, as in Patricia K. Meszaros' article on <u>Pericles</u>, can lead to conclusions ranging from practical to thematic. Catherine M. Shaw's consideration of masques in Shakespeare's plays also enlarges our understanding. Masques, with their combination of music, spectacle, dance, and contrapuntal thematic organizations, reinforce the focus of this collection on the interrelationship of the arts. In addition, Lois Ziegelman considers Shakespeare's relation to the period's aesthetic temper, which she takes to be mannerism.

It could with some justice be argued that Panofsky's work in iconography has revolutionized Shakespeare criticism. Professors Truax and Davidson explore the resources of painting, sculpture, emblem books, manor houses, tapestries and embroideries in order to translate the speaking picture to our provincial eyes.

CWC

PERICLES: SHAKESPEARE'S DIVINE MUSICAL COMEDY

Patricia K. Meszaros

In *The Shakespearian Tempest* (1932) and *The Crown of Life* (1947), G. Wilson Knight organized his interpretations of Shakespeare's last plays around their recurring, dichotomous images of tempests and music--the former representing ultimate disorder and chaos, the latter universal harmony. Knight's reading of the romances as immortality myths in which restoration and reconciliation are symbolized by the final victory of music over tempest has informed nearly all subsequent criticism, and although John Hollander has rightly pointed out that Knight's "insistence on symbolic music ignores conventions of musical imagery and exegesis in Renaissance literature,"[1] it is nevertheless true that Knight's initial premise, that tempest and music are the two poles of a single force, is valid in terms of Elizabethan thought about music. In the work of Hollander and others, moreover, we now have studies of the music in Shakespeare's plays which go well beyond the *symboliste* suggestiveness of Knight's analyses to satisfy both the historian of the theater (not to mention the modern director) and the historian of ideas--studies of what the Elizabethans would have called *musica practica*, and of what they would have called *musica speculativa*.[2]

Among the discussions of the music called for in the last plays, however, and of what its being there *means*, there is none which to my mind satisfactorily resolves one of the problems about the nature and meaning of music in *Pericles*. I refer to the oddly anticlimactic sequence of recognition and reconciliation scenes in Act V, in which Pericles, after being reunited with his daughter Marina, seems to hear the music of the spheres, *then* has a vision of the goddess Diana (accompanied by music), and only then, after receiving the goddess' instructions, is reunited with his wife Thaisa, whom he had believed dead and buried at sea. The problem of the music of the spheres in *Pericles* has both speculative (i.e., critical) and practical (i.e, theatrical) dimensions. The first is a matter of placement and causality: if the music of the spheres expresses *universal* harmony, why does Pericles hear it after the lesser miracle but before the greater; that is, before the theophany and before his wife is restored to him? The second is a matter of staging, but one of interpretive significance: clearly Pericles is the only character on stage who hears the music of the spheres, but does the audience hear it with him, and if so, what does it sound like? Both dimensions of the problem must be considered together, and the problem itself must be considered with reference to other instances of music in the play, and within the context of the play as a whole.

This last is not easy to do, given doubts about the play's authorial integrity and the degree and nature of the corruption of the 1609 Quarto text. As the author of the most recent detailed textual study of Pericles concludes, the text we have is "made up of material of varying authority and diverse origins" into a "difficult manuscript" which was also "printed carelessly."[3] Yet we know that Pericles, probably presented at the Globe in a form bearing a close resemblance to the Quarto text, was among the most popular plays of its time (more popular, apparently, than was King Lear), and we also know that it has been revived occasionally in recent years with considerable success, as a triumph of stylized and self-reflexive theater. It seems reasonable, therefore, to set aside for the moment vexed questions of authorship and textual validity, and to adopt instead an audience-centered approach to the play, following the text we have.[4] I should like us to imagine, then, a performance of Pericles in the Globe Theatre, following the text from the 1609 Quarto, as prepared by James G. McManaway for the Pelican Shakespeare.[5] It is obvious that the words of the text must be supplemented by the spectacle and music that are integral to the play's effect, and yet it is not at all clear that the generalized pattern articulated by Knight, "from normality and order, through violent conflict to a spiritualized music and thence to the concluding ritual" comfortably fits the play.[6] We shall see.

"To sing a song that old was sung": the first words we hear are chanted, in sing-song tetrameter, by a figure dressed in a cloak and carrying bays.[7] He is the long-dead poet Gower, returned "from ashes," he tells us, "To glad your ear and please your eyes."[8] All his emphasis in on the antiquity of the story (he himself has read it in the work of other authors) and on the refined pleasure it will bring us (lords and ladies

have read it "for restoratives"). Yet the tale Gower
narrates in his archaic rhythm, with an occasional awkward shift for a line or two into iambic pentameter (as
if the immediate seriousness of the material will break
through), is a horrifying story of incest and murder,
and the first spectacle he calls to our attention to
"please" our eyes is the "grim looks" of the severed
heads of unsuccessful suitors upon the walls of Antioch.
We must trust the authority of the poet, of antiquity,
and of tradition, but how is this tale, this spectacle,
to edify and please us? Almost before we can formulate
the question, Gower himself seems to abandon his professed cause. No longer chanting, he tells us in an
iambic pentameter couplet that we must depend on what
he calls "the judgment of your eye" (I.Cho.41) from
this point onward.

But in fact another of our senses is called upon.
No sooner have the identities of Antiochus, the incestuous king, and Pericles, another in the succession of
suitors, been introduced in a few lines of dialogue
than we have an opportunity to listen to music,
commanded by Antiochus (I.i.6) for his daughter's entrance.[9] Since she is "clothèd like a bride" (I.i.7)--
that is, a virgin--and since Antiochus asserts that the
planets themselves, from her conception to her birth,
"did sit/ To knit in her their best perfections" (I.i.
11-12), the music arranged by her father to accompany
her appearance must be not the earthly, sensual music
of reed and wind instruments, but the heavenly, spiritual music of strings, probably a consort of viols.[10]
As we know (because we have heard Gower's introduction),
but as Pericles does not, the music masks and falsifies
the reality of father-daughter incest, providing a
setting for the daughter's beauty that encourages the
innocent suitor to find in her "every virtue [that]
gives renown to men!" (I.i.15). But this ethereal
music, invented by man in imitation of divine harmony,
can also be used by man as he sometimes uses language
and costume (and as Antiochus does here), to whiten the
sepulchre--to lie. Thus, when Pericles reads aloud the
riddle that blatantly reveals the ugly truth hitherto
so artfully concealed, he recoils in disgust not only
from the fact itself but also from the shock sustained
by his aesthetic sensibilities. In a brief, meditative
aside before he responds to Antiochus, Pericles dwells
upon the way in which the riddle's revelation has violated the evidence of his eyes and ears. The daughter

still appears to him to be a "fair glass of light" (I.i.77) and a "glorious casket," but one "stored with ill" (I.i.78). The musical setting for the woman's appearance leads him to reflect in a more extended metaphor:

> You are a fair viol, and your sense the
>   strings;
> Who, fingered to make man his lawful
>   music,
> Would draw heaven down, and all the gods,
>   to hearken;
> But being played upon before your time,
> Hell only danceth to so harsh a chime.
>   (I.i.82-86)

As we witness Pericles' confusion and empathize with his shocked revulsion, we ourselves are more than ever confused by Gower's promise to delight our eyes and ears and by his injunction that we rely upon the "judgment" of our eyes. The scene we have just witnessed has demonstrated that delights for the eyes and ears mislead us; truth appears in a gnomic riddle that places the only character with whom we can identify in a classic "double bind": not to "solve" the riddle is to incur execution as punishment, but to interpret it aloud will also mean certain death. Gower's introduction to his tale thus at this point seems quite inadequate--the story is neither pleasant nor edifying, and its "truth" is both figuratively and literally unspeakable. So far, Gower seems to be something of an "unreliable narrator."

Since escape from Antioch is the only course of action available to Pericles, the audience is called upon now to follow a plot of flight and pursuit through a series of scenes (from the end of I.i. through I.iv.) in which new characters and situations are introduced abruptly and as quickly dropped, so that we have time to register our perceptions only in the simplest abstract terms--the loyalty of Helicanus; the treachery of Thaliard; the destitution of Tharsus (to be contrasted, perhaps, with the corrupt opulence of Antioch). Still unable to exercise the "judgment" Gower has recommended, we experience instead bewilderment and disorientation mirroring Pericles' own. It is with something akin to relief, therefore, that we hear Pericles' decision to accept Cleon's welcome, to "feast here awhile,/ Until our stars that frown lend us a smile"

(I.iv.106-07). Perhaps we will see more of Pericles now, listen to his thoughts about the harrowing experience he has just gone through, get to know him better.

The impatience we feel, however, when it is Gower and not Pericles who returns, seems to have been anticipated by the old poet, who tells us to "Be quiet then, as men should be" (II.Cho.5), just as Helicanus had earlier counseled patience in adversity to Pericles. In the same chanted tetrameter we heard earlier, Gower summarizes, hints at a moral--"I'll show you those in trouble's reign,/ Losing a mite, a mountain gain" (II.Cho.8-8)--calls upon spectacle (this time a dumb show) to supplement his words, and finally, having described a storm and shipwreck to which Pericles has fallen victim, excuses himself.

The following scene with Pericles and the fishermen offers the most sustained dialogue of the play to this point, and full of the conventional wisdom of the common folk as it is ("I can compare our rich misers to nothing so fitly as a whale"), puts us ashore on familiar dramatic territory. There is talk about happy kings and good government, and the well-known parallels are drawn between the commonwealth and the order of nature. Thematically oriented at last, we can reflect upon the wickedness of Antiochus and the goodness of Pericles. We can also move with ease and assurance into the next scene, in which another princess is presented by her father with music and pageantry. What a satisfying repetition! What a satisfying contrast to the scene in Antioch, for this princess is all that she appears to be on the surface--not only beautiful but also virtuous--and learned as well, to judge from her skill in heraldry and her ability to interpret the mottos in Latin and Spanish upon the knights' shields. The tournament, an honest contest unlike the travesty arranged by Antiochus, naturally and satisfyingly results in the triumph of Pericles, the knight in rusty armor.

Significantly, the tournament is followed by the first music we have heard since the introduction of Antiochus' daughter: Simonides' court is all art and elegant ceremony representative of the harmony of the well-ordered state under a benign ruler. This music (presenting another contrast with the treacherous world of appearances in Antioch) is exactly right for the audience and the occasion. First, all the knights who had participated in the tournament perform a soldiers' dance, or <u>almain</u>,[11] followed by a dance performed by the soldiers and ladies together, and joined by Pericles and the lady Thaisa at the urging of her father. The old king, with his rough humor and his "Unclasp, unclasp!" (II.iii.106), is completely in control of the action, so that the banquet hall represented by the stage becomes a microcosm of world order. The king calls for music and sets his guests to dancing, just as the Creator ordered the cosmos and set the planets in a dance.

In this scene of social grace and harmony we find such a satisfying sense of rest and closure that we are not distressed when we are called upon next to give our attention once again to Helicanus. His news, indeed, adds another important element of resolution: Antiochus and his daughter are dead, consumed by a fire from heaven. Pericles need no longer flee the assassin; he can return to Tyre, taking Thaisa with him as his bride.[12]

So, as Gower had promised, an early misfortune has been overshadowed by subsequent and unexpectedly great good fortune; the bride Pericles has won incomparably exceeds in merit the one he initially sought. As Gower had predicted, too, our eyes and ears have indeed been delighted by spectacle and music. He is not such an unreliable narrator after all. When he makes his third appearance, a familiar and more trustworthy figure now, his tetrameter couplets and archaic diction seem just right for the little epithalamion he recites.

But then we are thrown badly off-balance again, as the happy sing-song tetrameter turns by degrees into another tale of woe. The stability and calm produced by the music, the dancing, and the plot resolutions of the preceding scene have left us unprepared for what follows now. Nothing in the play so far, in fact, has prepared us for the drama, the poetry, of the scene in which Pericles, amidst a storm at sea, greets his newborn child and prepares to commit the body of his wife to the deep. It is as if we have been leafing through an album of snapshots, to come suddenly on an unsettling close-up, a portrait blazing with character and pain. The desire we felt earlier to know Pericles better, and which we have since forgotten, is now unexpectedly fulfilled. We hear the intimate voice of the private men:

> A terrible childbed hast thou had, my dear;
> No light, no fire, Th' unfriendly elements
> Forgot thee utterly . . . . (III.i.56-57)

Almost immediately, however, our renewed interest in Pericles is diverted again, this time to the physician Cerimon and his wonderful skill, as the sounds of tempest give way to the sounds of music.

This is medicinal, restorative music, played by a viol (III.ii.89) because the vibrating string is most like the veins and nerves of the body, and because strings produce the most ethereal music accessible to mortals, thus calling the spirit back to the body and composing the senses. But that single viol, theories about music aside, also strikes an echo from the harmonies of the court of King Simonides, and that in itself may be a restorative for Thaisa. In any case, the music is efficacious: after calling, "The music there!" Cerimon says, "I pray you, give her air./ Gentlemen, this queen will live" (III.ii.93-94).

In the first movement of the play, we can see in retrospect, evil and treachery forced Pericles to take ship, but a storm at sea brought him to good. Now, it seems, we are witnessing an opposing sequence: a happy series of events having brought Pericles to sea again, disaster and then more treachery follow, this time in Tharsus, with the abortive plot of Dionyza to have Marina murdered. The audience can watch these new events with some equanimity, however, because we have come to accept the play's pattern of discontinuous scenes broken by the dumb shows and Gower's appearances, because we have come to trust Gower, and most of all because we share with Gower a knowledge superior to that of Pericles--neither Thaisa nor Marina is dead. The latter, indeed, clearly bears a charmed life. So much attention is given by Gower to her graces and accomplishments that she seems a paragon, and although she is captured by pirates and sold into a brothel, the comic tone of these scenes tells the audience that she is never really in danger.

Like her father, Marina is a talented musician: "by Cleon trained/ In music's letters" (IV.Cho.7-8); according to Gower, "She sings like one immortal, and she dances/ As goddess-like to her admirèd lays" (V.Cho. 3-4). It seems not only right but inevitable, then, that Pericles in his wanderings should eventually arrive at Mytilene, and that Marina should be brought before him to sing, in an attempt to arouse him from the deep melancholy and silence into which he has fallen upon being told by the false Cleon and Dionyza that his daughter is dead.[13]

Pericles seems to those watching on stage not to hear Marina's song, but in fact the audience sees that he is rapt, concentrating totally on his attempt to recall an almost-forgotten melody and the larger harmony it evokes. Marina next resorts to speech, and her powers of persuasion (as we know from the brothel scenes) are as impressive as her musicianship. Still, it is <u>what</u> she says that restores Pericles to health; here <u>music</u> is only an ancillary restorative. Marina's song has aroused in Pericles the <u>memory</u> of harmony, but her story renews his <u>faith</u> in harmony. Convinced at last that she is his <u>own</u> child, he calls her "Thou that beget'st him that did thee beget" (V.i.195), stating a paradox that is the antithesis of the paradox of Antiochus' riddle. Indeed, the therapeutic harmonies of Marina's musical performance have finally countered the dissembling harmonies of the music which had been used to introduce Antiochus' daughter, and the silence with which Pericles was forced to respond in untying the riddle of her relationship to her father is countered in the speech by means of which he and his own daughter untie the riddle of <u>their</u> relationship. We remember that Pericles has been speechless since hearing of his daughter's supposed death, and we realize that in this play silence (i.e., the absence of music and language) as well as tempest can be a manifestation of the forces of chaos. But in Marina's song and her marvelous story, Pericles has found good and harmony and order enough to balance the evil and chaos he has known in the world.

As for the audience, it has once again had its faith in Gower confirmed, and has been delighted and edified by spectacle and poetry, and especially by music. Moral and physical evil have occurred repeatedly without rational motivation or apparent cause in the world of the play, but human speech rises above the noise of the storm and untangles the knots of unhappiness wrought by human malice, and recurring music as outward manifestation of internal social harmony and as restorative of physical and mental health prevails again and again over chaos.

Pericles himself, however, now attains a degree of awareness of universal harmony transcending that of the audience, for it is granted to him to hear the music of the spheres. Originating with Pythagoras, adopted by Plato, and kept alive in Christian neoplatonic tradition, the concept of the music of the spheres was the central image of the doctrine of universal harmony prevalent in Shakespeare's time. In the Pythagorean sense, music is mathematical proportion bearing no resemblance to earthly music except as that music also is based upon proportion and degree; the music of the spheres comes from the vibrations of the planets moving at varying distances from each other, proportional to musical ratios. Symbols of this divine harmony, strictly speaking, are to be found only in such phenomena as "the . . . variety of Seasons, the concorde of the Elements . . . the politike Lawes . . . the love of the King" (Stephen Gosson, The School of Abuse, 1579); the divine harmony itself is not directly accessible to fallen humanity. In the words of Shakespeare's Lorenzo in The Merchant of Venice,

> Such harmony is in immortal souls;
> But whilst this muddy vesture of decay
> Doth grossly close it in, we cannot
>   hear it.   (V.i.63-65)

That a living man should hear the music of the spheres is thus exceedingly unlikely. Such an experience could probably come only to a good and noble man with an understanding of all the manifestations of earthly harmony, and then only at a moment when that man's spirit was peculiarly sensitive to the existence of a sublime and perfect harmony transcending that of this world. To hear the music of the spheres is to have a mystical experience. Obviously, Pericles alone of all characters on stage is capable of such sensitivity to harmony, and the text is clear on the point that he alone hears it:

> PERICLES
> Give me my robes. I am wild in my beholding.
> O heavens bless my girl! But hark, what
>   music?

> Tell Helicanus, my Marina, tell him
> O'er, point by point, for yet he seems to doubt,
> How sure you are my daughter. But what music?

HELICANUS

> My lord, I hear none.

PERICLES

> None?
> The music of the spheres! List, my Marina.

LYSIMACHUS

> It is not good to cross him. Give him way.

PERICLES

> Rarest sounds! Do ye not hear?

LYSIMACHUS

> Music, my lord? I hear.

PERICLES

> Most heavenly music!
> It nips me unto list'ning, and thick slumber
> Hangs upon mine eyes. Let me rest.
> (V.i.224-36)

The responses of the bluntly honest Helicanus (229) and the more politic Lysimachus, who thinks it best to humor Pericles with a "white lie" (232, 234) are evidence that they hear nothing. The short lines (229, 230) are silences to be filled by intent listening, spaces into which both the characters on stage and the audience pour their collective concentration, trying to experience what Pericles experiences.

Having come this far with Pericles, having empathized with his sufferings and rejoiced at his reunion with Marina, bearing the knowledge that more happiness is to come (for Pericles still does not know what the audience knows, that his wife, too, is alive), the audience is nevertheless cut off from sharing with Pericles this transcendent experience. We shuffle our feet restlessly: what are we to make of this moment? Our rapport with the character is momentarily broken;

the play has left us once more, unexpectedly, without bearings.[14]

But then Pericles, exhausted by emotion, falls asleep. One by one the other characters leave the stage, and almost inaudibly at first, then gradually louder, the sound of broken chords on lutes and harps is heard, introducing the goddess Diana, who instructs Pericles to repair to her temple at Ephesus to sacrifice and to tell his story.[15] These sounds, however celestial, cannot be more than a pale shadowing forth of the total divine harmony of the spheres, for they accompany the earthly appearance of only one of the goddesses in the pantheon. Nor is it possible for Pericles to remain permanently attuned to the celestial harmony. Man cannot remain long in a state of spiritual ecstasy, but the memory of such a state can sustain and uplift him long after the experience is past. Pericles' sublime experience has reassured him that the world is ordered harmoniously. Thus, though he no longer hears the music of the spheres, he is receptive to divine guidance from the goddess.

If the audience cannot share Pericles' mystical experience, we can nevertheless share his dream-vision, and we have, moreover, regained our bearings, for we know why the goddess directs Pericles toward Ephesus. Our recent momentary confusion put aside, we revel in pleasurable anticipation of the reunion of Pericles and Marina with Thaisa. The sense of power which our knowledge of the outcome seems to confer on us is reinforced by Gower, who addresses us this time to flatter us by reminding us of the control we exercise through our imaginations. It is we who

> aptly will suppose
> What pageantry, what feats, what shows,
> What minstrelsy and pretty din
> The regent made in Mytilin
> To greet the King. (V.ii.5-9)

It is also our imaginations that will encompass the time and space necessary to bring Pericles and his company to the temple of Diana at Ephesus:

> That he can hither come so soon
> Is by your fancies' thankful doom.
> (V.ii.19-20)

It is significant, perhaps, that Gower began his addresses to the audience by promising us edification and pleasure, as if we had to be coaxed into paying attention, and by asking us to listen and watch patiently and passively, but that he ends by praising our imaginations and by inviting us to participate more actively in bringing the story to its conclusion.

For the audience, <u>Pericles</u> has been an experience by turns bewildering and satisfying. We have been asked to attend to a succession of shifting scenes and characters, often following one upon another without apparent reason, but we have also found moments of delightful repose in musical harmony and of intense emotion expressed in moving language. We have been led to expect a moral, but none has been pointed, and no obvious one has emerged. We have followed the fortunes of the hero at varying distances--watching him objectively at the beginning as he learns the horrible truth we ourselves have only just learned, feeling with him intensely as he buries his wife at sea and again as he finds his lost daughter, observing him from a superior distance as he is brought innocently toward the reconciliation we ourselves have long anticipated. Occasionally, as an audience, we feel secure in our imaginative understanding of the unfolding story. Most strangely, however, we have not been able to share with Pericles the experience that might have been the climax of the play: we have not heard the music of the spheres.

Perhaps it is somewhat comforting, given our inability to make of <u>Pericles</u> a coherent play and our lack of understanding of <u>one of</u> its crucial episodes, to have a fall-back position in which we remind ourselves that Shakespeare probably took over the authorship of a botched play at about III.i., and that even in writing the remainder he paid scant attention to the sections that did not readily excite his interest; this way we can reject everything except those parts that remind us most of what we think a Shakespearean play <u>should</u> be. This argument, too, gives us authority for <u>imagining</u> the play as something other than it is. If only the music of the spheres occurred at the <u>end</u> of the play, for instance, we could view the play <u>as an</u> allegory of man's progress from earthly passion to divine love and harmony. Or if interludes of peace and harmony did not so prominently figure at the <u>center</u> of the play, we could find satisfying Knight's formula of normality--violent conflict--ritualized, spiritualized order. And if the formula still did not fit Pericles very well, we could say that the author was only practicing to write The Winter's Tale and The Tempest.

But these attitudes (which I have presented only a little unfairly, and which do inform much criticism of Pericles) seem to me to be false to our theatrical experience of the play. That experience, always interesting and occasionally quite moving, is difficult to describe because it cannot be summarized or organized as a unity. Again and again we have seen that events in this play are not linked causally, that Pericles does not suffer because of a tragic flaw or even because of any wrong action. His suffering carries no moral overtones; indeed, it is so painful to see partly because it is (to borrow the phrase A.C. Bradley applied to Desdemona) mere suffering. Lacking causality and motivation, the play's sequence of events denies the coherence of beginning, middle, and end. The culminating spiritual event of Pericles' life is from an aesthetic point of view anti-climactic, and his reconciliation with his wife, though prompted by a goddess, is carried out without the appearance of supernatural harmony. A better or more attentive playwright, we might conclude, would have arranged things more logically. But a perceptive comment by Clifford Leech rings more true to our experience of the play. The ending, he says, "is not truly a point of finality." Pericles has won no immunity to fortune. "We have the sense of a life-cycle," Leech goes on, "which can be repeated both in other lives and, in its essentials, in the same life if our vision is extended."[16]

What Gower has presented, then, has been a "pattern" (in the sense of a universal or archetypal model) of "painful adventures," a parable of a life apparently as formless as the sea on which so much of it is lived, alternately wracked by storms and calmed by music, not subject to the false coherence of narrative or dramatic form, but presented, nevertheless, through the powerful magic of a poet musician.[17] In this setting, man's best virtue both as actor and as spectator is patience, fortified by faith in the real and eternal harmony underlying and ultimately transcending temporary chaos. The deliberate confrontation of evil and chaos with the formal beauty of art--ceremony, poetry, dance, music--

is an act of faith in the victory of harmony over chaos. Gower lets the audience discover that fact, and then sets it free to perform its own act of faith through the exercise of its creative imagination.

Some readers of <u>King Lear</u>--a play whose relationship to <u>Pericles</u> has not yet been adequately examined--find it intolerable to believe that Lear, when <u>his</u> "untun'd and jarring senses" have been restored to order through reunion with his daughter and through the therapeutic use of music, only to be finally destroyed by the most heartless evil of all, does <u>not</u> attain a single glimpse in this world of a transcendent justice and harmony. But audiences who watch and listen hear no music, and see only Lear dead, with the body of Cordelia in his arms. <u>Pericles</u> offers a degree of reassurance. Though man<u>'s life i</u>s as a lasting storm, there is evidence that harmony is real and unconquerable. Yet in this play, so much of which is concerned with art, particularly music, as an act of faith in harmony in the face of chaos, the audience itself is called upon to participate in an act of faith and imagination, for it must be willing to believe that Pericles <u>has</u> heard the music of the spheres, and yet it is not assured that the painful adventures of the Prince of Tyre have come to an end. We might paraphrase Jesus: "Blessed are they that have not <u>heard</u>, and have believed." For <u>Pericles</u> requires of us the virtues of its hero--faith in an ultimate harmony, courage and imagination to imitate it as best we can on earth, and patience to wait for its full revelation until the revels are ended.

NOTES

[1] *The Untuning of the Sky: Ideas of Music in English Poetry, 1500-1700* (Princeton: Princeton University Press, 1961), p. 147.

[2] See, for example, John H. Long, *Shakespeare's Use of Music: The Final Comedies* (Gainesville: University of Florida Press, 1961); Gretchen L. Finney, *Musical Backgrounds for English Literature: 1580-1650* (New Brunswick, N.J.: Rutgers University Press, 1962); F.W. Sternfeld, *Music in Shakespearean Tragedy* (London: Routledge & Kegan Paul, 1963); *Shakespeare in Music*, ed. Phyllis Hartnoll (London: Macmillan, 1964).

[3] S. Musgrove, "The First Quarto of *Pericles* Reconsidered," *Shakespeare Quarterly*, 29 (Summer 1978), 406.

[4] I am indebted for method to the brilliant essay by Stephen Booth on another textually (and otherwise) problematic play: "On the Value of *Hamlet*," in *Reinterpretations of Elizabethan Drama: Selected Papers from the English Institute* (New York and London: Columbia University Press, 1969), pp. 137-76.

[5] *Pericles*, revised edition (New York: Penguin, 1977).

[6] *The Crown of Life* (London: Oxford University Press, 1947), p. 336.

[7] Gower appears this way on the title-page of George Wilkins' *The Painful Adventures of Pericles Prince of Tyre* (1608). The conventional elements in the presentation of Gower are discussed by Walter F. Eggers, Jr., "Shakespeare's Gower and the Role of the Authorial Presenter," *Philological Quarterly*, 54 (1975), 434-43.

[8] I.Cho.4. All quotations and line numbers are from the McManaway edition cited above.

[9] Some editors interpret the first word of Q's "Musicke bring in our daughter" as a stage direction rather than as a command. The effect of either, from the audience's point of view, is the same: the music

does begin at this point, and Antiochus is clearly acting as stage manager.

[10] The Jacobean audience would probably have been quite familiar with this distinction, which, according to Sternfeld's <u>Music in Shakespearean Tragedy</u>, was commonly made in the Renaissance and earlier (p. 227).

[11] See Long, pp. 40-41.

[12] In the scene in which Simonides gives Thaisa to Pericles in marriage, he also refers to the musical entertainment Pericles had provided on the previous evening, saying, "Sir, you are music's master" (II.v.30). Although this passage may be a vestigial remnant of an episode from the <u>real</u> Gower's "Apollonius of Tyre" in which Apollonius gives the princess a music lesson, it is possible that <u>Pericles</u> as acted contained an interlude between II.iii. and II.iv. in which Pericles, represented as being alone in his chamber, plays the lute and sings, to the delight of Simonides, who overhears him. Wilkins' prose version, which was very likely based on the play as performed, contains such a scene. There is certainly charm in the idea that Pericles is himself a musician, and appropriateness in the setting: a gentleman would not perform in public before strangers. If such an interlude is added, the sense of a restoration of peace and harmony through music will be even more pronounced than that I have noted.

[13] The text gives no indication about the song Marina is to sing; it may be that she sings a contemporary popular song instead of one written for the play. In this case my own favorite candidate is "Come, heavy Sleep," from Dowland's <u>First Book of Ayres</u> (1597). It would be especially appropriate if this song had been sung earlier by Pericles in an interlude following the banquet in II.iii., as I have proposed.

[14] My interpretation of this scene places me in a distinct minority, for most editors interpolate at V.i.225 a stage direction for music. In the New Arden Edition of <u>Pericles</u>, for example (London: Methuen, 1963), F.D. Hoeniger says that the music of the spheres "must be shared by the audience from the beginning, to avoid the absurd impression of Pericles being deluded" (p. 153). In generalizing about instances of celestial

18

music in the Renaissance theater, on the other hand, F.W. Sternfeld concludes that it was played by theater musicians only when it was heard by <u>all characters on stage</u> (p. 246). I argue that everything in the play up to this point directs us toward an interpretation of the music of the spheres as inaudible to everyone but Pericles, in a deliberate temporary alienation of the audience--a daring <u>coup de théâtre</u>, perhaps, but one that is not inconsistent with other strange touches in this odd, possibly experimental play. Some indirect support, moreover, may be found in Inga-Stina Ewbank's convincing argument pointing out that Marina's therapeutic use of <u>language</u> here has provided a "unique demonstration of the power of words," since Pericles "begins as an apathetic deaf mute and ends up hearing the music of the spheres." Professor Ewbank concludes that this is "a scene about the readiness to accept the impossible, a scene hinting at knowledge which passes understanding." (See "'My name is Marina': The Language of Recognition," in <u>Shakespeare's Styles</u>: <u>Essays in Honour of Kenneth Muir</u>, ed. Philip Edwards, Inga-Stina Ewbank and G.K. Hunter [Cambridge: Cambridge University Press, 1980], p. 115, p. 129.) My staging of the scene, I believe, would best convey to the <u>audience</u> that sense of a "knowledge which passes understanding."

    [15] The music to accompany a theophany, unlike music of the spheres, has justification in Shakespearean stage convention. John H. Long observes that the appearance of the supernatural in Shakespeare's plays is usually preceded and accompanied by stage directions for music (p. 47).

    [16] "The Structure of the Last Plays," <u>Shakespeare Survey</u>, 11 (1958), 22.

    [17] Others have also recently noted the degree to which Gower's presence organizes and unifies our experience of the play. Eggers, for instance, remarks on his "almost continuous control" (p. 438) and on the fact that his eight appearances give him a more dominant role than any other authorial presenter in an Elizabethan play. In a tantalizing brief summary of a paper given at the 1975 MLA meeting, F.D. Hoeniger is reported to have departed sharply from the Introduction to his own New Arden Edition to argue that "a dramatic decorum for the differences in [the play's] style can be experienced, on the stage at least, once one becomes fully aware of Gower's dominating role from beginning

to end." The summary of the talk, "Gower's Dramaturgy fitfully improved by Shakespeare," is by David Bevington, in _Research Opportunities in Renaissance Drama_, 19 (1976), 1-2. A promised longer essay by Hoeniger on the subject has to my knowledge not yet appeared.

THE VISUAL AND THE SYMBOLIC
IN SHAKESPEARE'S MASQUES

Catherine M. Shaw

Although I will discuss but four of Shakespeare's plays in detail in this study--Romeo and Juliet, Merchant of Venice, Timon of Athens, and Henry VIII--let me begin by saying that masque appears, in whole or in part, in about a third of Shakespeare's plays and not once is it used as gratuitous entertainment.[1] I exclude from this number those plays in which Shakespeare relies on the mere word masque to conjure different receptions depending on dramatic circumstances. Connotations of shallowness and insincerity, for example, are assumed when, in 3 Henry VI, the French king substitutes the word masquers for soldiers. "Then England's messenger, return in post,/ And tell false Edward, the supposed King,/ That Lewis of France is sending over masquers/ To revel it with him and his new bride" (III.iii.223-5).[2] The words are spoken in contempt for the wanton revels of the English king, "sportful Edward," whose declarations of loyalty and love are worth no more than flirtacious whisperings behind visors. In the company of Sir Toby Belch and Andrew Aguecheek, on the other hand, a masque is a "kickshaw" (Twelfth Night, I.iv.115), a trifle which, like the lank-haired knight, is of pretended elegance, silly and insubstantial.

The masque in Love's Labour's Lost relies upon a combination of such connotations. Ostensibly, the performance is to entertain and to advance the suits of these young men who woo by the book. But their attitude toward courting, like their attitude toward immortality, is make-believe just as the masque is make-believe, and both break down before the ladies' determination to have nothing to do with such insincerity. The wit of the ladies with its edge of reality cuts through the artifice and emerges victorious. These are not lovers but clowns and the masque-burlesque presents them to the audience as just that.

Such uses as these do not mean that the masque had lost its association with the revelry of joyous and harmonious occasion. The masque elements which close As You Like It serve as the direct visual representation of the triumph of young lovers over adversity, reunion of child with father, reconciliation of brothers, and the restoration of rightful authority. The surprise entry and songs of Hymen, and unmasking of Rosalind, the patterned pairing of the lovers, lead up to the Duke's call for revels. The melancholy Jaques, the last alien element, is for "other than dancing measures," but his exit line, "To see no pastimes I" (V.iv. 193, 195) confirms that Capell and editors who have followed him are right in seeing the play end with a dance as a further visual expression of new-found harmony before the company sweeps off-stage.

Structurally and visually, the masque-like ending of As You Like It provides the play with a grand, full-ensemble, full-stage finale. Its relation to the audience is simple and straightforward. Discord has been resolved, the movement from disorder to order completed and, therefore, what Stephen Orgel has called with relation to the formal Court Masque, "the unmediated confrontation"[3] of actors and spectators may take place.

Of much greater complexity is the way masque operates when it is at once part of and framed by a continuing dramatic action. And this is as true in The Merchant of Venice in which the actual performance never materializes as it is in Romeo and Juliet, Timon of Athens, and Henry VIII in which the masques not only take place but are provided with on-stage viewers to their performance. In each play the masque sequence is as complete as dramatic circumstances require; and in each the form of the entertainment itself and the performers involved become visual projections of the central concerns of the play and symbols (directly or indirectly) of the world view which it ultimately presents.

In Romeo and Juliet, Benvolio has conveniently set aside the necessity of a Presenter for the surprise entry, and therefore the masquers can be on the acting platform, standing to one side, when the Capulets and their guests enter. Romeo, having isolated himself from the others in the role of a torchbearer, is presumably standing furthest into the theatre, let's say downstage right, and thus, like the audience, is observer to the scene. Capulet jovially welcomes the masquers and encourages the ladies to dance. As he, like "good cousin Capulet," is too old for measures, he also moves

front stage out of the way of the dancers. At this
position, the angry Tybalt joins him.

Both Neville Coghill and J.L. Styan have dealt with
Shakespeare's skillful blocking of his characters in
this scene[4] in which there is a full-complement projection from the stage. Against the patterned movement of
Montague masquers dancing with Capulets, the audience
sees and, because of its proximity to Romeo and Tybalt
standing front stage, feels renewed the opposing forces
which are central to the play. The soft lyricism of
Romeo's expression of new-found love set against the
counterpoint of Tybalt's punctuated rage heightens the
expectation of "new mutiny." At this precise moment,
however, Shakespeare reverses direction. Capulet meets
Tybalt's threat of violence with reason and the demand
for moderate behaviour. In subtle detail, Capulet's
anger with his nephew for challenging his authority may
foreshadow his reaction to Juliet's later defiance, but
as this point Tybalt is driven out and the meeting of
the lovers in a delicate and youthful duet of patterned
quatrains becomes the focus of attention. Thus, in the
larger view, what should be the ideal outcome of the
play is symbolically and visually projected from the
stage--the torches of love burn bright and violent
hatred is curbed by reasoned judgement.

Some years after Romeo and Juliet was written, Ben
Jonson was to speak of the "body" and the "soul" of
masque.[5] In Shakespeare's play, the structural form of
the masque, its "body," has brought together the young
lovers (albeit under an alien roof) and it has provided
the spark to re-flame the "ancient grudge." Briefly,
however, it also envisions the "more remov'd mysteries"
which Jonson saw as the "soul" of masque--"rude will"
held in check and "grace" allowed to dominate the stage.
Only then comes the unmasking of the lovers' identities
after which the narrative action picks up and sweeps
them to their "piteous overthrow." The masque then is
allowed to project that movement from disorder to order
which is central to its nature, to resolve discord, and
to forestall ever so briefly the tragic inevitability.

That the lovers ultimately die as sacrifices to
enmity, however, does not mean that the masque vision
is lost. As Nicholas Brooke has pointed out, Romeo and
Juliet is, overall, "suspended between two major ceremonies: the dance-betrothal of Act I [in other words,

the masque] and the wedding-funeral of Act V."[6] Although the final scene in the tomb is not a masque, the repetition of elements from that earlier ceremonious occasion nonetheless stimulates in the mind and the sensibilities a recall of the masque vision.

Once again, a torch lights Romeo's way into Capulet territory and he approaches Juliet under a roof alien to love. Tybalt, his irrationality stilled by death, is a silent onlooker as Paris, his surrogate, takes up the Capulet cause and accuses Romeo of insult to their house. Romeo's plea to him, "O, be gone!/ By heaven, I love thee better than myself" (V.iii.63-4), recalls his similar words to Tybalt, "I do protest I never injured thee,/ But love thee better than thou can devise" (III. i.68-9). Juliet is masked by the Friar's potion and Romeo by the dark of night. Again two kisses are exchanged as the lovers, joined in purpose, find immortal life together. The apothocary's poison is "quick;" Romeo's dagger a "restorative;" the pulse of love beats as strongly as it did in the masque and again transforms their world. Finally, and of greatest importance, the recall of that masque vision of ideal harmony provides for Romeo and Juliet that which is demanded of all tragedy--that sense of tragic waste of all that might have been.

That triumph of harmony over discord which is projected from the masque in Romeo and Juliet and from its companion scene, the wedding-funeral, is almost always at the heart of Shakespeare's adaptation of masque to his theatrical purpose even when the triumph is an illusion broken by the play as a whole. In The Merchant of Venice, Bassanio, ignoring Shylock's earlier refusal to break bread with him, sends another invitation to join in social amenities. To all intents and purposes, Jew and Gentile will celebrate the accord of the bond, and what better symbol for the movement from former antagonism to apparent order and harmony than the masque. The lead-up to or anticipation of this conviviality is spread over the first four scenes of Act II. Jew in scene v, however, and Gentiles in scene vi dispel any expectation of concord, and the two abutting scenes forecast the inevitability of the climactic confrontation of opposites in the trial scene.

Shylock's mood at the beginning of the scene is sour and suspicious because he mistrusts Bassanio's tendering of an open hand. Nonetheless, as he had previously determined to catch Antonio "upon the hip" in retaliation for the Christian's railing against moneylending and against the Jewish nation, now he resolves to respond to what he sees as Gentile sham and condescension by going to dinner "in hate" to order "to feed upon/ The prodigal Christian" (II.v.14-15). When Lancelot Gobbo announces there is to be a masque for the entertainment of the guests, Shylock's sudden and violent response firmly establishes him as an antimasque figure--an adversary to revelry and a hater of music.[7] Such "shallow fopp'ry" is for Shylock equated with Christian duplicity against which he would lock his house. His repeated injunctions to Jessica, says Styan, "transform the facade of the tiring-room into the facade of his house, all in preparation for the scene which follows."[8] And, indeed, although the Jew is an object of laughter at this point, the next scene shows he is right to be fearful of knavery. Shylock's mere absence from home would be enough to allow the youthful Christians to accomplish the elopement of Jessica with Lorenzo. They go further than this out of sheer malice toward the Jew. With Jessica as torchbearer, they plan to parade her before her father's very eyes. In their own way, they are also antimasque figures because their scheme is to subvert the occasion of masque good fellowship for their own mockery. Only the sudden calling off of the masque prevents this. Shylock's public humiliation must wait.

Of more importance at this point in the play, however, is that the young masquers who invade that "house" for which Shylock shows such concern do much greater injury to Lorenzo's "father Jew" than he ever received on the Rialto. That "house" symbolizes those things which Shylock holds most dear--his money and his daughter--and it doesn't take long to find out which he values most. When, in the opening scene of Act III, the saucy Christians question him, "How now, Shylock, what news among the merchants?" he replies, "You knew, none so well as you, of my daughter's flight." And when they continue to mock, he cries, "I say, my daughter is my flesh and blood" (III.i.23-25, 38). This scene is singled out by Norman Rabkin to show how Shakespeare evokes complex responses from his audience, "kaleidoscipic shift[s] of emotion."[9] The audience which previously laughed at his isolation and rigidity is now genuinely touched by Shylock's grief because it

knows the depth of the injury inflicted in the masque
ruse and the shallow Christians do not. Jessica is
Shylock's house. In terms of his flesh and blood she
is both his daughter and the continuation of his Jewish
line.[10] The reminder of his dead wife not only points
up Jessica's thoughtlessness in taking her father's
ring but also that she is his only legacy to his tribe.

    The trial scene in Act IV, although having no
masque features, brings to a climax those polarities
established by the masque preparation and its aftermath
and achieves again that very complexity of audience
response which Rabkin explores. Shylock, when he is
offered double the amount of money lent, even "ten times
o'er" (IV.i.211), refuses it. His revenge for injury to
his personal and racial pride will only be sated by the
Christian flesh promised him in the bond. Adamant, merciless, antagonistic to any sort of harmonious compromise with the Gentiles, he is again the outsider, the
object of scorn. Then, as Christian guile in the masque
ruse motivated the revenge which Shylock seeks, so
Christian guile prevents him from achieving it. The
audience has short time, however, to cheer his defeat
because again the treatment accorded him by the Gentiles
causes a shift in emotional response. Perhaps
Bassanio's generous willingness to settle the bond issue
within its own terms is the act we might wish would
represent Christian mercy, but that is not what we get.
Once again the tremendous sense of Shylock's isolation
projects from the stage and his words recall for the
audience injuries which his on-stage antagonists do not
comprehend:

> Nay, take my life and all, pardon not that:
> You take my house when you do take the prop
> That doth sustain my house; you take my life
> When you do take the means whereby I live.
>   (IV.i.374-77)

    Following this, as Styan has noted, Shylock is not
even given a strong theatrical exit. Rather, it is
"quiet, even pathetic."[11] Without money and, more particularly, without Jewish progeny Shylock has no
"house," and the total humiliation creates for the audience that same sense of disquiet or uneasiness as
occurred after the masque ruse. The masque, then, in
addition to serving dramatic functions on a narrative
level, also sets up early in the play those "ambivalent

signals,"[12] to use Rabkin's term, upon which is based much of the tension of the whole play.

The body of the masque in Timon of Athens, that is, its staging and immediate dramatic effect, is different from that of the masque in Romeo and Juliet and Merchant of Venice because, in this case, none of the main characters takes part. Timon and his attendant lords enter and take their positions to one side of the acting area. They must be dressed in ceremonial robes as Apemantus, who comes "dropping after all," is described as being "like himself" or plainly dressed to distinguish him from the others. Because of his churlish humour, Apemantus is ordered to a table by himself "yonder" or on the other side of the stage. Thus, plain-clothed and plain-spoken, he is in a position to pursue his caustic comments in asides. J.L. Styan sees this physical arrangement as part of Shakespeare's anti-illusory stage.[13] This blocking, however, allows the audience a number of simultaneous levels of representation. It is able to see the masque in a purely theatrical sense, to observe Timon taking pleasure from it, and also to hear Apemantus' bitter and cynical undercutting. In other words, the broader view projected from the stage is not only what is going on in the masque but also what it represents to its on-stage viewers and, under the realistic promptings of Apemantus, what ironic juxtapositions are established between that large-sightedness afforded the audience and the short-sightedness of Timon.

As soon as the "extremities of both ends" are settled in their seats, Cupid enters between them as Presenter. Moelwyn Merchant is one of the few commentators to pay attention to the divided Folio directions for stage entrances, and I think he is right in seeing the next sequence to be a dumb show of the senses who, during Cupid's prologue, acknowledge Timon as their patron and "gratulate" his "plenteous bosom."[14]

Next come the "Maskers of Amazons" who perform dances which, from Apemantus' description, are somewhat antic. There follows further honoring of Timon by the lords before they take out the Amazon women for the revels. At their close, Timon compliments the masquers and invites them to further "eating." With that, the ladies leave the stage. Significantly, the only part of the performance missing is the unmasking. But dramatically this cannot take place until after Timon becomes aware that he has been seeing but outward appearance and not the true nature of those who frequent his house.

Apemantus' attitude to the masque is to be expected--he sees it as the self-indulgent sport of madmen and fools. Timon sees it as a compliment to his banquet, as emblematic of concord and generosity. Each sees the masque as mirroring his own particular conception of mankind. What the audience sees, however, is a visual extension of the problem inherent within the paragone between the Painter and the Poet in the first scene--the question of the competence with which art renders "appearance" as a revelation of "reality." And indeed, the masque, itself an art form, projects the true image. The elements of Timon's life--lavish expenditure, ceremony, and ostentation--are symbolically characterized as effeminate and bizarre. And the lords, by joining in the spectacle, show themselves to be as much impersonators as the adoring senses and the dancing Amazons.

In his article, "Timon, Cupid, and the Amazons," Robert C. Fulton has added much to our understanding of the symbolism of the allegorical figures Shakespeare chooses for this masque--what Fulton calls their "iconographic doubleness."[15] Cupid and Amazons were, of course, familiar to renaissance entertainments, and indeed Timon sees the joining of these symbols of love and war as that idealized reconciliation of opposites which was necessary to those masques presented in aristocratic houses. For Apemantus, on the other hand, and for the theatre audience, this masque is set against and is part of an Athenian world of wanton and licentious liberty. Against this background, Cupid becomes equated with the blind Eros who plays with sparrows, an image of inordinate and indiscriminate appetite. In addition to this, Celeste Wright has shown that "Amazon" was an Elizabethan cant word for prostitute.[16] (Queen Margaret, it will be remembered, is called an "Amazonian trull" in 3 Henry VI [I.iv.114].) And, indeed, even if the dances shared by the Athenian Lords and these unnatural creatures are not suggestive in themselves, Apemantus' repeated images of eating, consuming, and rotting underscore the doubleness in their symbolic representation. Timon, who both offers and enjoys these delights of the senses, is both procurer and whore. Athens feeds on Timon both literally and metaphorically. And the audience is not allowed to forget this association of Timon's house with whoredom. A senator later describes it like to a brothel.

> No porter at his gate, [he says,]
> But rather one that smiles and still invites
> All that pass by.   (II.i.10-12)

The corresponding later scene to the actual banqueting in Timon's entertainment is obviously the mock banquet in Act III, scene vi. For the correspondent to the masque, as Fulton has observed, we look later in the play. "In Act IV, scene iii, [he says,] Timon, the metaphorical whore and bawd of Athens, comes face to face with two literal prostitutes. . . . The confrontation is charged with bitterness, filled with vile and scathing language." "The masque of Act I, scene ii," Fulton goes on, "has undergone a complete metamorphosis. The bright shapes and sparkling figures of that first banquet have given way to images of chaos and destruction. Cupid has become the presiding genius at a feast of death. The brave habits of the dancing ladies have fallen away to reveal a pair of poxy Amazons."[17] The tables are turned, and now Timon will, with his surrogate whores, eat and destroy Athens.

In order then, to understand the manner in which Shakespeare employs masque in Timon of Athens to serve the dramatic ends of the whole play, it must be envisioned not just as performance in itself but within the larger view of the total stage impression. Seen within its dramatic framework, the masque provides a visual miniature of and a symbolic paradigm for the moral thrust of the whole play.

Henry VIII provides an example of how Shakespeare used that kind of masque which best served particular dramatic requirements of the play, regardless of the increasing sophistication of the aristocratic Court Masque. Although framed by a different social occasion, for the masque in Henry VIII Shakespeare returns to the same simple form as that in Romeo and Juliet. In fact, even the brilliance described in Shakespeare's source is stripped away. Indeed, although explicit directions are given for fine costumes and stage elaboration for other ceremonious scenes in Henry VIII, Shakespeare's masquers enter merely "habited like shepherds" onto a stage with no more properties than might be found in any play which does not include a masque. What we have, then, is a sequence which allows the audience to concentrate solely on what is going on in the masque, undisburbed by spectacle.

And what does the audience see? At one side of the downstage area is a long table for Wolsey's banquet guests, among them Anne Bullen. Wolsey enters and takes his place at a small table opposite them. After a flurry of trumpets and the discharge of cannons have surprised the gathering to attention, Wolsey reassures the women, "Nay, ladies, fear not;/ By the laws of war y'are privileged." His words set up the ideal of assault which was a common disguising pattern and eminently suitable for the sweeping courtship which follows. A servant announces the "noble troop of strangers" who have arrived "as great embassadors/ From foreign princes" (I.iv.53-56), and the masquers enter. To the music of oboes they move quickly downstage and with bows they salute the Cardinal who sits alone under a large canopy designed to set him apart from the others and to indicate his high position. (Perhaps the audience is meant to see irony in the secular shepherd of his flock in plain attire confronting the spiritual shepherd in his ceremonial robes.) There are no masque dances and no songs but, with the Cardinal's permission, the masquers take out the ladies. With the words, "Oh Beauty, Till now I never knew thee!" (I.iv.75-76), the disguised King chooses Anne Bullen for his partner and dances her furthest front stage in full view of the Cardinal and the audience.

The narrative function of the body of the masque is still quite simple. It provides the opportunity for the King to meet his next Queen, an opportunity arising out of the commoning, a situation long associated with intrigue and which Shakespeare had relied upon before in <u>Much Ado</u>. Shakespeare adds to this the irony of having the meeting take place under the roof of the man who was to become the antagonist to the union. This irony is compounded by the larger view presented to the audience eye. Seated in his great red Cardinal's robe, the most politically powerful man in England is seen at the height to which his greed for material possessions and his ambition for authority have brought him. What better moment, dramatically and visually, for the romantic meeting which will lead to the downfall of Wolsey and the church which he represents in England! Perhaps, as they dance and kiss before him, he smiles benignly.

After the unmasking, the company prepares to retire to the next chamber where the fresher air may cool the King's heat. Shakespeare, however, does not let go of the scene so easily. Henry's closing lines first send the other dancers off stage, "lead in your ladies ev'ry one." This leaves Anne, Henry, and Wolsey alone on stage at the front of the acting area. His words to Anne, "Sweet partner, I must not yet forsake you," suggest that he takes her hand again. Next, the King addresses Wolsey, "Let's be merry,/ Good my Cardinal: I have a half a dozen healths/ To drink to these fair ladies, and a measure/ To lead 'em once again." Then, on Henry's magnificently ambiguous line, "And then let's dream who's best in favour" (I.iv.103-8), the three turn their backs on the audience and move up and off stage--Henry and his lady through one door, the Cardinal through the other.

Thus, the <u>un</u>spectacular masque has projected four vivid stage impressions--the Cardinal as smiling host welcoming his guests and permitting their revels; the meeting of Henry and Anne directly under Wolsey's eye; the King revealed and taking over the position of authority; and the magnificent exit tableau. In the larger view, this succession of images presents the audience with a visual shift of power which presages the fall of Wolsey and, ultimately, the firm establishment of the monarch as head of state and church in England.

The later scene with which the masque most clearly corresponds in <u>Henry VIII</u> and with which it has strong visual and symbolic links is the christening scene which closes the play. There are, however, other scenes of high ceremony which come in between; which intrude and, because they project continuing conflict, postpone the vision of state harmony which the masque anticipated. The trial of Queen Katherine juxtaposes the dignity of her established position with the continuing and insidious power of Wolsey. The pageant of crowned figures which accompanies the diademed Anne in her coronation procession is immediately followed by Queen Katherine's vision of white-robed figures who honour her with garlands. Regardless of the audience's pre-knowledge of historical outcome, its responses are kept unsettled by these antagonistic demands on its sympathies.

The christening scene is equally if not more elaborate than any other in the play. Indeed, in this instance, Shakespeare makes full use of the brilliance of the occasion described in his source. There are still, however, the same two visual focuses as were in the masque--temporal and divine authority--and the way that those two powers are projected from the stage in the christening scene finally confirms what the earlier masque scene had only augured. This time it is the infant Elizabeth "richly habited" (V.iv.s.d.), who is kissed by the King as he joins her under a canopy of state. Before them, doing obeisance, kneels Cranmer, Primate of England. The threat of Popery and ambitious governance personified in Wolsey and later in Gardiner has been broken. As the new heir is placed in the arms of the Church of England, historical past merges with historical present for Shakespeare's audience, and present projects into future. There is no conflict left and no doubt as to who stands as supreme head of established church and secular law in Protestant England.

In conclusion, let me point out that by the time Shakespeare began writing, masque, whose essence is essentially the projection of concord, had already gathered about it other dramatic connotations upon which the playwright could rely to stimulate certain audience responses to its immediate performance--romantic intrigue, ironic juxtaposition, excess, and so on. In Shakespeare's plays, however, at the same time as the realistic mind is accepting masque as part of the immediate social environment of the action, the sensibilities of the "inward eye" touched by symbolic vision, allegorical or otherwise, pick up those impulses which inform the whole play, masque and all. The plays with which I have been concerned are examples of Shakespeare's successful assimilation of masque as a visual theatrical device, with masque as a symbolic contributor to dramatic totality so that a union is established between what is shown immediately and what is intended to be comprehended in the mind and felt in the imagination.

NOTES

[1] All of Shakespeare's plays which include masque are discussed in my book, "Some Vanity of Mine Art": The Masque in English Renaissance Drama, 2 vols., Jacobean Drama Studies, 81 (Salzburg: Institut für Englische Sprache und Literatur, 1979). Although the emphasis of that work is primarily generic, of necessity some material from it is repeated here.

[2] The Riverside Shakespeare, ed. G.B. Evans et al. (Boston: Houghton Mifflin, 1974). All quotations are from this edition.

[3] Introduction to The Complete Masques, The Yale Jonson (New Haven: Yale Univ. Press, 1969), p. 2.

[4] Shakespeare's Professional Skills (Cambridge: Cambridge Univ. Press, 1964), pp. 29-31; Shakespeare's Stagecraft (Cambridge: Cambridge Univ. Press, 1971), pp. 82-84.

[5] Introduction to Hymenaei, in The Complete Masques, pp. 75-76.

[6] Shakespeare's Early Tragedies (London: Methuen, 1968), p. 106.

[7] Shylock looks different than all the others on stage from the time he first appears. A distinctive costume and gestures such as the "patient shrug" demanded by the dialogue set him visually apart.

[8] Styan, p. 21.

[9] Shakespeare and the Problem of Meaning (Chicago and London: Univ. of Chicago Press, 1981), p. 6.

[10] In an earlier article, "'Dangerous Conceits Are in Their Natures Poisons': The Language of Othello," I pointed out the similarity between Shylock's and Brabantio's grief at the loss of their daughters to someone they consider unsuitable (University of Toronto Quarterly, 49 [1980], 308-9, n. 20.)

[11] Styan, p. 79.

[12] Rabkin, p. 28.

[13] Styan, p. 102.

[14] *Shakespeare and the Artist* (London: Oxford Univ. Press, 1959), pp. 168-69.

[15] "Timon, Cupid and the Amazons," *Shakespeare Survey*, 9 (1976), 283.

[16] "The Amazons in Elizabethan Literature," *Studies in Philology*, 37 (1940), 449.

[17] Fulton, pp. 292, 294.

Venus, Lucrece, and Bess of Hardwick:
Portraits to Please

Elizabeth Truax

Shakespeare, as a man of the theatre, knew the importance of an audience. So when the theatres were closed in the summer of 1592 because of an outbreak of plague, he temporarily abandoned writing plays and began to compose his two narrative poems, Venus and Adonis and The Rape of Lucrece, with a new audience in mind. His choice of Henry Wriotheseley, third Earl of Southampton, to be his patron suggests that he anticipated this new audience to be composed of well read and broadly educated noblemen and noblewomen who would be familiar with the Latin classics and would enjoy an erotic interpretation of the Ovidian tales that had become such popular subjects for contemporary artists and poets on the continent. Nor could Shakespeare ignore the fact that this courtly group knew its Bible and was accustomed to temper entertainment with moral instruction.

In 1952 London bookshops already offered the reading public accounts of the amorous adventures of pagan gods and goddesses, translated and moralized to appease Puritan sensitivities by Arthur Golding, Abraham Fraunce and others.[1] Trade with the Flemish city of Antwerp was brisk, and printed books, often with wood-cut illustrations, most likely reached English shores.[2] English travelers visited the wonders of the ancient world and the new wonders of the Renaissance (Venice was the favorite city) and returned home with engravings and pattern books which they submitted to English craftsmen and immigrant Flemish artists to use as models in elaborate decorative schemes for the manor houses which were a-building everywhere.[3]

Because the Renaissance came late to England, almost two hundred years late, the art which the English nobility enjoyed in architecture, painting, decoration--and poetry--does not reflect the style of the early Italian Renaissance, but becomes instead a curious blend of Gothic and later Renaissance or Mannerist style, characteristic of Northern Italy, France, and Flanders. Mannerist compositions are complex, frequently highly dramatic in nature, and demonstrate virtuoso skills. Although the mood may appear balanced and confident, beneath the surface calm, irony and paradox are ever present. In both literature and the visual arts, a contrariety often results from the juxtaposition of sensuous naked or semi-naked figures in scenes of amorous encounter, set precariously within a framework of allegory and moralization.[4]

Contrariety of amorousness and allegory is the fabric of Shakespeare's narrative poems. If Venus is Lust; Lucrece is Chastity. Yet Venus is redeemed by suffering at the death of Adonis, while Lucrece must die to preserve her honor. Shakespeare dedicated these poems to the young university-educated Earl of Southampton, but he must have had in mind a circle of readers, male and female, who would find such a provocative and paradoxical treatment of stories from classical times engaging--both as an example of erotic literature, and as a subject for moral contemplation.[5]

Bess Talbot, Countess of Shrewsbury, may have been a member of that audience. Following the example of many distinguished members of the upper-classes, such as Sidney, Leicester, Essex, and Southampton, Bess encouraged the promulgation of the arts--but she did so in her own highly individual way. She employed countless artisans, craftsmen and ladies trained at needlework to build and decorate Hardwick Hall, that jewel of the English Renaissance which remains today, by some miracle, virtually intact.[6] Hardwick Hall contains many pictures inspired by biblical and classical sources, especially on subjects related to women, drawn (without extraordinary skill) from engravings probably imported from Flanders. Among the embroideries executed by Bess's ladies is a series of panels demonstrating the triumph of Virtue over Vice. A tapestry depicts the adventures of Ulysses, and a painting records his return to his faithful wife, Penelope. The Great High Chamber is decorated by a huge frieze of Diana, Goddess of Chastity, and her court; in another place is a tiny cushion-cover narrating the misfortune of Actaeon who, as Golding points out in his translation of Ovid's <u>Metamorphosis</u> (1567), spent too much money on venery and gambling, and hence was transformed into a stag and killed by his own dogs. Bess also commissioned pictures of Venus and Lucrece. These pictures, viewed in the context of Shakespeare's narrative poems, provide a rare and illuminating illustration of how visual and literary arts delighted and instructed English courtly audiences in the late sixteenth century.

Shakespeare, in the new manner he may have learned from Marlowe, composed both poems with the vivid imagery associated with Renaissance painting, and without the moralistic gloss so often appended to earlier English literary interpretations of Ovid. Nonetheless, by an innovative approach to characterization, plot development, and imagery, he suggests ethical concepts that sometimes are at variance with the dramatic action of the poem, but which nonetheless appear consistent with the attitudes of his readers. He functions like a Mannerist artist, who freely introduces erotic images of bizarre behavior, subtly wooing his courtly audience into believing that such entertainment is indeed educational.[7]

In these narrative poems, Venus and Lucrece, like protagonists elsewhere in Shakespeare's plays, experience a series of metamorphoses that convey gradual shifts in characterization and prepare the reader for an ultimate affirmation of ethical values.[8] At first Venus appears as the goddess of Love and Beauty who strives to seduce the youthful Adonis. She has the sensual animal beauty of Venus in paintings by Titian, Giorgione or Corregio. Usually in these pictures Venus is nude or lightly draped, and she is shown either at moments of anticipation of an amorous encounter, as in the pictures of Venus at her toilet, or later in a moment of pleasing satisfaction in the company of Mars or Adonis.[9]

Shakespeare tells little of Venus' appearance other than that she is beautiful. He does not mention whether she is clothed or naked, but Ovid writes in Book X of the Metamorphosis that Venus roams the wood dressed in a short costume like Diana (533-536), a notion which Golding reiterates. Here, certainly, draped or naked, Venus is the huntress, not the chaste huntress Diana, but the lustful huntress whose arrows are Cupid's darts that Renaissance classical dictionaries deplored and Renaissance painters celebrated. She is also of substantial size, as she is strong enough to pluck Adonis from his horse and drag him to the ground. Perhaps her monumental stature was suggested by the columnlike statues of Venus depicted on frontispieces of books such as John Harington's translation of Orlando Furioso (1591).

Not only is Venus larger than life, everything

about her behavior in Shakespeare's poem is hyperbolic. In the opening stanzas she reveals her determination to woo Adonis despite his equal determination to resist. There is nothing modest in her language of love. "Here come and sit," she coos to Adonis, "where never serpent hisses,/ And being set, I'll smother thee with kisses."[10] Here is no moment of tranquil ease characteristic of Renaissance paintings of the lovers, but one of violent passion and attempted rape that may have been suggested to Shakespeare by pictures of the leave-taking when Adonis struggles to free himself from Venus' embrace and resume the hunt for the fatal boar. The best known illustration is the painting by Titian, but numerous engravings of the episode were also executed, among them one by George Ghisi.

A similar iconographic treatment of Venus' passionate lovemaking can be seen in an engraving by Flemish artist Philip Galle, after a painting by Antonie Blocklandt (Fig. 1). The lovers are portrayed in a woodsy setting overlooked by Cupid. Venus lies, her back to us, and reaches towards Adonis, drawing him to a deep embrace. Adonis bends towards her, his spear still in his hand as if he is torn between the lure of the hunt and the lure of Venus. The picture, in effect, describes the protracted goodnight kiss Shakespeare's Venus gives Adonis when he momentarily submits to her will:

> "Now let me say 'Good night,' and so say you;
> If you will say so, you shall have a kiss."
> "Good night," quoth she, and ere he says
>   "Adieu,"
> The honey fee of parting tend'red is;
>   Her arms do lend his neck a sweet embrace;
>   Incorporate then they seem, face grows to
>   face;
>
> Till breathless he disjoin'd and backward drew
> The heavenly moisture, that sweet coral mouth,
> Whose precious taste her thirsty lips well
>   knew,
> Whereon they surfeit, yet complain on drouth;
>   He with her plenty press'd, she faint with
>   dearth,
>   Their lips together glued, fall to the
>   earth.   (535-546)

This Venus is not a calm seductive goddess, but a lustful courtesan, driven almost mad by love melancholy. Her pursuit of Adonis is relentless, even vicious, and she is repeatedly characterized by unpleasing images of failed birds of prey and scavengers. She is "an empty eagle/, Sharp by fast" (45), and later when she holds Adonis tightly in her clutches, she becomes a vulture feeding gluttonlike on dead carrion (547-552). Marsilio Ficino terms such behavior <u>amor ferinus</u> (bestial love).[11] Shakespeare calls her a "love-sick queen" (326). She insists that if she were not immortal she would die (197), and she aims to "smother" Adonis with kisses (18).

Yet all the while Venus pursues Adonis with apparently unmitigated passion, Shakespeare conveys something warm and compelling in this bizarre courtesan. Something very human and a little pathetic. Her wanton beauty seems transformed into that of an aging maternal English woman. Even when she is most assertive and most demanding, she touches Adonis "with her fair immortal hand" and attempts to entice him with an account of her fading, but still vibrant beauty:

> "Thou canst not see one wrinkle in my brow;
> Mine eyes are gray and bright and quick in
>   turning;
> My beauty as the Spring doth yearly grow,
> My flesh is soft and plump, my marrow burning."
>   (139-142)

In this role, she functions as Venus, genetrix of new life. According to Erwin Panofsky's interpretation of Ficino, she can be seen in platonic terms as <u>Venus Vulgaris</u>, the robed Venus of Titian's <u>Sacred and Profane Love</u>.[13] She is ennobled by grief and for a moment seems like the grieving mother, the bereft Virgin Mary, the saintly goddess. She is consoled by the little red and white flower that has sprung up beside the body of Adonis--generation will continue despite her loss--and then prophesying that "Sorrow on love hereafter shall atone" (1137), she climbs into her chariot and is wafted away by her swans and doves.

The Earl of Southampton and his gentlemen friends might be expected to enjoy such an amorous poem, but what about the Elizabethan ladies of the court? To them the libidinous Venus of the opening scenes could have been an anathema (unless the ladies secretly admired the goddess of love and beauty), but the remainder of the poem has redeeming features. As lecherous Venus fails at her quest, the ladies may applaud and shift their attention to pure spotless young Adonis. Then, as Adonis persists in rejecting love, he may lose their sympathy (after all, what woman likes to be rejected?). When Venus begins to offer motherly advice, the feminine readers may now begin to take her side (certainly all mothers understand the problem of disciplining young children, especially impetuous boys!). Then at the sad denouement, how easy it is to forget the earlier courtesan--or, if she is remembered, to affirm that Venus has justly received the misery she has earned. The lament over the dead body of the beautiful youth, the symbolic metamorphosis of the little flower sprouting at his side, a reminder of the cycle of birth and death of all nature, and Venus' ascension to heaven all serve to elevate the tone and concerns of the poem so that an enlightened literature-loving English woman could read and enjoy the poem confident that she was being taught as well as delighted.

And so it was perhaps with Bess of Hardwick, Countess of Shrewsbury. Ironically, however, although Bess, a staunch Protestant, would have condemned the initial image of Venus, the lusty, lecherous would-be seducer of innocent young men, her own amorous conquests are surprisingly comparable with those of Venus. In her youth Bess was beautiful and clever enough at the skills of courtship to achieve a succession of four husbands, each richer than his predecessor, and thereby advance from a background of impoverished nobility to become one of the wealthiest and most important ladies of her day. In later years, by skillful craft Bess was able to trap her Adonis, not for herself, but as husband for her daughter, Elizabeth Cavendish, and the issue of that marriage, Arabella Stuart, stood after James, her cousin, in line for the throne of England. Certainly Bess would never acknowledge a lustful nature like Venus, nor did she choose any picture expressing blatant, vicious sexuality to decorate her home. However, she was not insensitive to the beauty of the human body, for Hardwick Hall has several nude pictures of seductive ladies reminiscent of Venus as both ideal and generative love and beauty.

On one of the walls of the Great Chamber there is a stucco relief after an engraving by Martin de Vos

(Fig. 2). Here Spring (Venus) like the illustrations in emblem books appears to chastize her son, Cupid, whose enthusiasm for play with his little bow and arrow has apparently been excessive. The female figure is nude with a ribbon-like drape across her thigh. She holds flowers in her right hand (the left is censuring Cupid) and fruits and vegetables grace her head. The background of the picture shows more images from nature to firmly establish the concept of Spring and the renewal of nature. Another picture of a nude figure is a stucco overmantel relief of Ceres (Venus) in the Paved room where Bess customarily enjoyed her breakfast (Fig. 3). This figure is holding a cornucopia filled with spring flowers, a sun smiles above, a moon face peers from the left, and trees, flowers, a stag, a lion, and even a unicorn complete this ensemble of allegorical images of virtue and abundance. An engraving by a Fontainbleau artist shows Venus, standing in a similar position, but her feet are set in a seashell, suggesting Venus' birth from the sea. In both of these pictures, images of birth and renewal, associated with Venus' role as goddess of love and beauty are repeatedly expressed.

The Rape of Lucrece would be especially attractive to Bess's tastes. Lucrece's tragedy Bess knew and admired so well she named one of her daughters Lucretia. Hardwick Hall is replete with pictures of domestic virtue. Penelope, that loyal wife who waits twenty years faithfully for her errant husband, appears to be Bess's favorite exemplum of wifely fidelity. Bess, however, was a lady of contraries--after a series of marital spats, she left her fourth husband in 1582, never to return, and moved back to her childhood home in Derbyshire to build Hardwick Hall, bringing with her many of the treasures of art she had commissioned for her earlier residence at Chatsworth where her husband had been custodian for Mary, Queen of Scots.

It has often been suggested that Shakespeare chose this tragic tale of Lucrece because he wished to please his audience by balancing the erotic tale of amorous Venus with a melancholy tale of chaste Lucrece. At the outset Lucrece appears neither bestial nor maternal nor divine. As Venus is characterized as the immortal goddess of Love and Beauty, so Lucrece is shown as the mortal paragon of Chastity.[14] Paradoxically, however, from the beginning of the poem, Lucrece's beauty is described in sensuously provocative language and her idealized beauty is gradually eroded by Tarquin's assault until she eventually becomes intensely melancholy and violent. Precisely the reverse of the pattern of metamorphoses experienced by Venus in the earlier poem.

For Bess of Hardwick and her friends, the poem could inspire a frenzy of sympathy for the chaste and loyal wife so brutally violated. Yet, ironically, Shakespeare's treatment of Lucrece is expressly erotic. The reader, like a voyeur, sees the chaste body on the stainless bed and watches as Lucrece's immaculate petrarchan beauty is gradually tarnished by Tarquin's "greedy eyeballs" and becomes that of a wanton seductress:

> Her hair, like golden threads, play'd with her breath;
> O modest wantons! wanton modesty! . . .
> (400-401)
> * * *
>
> Her breasts, like ivory globes circled with blue
> A pair of maiden worlds unconquered . . .
> (407-408)

However, Shakespeare carefully structures the rape sequence so that the reader need not be corrupted by vicarious pleasure for he/she is reminded that Tarquin is a "devil" and Lucrece a "heavenly beauty" and "earthly saint". Lucrece is called Chastity; Tarquin, Lust, Selfwill and Desire.[15] The rape scene was frequently represented by sixteenth century artists in just such a manner--eroticism augmented with moralistic iconography. Titian's painting of The Rape of Lucrece is, of course, the most famous example, but innumerable other artists made engravings that were widely circulated: among them Philip Galle (after Glotius) and H. Aldegrever and George Chisi, and engravings by Enea Vico and Agostino Veneziano (after a sketch by Raphael, Fig. 4).

The iconography of these pictures is strikingly similar. A curtained bed is center stage. In some instances Tarquin is fully dressed, in others, nude; Lucrece is almost always naked. In each picture the degree of dress or nudity serves to intensify images of sensuality, simultaneously with those of horror and

revulsion. Lucrece's mortal danger is stressed as
Tarquin holds a sword or knife in his right hand and
his left hand clutches her arm or her shoulder or her
breast (as Livy describes). Frequently, a third character, an observer, is included in the scene who may
have been introduced to bear witness that Lucrece is
indeed an innocent victim of Tarquin's lust. The Vico-
Veneziano engravings have curious additions. In one
corner we see a pair of copulating dogs, on a wall a
basin with a towel: small details that serve ironically
to emphasize both Lucrece's sexuality and her purity.

Following the rape, the lovers do not repose like
the satiated Mars and Venus of so many Renaissance
paintings, but separate, each in his own agony. In the
manner of the artists of his day, Shakespeare makes the
scene absolutely clear in allegorical and tropological
terms: "Pure Chastity is rifled of her store,/ And Lust
the thief far poorer than before," (692-693). Tarquin,
faint and guilt-ridden, slinks away; Lucrece, tainted
by the pollution of his barbarous act, grows in passion
and lust. She (like Venus in the earlier poem) has
become infected with amor ferinus, love melancholy.
She tears at her own flesh and vows revenge and self-
slaughter, acts of violence that are contrary to
Christian dogma and threaten to annihilate chastity and
virtue.[16]

Bess owned no rape pictures. However, she did own
a picture of another episode of the Lucrece story that
Shakespeare celebrates in the poem--the suicide.
Pictures of Lucrece stabbing herself were frequently
executed and widely circulated in sixteenth century
Europe. Often Lucrece is portrayed nude--but her nakedness is intended to demonstrate innocence not concupiscence. The scene was particularly popular in England
where it served time and again for moral affirmation.
Thomas Purfoot, a printer of sermons and books of moral
instruction, used a picture of Lucrece stabbing herself
as a sign for his print shop and a press mark for his
publications.[17]

The standard iconography of Lucrece's suicide,
which stresses her chastity more emphatically than
Shakespeare does, is fully illustrated in Bess's Lucrece.
In the entry hall at Hardwick Hall stands an embroidery
of Penelope, flanked by Patience and Perseverance (c.
1575) and adjacent to it is one of Lucrece, flanked by

Chastity and Liberality (Fig. 5).

Lucrece has bared her breast, as customary in these suicide pictures, and she is about to insert the knife. Here, again, nudity is not a sign of licentiousness, but of maternity and nurture, and reinforces the concept of Lucrece as chaste and virtuous. Furthermore, Lucrece holds the knife in her right hand which she will soon plunge into her right breast--a nearly impossible and certainly unnatural feat. The purpose clearly, is to ease the stigma of Lucrece's culpability and to reinforce the image of Lucrece's liberality, her willingness to sacrifice herself for her husband's honor. This iconographic treatment is frequently found in sixteenth-century visual art as seen in pictures by Jacobo Francis, Frans Floris and others.

Shakespeare's Rape of Lucrece contains other pictures, not all of which can be found at Hardwick Hall. The long passage of the picture of the Sack of Troy, which is an extended metaphor for the assault on Lucrece's own person, I have discussed elsewhere.[18] The pictures which tell the story of Lucrece through the iconography described here are most frequently achievements by Italianate mannerist artists either from Northern Italy or Flanders, or in some cases from Germany and France.

At the end of the poem Lucrece is not, in the view of this reader, as blameless as Shakespeare's courtly audience may have wished to believe. This Lucrece is not the stoical, almost passive woman of Bess's embroidery or the engravings that inspired it. She is a woman hell-bent for revenge--a revenge which Bess, a woman of strong feminist sympathies, would applaud.[19] But Lucrece's cry for revenge, like her suicide, must be reconciled with Christian values. A goddess like Venus can escape punishment; a mortal--Lucrece, Hieronimo, Hamlet, no matter how just the cause, in Renaissance iconography (in both the visual arts and in literature), must die to reestablish justice, virtue, right thinking, and to restore moral order.

Shakespeare, the poet, like so many Northern European artists of the Sixteenth Century, is Mannerist to the core. Paradox and irony abound in these poems. Absolute values confidently stated seldom hold up firmly under close analysis. If Venus, the lustful courtesan, becomes a saintly figure and Lucrece, the chaste,

generates a passion for revenge that parallels Venus'
passion for Adonis, the reader is not to worry. Like
the Mannerist artist of his day, Shakespeare has taken
well known, well loved stories and manipulated them
within an allegorical framework so that they appear to
reaffirm established values at the same moment that they
provide a courtly audience with pleasures that may be
profane.

Fig. 1 Ph. Galle (after Antonius Blocklandt), Venus and Adonis. Permission of Rijksmuseum. Ref. F. W. H. Hollstein, Dutch and Flemish Etchings and Engravings ca 1450-1700 (Amsterdam: Menno Hertzberger, 1949), VII. 78.289.

Fig. 2 The figure of Spring in the High Great Chamber freize. Hardwick Hall. The National Trust, photograph by the author.

Fig. 3 Overmantel relief of Ceres in the Paved Room. Hardwick Hall. The National Trust, photograph by the author.

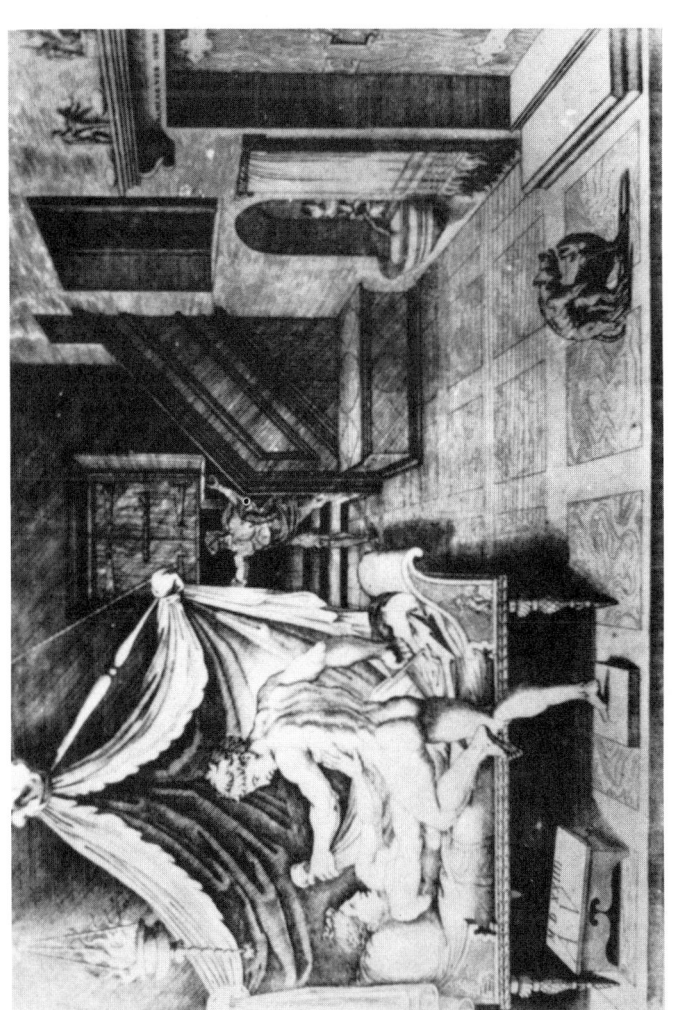

Fig. 4 Enea Vico (after a sketch of Raphael), The Rape of Lucretia. permission of Warburg and Courtauld Institutes Bartsch XV. 287.15.

Fig. 5 Lucretia flanked by figures depicting Chastity and Liberality. Hardwick Hall. National Trust, photograph by the author.

NOTES

[1] English translations of portions of Ovid's Metamorphosis began to appear in the early 1560's, culminating in Arthur Golding's complete work, the XV Bookes of P. Ovidius Naso, entytled Metamorphosis (London: Willyam Seres, 1567). Interpretations of Ovid's tales contained moralized comment as late as The Third Part of the Countesse ot Pembrokes Ivychurch, Entituled, Amintas Dale by Abraham Fraunce (London: Thomas Woodcocke, 1592). After 1592 moral interpretations of Ovid cease. Classical dictionaries followed a similar practice. For a complete list of poetry on mythological subjects printed in England from the beginnings to 1680, see Douglas Bush, Mythology and the Renaissance Tradition in English Poetry (New York: W.W. Norton, 1963), pp. 311-339.

[2] Printed books from publishing houses abroad such as Christopher Plantin's Golden Compasses in Antwerp and other houses located in Lyons, Venice, and elsewhere in Europe brought to England not only Latin texts by Roman and Humanist writers, but also contemporary books in a popular vein written in Italian and French which were often translated into English and sold in London bookshops. Many contained wood-cut illustrations, among them Geffrey Whitney's A Choice of Emblems (1586), the first English emblem book, which was printed in Leyden with plates from Plantin's extensive collection.

[3] Roy C. Strong's The English Icon: Elizabethan and Jacobean Portraiture (London: Routledge and Kegan Paul, 1969) provides a valuable study of painting in England during the Renaissance. For a general survey of the state of the arts in England see John Dixon Hunt, "The Visual Arts of Shakespeare's Day" in Shakespeare: Pattern of Excelling Nature, ed. David Bevington and Jay L. Halio (Newark: Univ. of Delaware, 1978), pp. 210-221. A general picture of the Elizabethan Society and the influence of Italian culture can be seen in the following: John Buxton, Elizabethan Taste (London: Macmillan, 1963), John Rigby Hale, England and the Italian Renaissance (London: Faber and Faber, 1954); Beverly Sprague Allen, Tides in English Taste (1619-1800), vol. I (Cambridge, MA: Harvard University Press, 1937); John Lievsay, The Elizabethan Image of Italy, Folger Booklets on Tudor and Stuart Civilization

(Ithaca: Cornell University Press, 1964) and The Englishman's Italian Books 1550-1700 (Philadelphia: University of Pennsylvania Press, 1969); Frank Ernest Halliday, Shakespeare in his Age (London: Gerald Duckworth, 1956), and Lewis Einstein The Italian Renaissance in England (New York: Burt Franklin, 1901).

[4] The term Mannerist evolved from Giorgio Vasari's discussion of "la maniera" or fine style in The Lives of Painters, Sculptors, and Architects, trans. William Gaunt (London: Dent, 1927), II, 151-153. For discussion of the character and implications of Mannerism, see Franzepp Wurtemberger, Mannerism, Trans. Michael Heron (New York: Holt Rinehart and Winston, 1963); John Shearman, Mannerism, Style and Civilization (Middlesex, England: Penguin Books, 1967); and Robert Eric Wolf and Ronald Miller Renaissance and Mannerist Art (N.Y.: Harry Abrams, 1968). Henri Zerner's The School of Fountainebleau: Etchings and Engravings, trans. Stanley Baron (London: Thames and Hudson, 1969) contains numerous examples of Mannerist etchings and engravings on profane subjects. Wylie Sypher's Four Stages of Renaissance Style (Garden City, N.Y.: Doubleday, 1955) is an interesting study of literature and the visual arts.

A recent study of value, although it does not deal specifically with iconography, is Robert Grudin, Mighty Opposites: Shakespeare and Renaissance Contrariety (Berkeley: University of California Press, 1979).

[5] The general history of Christian attitudes to the pagan gods is discussed by Douglas Bush in Mythology and the Renaissance Tradition in English Poetry, New Rev. ed. (New York: W.W. Norton, 1963), pp. 11-16 and Pagan Myth and Christian Tradition in English Poetry (Philadelphia: American Philosophical Society, 1968). pp. 71-80; Rosamund Tuve, Allegorical Imagery (Princeton University Press, 1966), pp. 305-314; Don Cameron Allen, Mysteriously Meant: The Rediscovery of Pagan Symbolism and Allegorical Interpretation in the Renaissance (Baltimore: John Hopkins Press, 1970), pp. 163-66: Clyde Barnes Cooper, Some Elizabethan Opinions of the Poetry and Character of Ovid (Menasha, Wis.: George Banta Publishing Co., 1914). See also Jean Seznec, The Survival of the Pagan God, trans. Barbara Sessions (New York: Harper & Brothers, 1961, first pub. 1940) and Edgar Wind, Pagan Mysteries in the Renaissance (London Faber and Faber, 1958).

⁶ Biographies of Bess of Hardwick which place emphasis on the character of Bess and comment on the artistic achievements of her unique home are: David N. Durant, Bess of Hardwick (London: Weindenfeld and Nicolson, 1977) and E. Carleton Williams, Bess of Hardwick (London: Longman's, 1959). Pictures of her home are reproduced in Hardwick Hall by Mark Giroad (The National Trust, 1976).

⁷ Studies which explore the interrelationships between the arts in the Renaissance include: Mario Praz, Mnemosyne: The Parallel Between Literature and the Visual Arts (Princeton University Press, 1970) and Studies in Seventeenth-Century Imagery (Roma: Edizioni di storia & letteratura, 1964): Samuel C. Chew The Pilgrimage of Life (New Haven: Yale University Press, 1962) and The Virtues Reconciled: An Iconographic Study (Toronto: University of Toronto Press, 1947); and Jean Hagstrum, The Sisters Arts: The Tradition of Literary Pictorialism and English Poetry from Dryden to Gray (Chicago: University of Chicago Press, 1953).

⁸ For commentary on Shakespeare-Venus relationship with literature and the visual arts, see T.W. Baldwin, On the Literary Genetics of Shakespeare's Poems and Sonnets (Urbana: University of Illinois Press, 1950), pp. 1-153. In Mythology and the Renaissance Tradition in English Poetry, new rev. ed. (New York: W.W. Norton, 1963), Douglas Bush provides a list of books on mythology printed in the sixteenth century, pp. 310-399.

Among recent discussions of Venus and Adonis which include some iconographic analysis are: William Keach, Elizabethan Erotic Narratives (New Brunswick, N.J.: Rutgers University Press, 1977); pp. 35-84, Heather Asals, "Venus and Adonis: The Education of a Goddess," Studies in English Literature, 13 (1973), 31-51; Don Cameron Allen, Image and Meaning: Metaphoric Traditions in Renaissance Poetry (Baltimore: John Hopkins Press, 1968), pp. 42-56; S. Clark Hulse, "Shakespeare's Myth of Venus and Adonis," PMLA, 93 (1978), 95-105; Donald G. Watson, "The Contraries of Venus and Adonis" Studies in Philology, 75 (1978), 32-63; and Eugene B. Cantelupe, "An Iconographic Interpretation of Venus and Adonis, Shakespeare's Ovidian Comedy," Shakespeare Quarterly, 14 (1963), 141-51. Almost every critic who comments on Venus and Adonis wrestles with the problem of moral implications.

⁹ Studies touching the iconography of Venus that prove helpful here are Erwin Panofsky, Studies in Iconology: Humanistic Themes in the Art of the Renaissance (New York: Harper & Row, 1939) and Problems in Titian: Mostly Iconographic (New York: N.Y. University Press, 1969); and E.H. Gombrich, Norm and Form: Studies in the Art of the Renaissance (London: Phaidon Press, 1966) and Symbolic Images in the Art of the Renaissance (London: Phaiden Press, 1971). Also of interest is Paul Friedrich's The Meaning of Aphrodite (Chicago & London: The University of Chicago Press, 1978).

According to Panofsky, Iconology p. 160, pictures of sensuous Venus may be categorized as Recumbent Venus, Toilet of Venus, Feast of Venus, and Venus and Adonis.

¹⁰ Lines 17-18 in the Riverside Shakespeare, ed. G. Blakemore Evans, (Boston: Houghton Mifflin, 1974). All subsequent citations are from this edition.

¹¹ Marsilio Ficino's Commentary on Plato's Symposium, translation, introduction by Sears Reynolds Jayne (Columbia: University of Missouri, 1944), IV, 8 and VIII, 3; pp. 220-226.

In the introduction Jayne comments that although Ficino was not translated into English until recent years, his attempts to reconcile Plato's Symposium with Christianity were influential on the work of many poets and artists that may have been familiar to Shakespeare, p. 28.

¹² Ficino, II, 7, Panofsky, Iconology, p. 151.

In "Mother Venus: Temptation in Shakespeare's Venus and Adonis," Shakespeare Studies II (1978), 1-19, Wayne A. Rebhorn discusses Venus' motherly behavior at length and argues that it is more important to the poem than her lust.

¹³ Ficino II, 7, p. 142, Panofsky Studies in Iconology, p. 152.

¹⁴ The story of Lucrece was never as frequently illustrated as that of Venus and Adonis, but many of the same painters and engravers of the sixteenth century who depicted Venus, also depicted Lucrece. The nine

female worthies are found less frequently than the men. Philip Galle engraved a series after Martin de Vos which included: Lucretia, Iahel, Judith, Virginia, S. Helena, S. Brigita, Hester, Vervria, and S. Elizabeta.

[15] The use of capitalization emphasizes the allegorical implications that Lucrece is innocent that can be traced back to Ovid moralized (although, of course, Shakespeare's Ovid source is not the Metamorphosis, but the Fasti or Livy's Historia). Livy describes Lucrece as "castitas" (chaste) once in the text, but Ovid writes only that she "corrumpere non est" (is uncorrupted)-- The emphasis is Shakespeare's, and his intention is certainly to stress Lucrece's innocence and virtue; Tarquin's sin and guilt.

[16] In "Some observations on the Rape of Lucrece," Shakespeare Survey, 15 (1962), 80-98, Don Cameron Allen concludes that Shakespeare shared the general Christian evaluation of Lucrece's suicide and suggests that he may have intended to employ allegory. Coppélia Kahn argues to the contrary in "The Rape of Shakespeare's Lucrece," Shakespeare Studies IX (1976), 45-72. Kahn suggests that strong cultural forces in Roman society would support Lucrece's conviction that suicide was the sole means by which she could preserve her husband's family honor, and that Shakespeare deliberately poised these attitudes against the Christian ethic. S.E. Sprott, The English Debate on Suicide from Donne to Hume (La Salle, Illinois: Open Court, 1961), p. 1, asserts that the suicide was commonly abhorred in 1601, thereby reaffirming the traditional Christian view against self-slaughter. Alice Shalvi, The Relationship of Renaissance Concepts of Honor (Salzburg: Institut Für Englische Sprache and Literatur, 1972), p. 93, believes that the poem reflects the contemporary code of honor written in the chivalric romance.

[17] Ronald E. McKerrow, Printers and Publisher's Devices in England and Scotland (1485-1640) (London: Chiswick 1913), pp. 164, 176. Thomas Bertholetus also uses a picture of Lucrece committing suicide for his device (1554), p. 180.

[18] I have discussed the similarities between Lucrece's Troy picture and certain etchings from the School of Fontainbleau at length in "Lucrece, What hath your conceited painter wrought?" Bucknell Review, 25

(1980). Another recent article on the subject is: S. Clark Hulse, "A piece of Skilful Painting in Shakespeare's <u>Lucrece</u>," <u>Shakespeare Survey</u>, 31 (1978), 3-22.

[19] Clark Hulse sees Lucrece's death as strategy, not passion, because she recognizes that a weak and defenseless woman would be unable to carry out the execution of Tarquin alone, "A Piece of Skilful Painting," p. 20-21; however if that were the case Shakespeare could have taken the dramatic moment from Livy when Lucrece tells the story and demands the men "pledge your right hands and your words that the adulterer shall not go unpunished"--"<u>Sed date dextras fidemque haud inpune adultero fore</u>" (8). Shakespeare's Lucrece draws their attention more to her own misery and suicide. The impact of the promise is much less strong, and Brutus has to convince them to act after she has died. For a comprehensive study of Renaissance attitudes to Revenge, see Fredson Bowers, <u>Elizabethan Revenge Tragedy</u>, (Gloucester, Mass: Peter <u>Smith, 1959</u>), first published 1940.

HAMLET: SHAKESPEARE'S MANNERIST TRAGEDY

Lois Ziegelman

Among spectators and scholars alike, Shakespeare's Hamlet has often been considered a particularly uneasy play. In a departure from the traditional High Renaissance concern with balance, order, and clarity, it is filled with elements of tension, darkness, and ambiguity from beginning to end. T.S. Eliot declares: "In several ways the play is puzzling and disquieting as is none of the others. . . . Both workmanship and thought are in an unstable position. We are surely justified in attributing the play . . . to a period of crisis."[1] L.C. Knights finds that "the implicit evaluation [of Hamlet] is not so subtle or so sure as in the later plays, and one is forced to the conclusion that this play contains within itself widely different levels of experience and insight which, since they cannot be assimilated into a whole, create a total effect of ambiguity."[2] C.S. Lewis notes in the play a "curious groping and tapping of thoughts . . . [a] quality of darkness and misgiving. . . . The world of Hamlet is a world where one has lost one's way."[3] Theodore Spencer sees in the disenchantment of Hamlet himself a "partial expression of a general predicament. . . . His discovery of the difference between appearance and reality, which produced in his mind an effect so disillusioning that it paralyzed the sources of deliberate action, was a symptom that the Renaissance in general had brought with it a new set of problems, had opened new psychological vistas, which the earlier view of man had not explored."[4]

These problems and similar ones have tantalized critics for generations. Yet it appears that at least some of this mystification could be allayed by abandoning traditional norms of judgment and viewing Hamlet in a new context, that of a distinct aesthetic and ideological movement prevalent throughout Europe in Shakespeare's time. This tradition, the Mannerist tradition, with the many great works of art it produced, marked a movement of violent reaction to the stress on "objective" reality, a complete turning away from the harmony, clarity, and balance which characterized the art of the High Renaissance at its best.

It is true, of course, that the term Mannerism was first employed by art historians to refer to certain stylistic changes in the visual arts which characterized a period of disintegration falling between the High Renaissance and Baroque eras, two periods of relative stability. Yet, as the noted critic Wylie Sypher declares, "Because a style serves as a syntax of consciousness, many of the definitions of style in the visual and plastic arts should have certain uses in analyzing the structure of literary experience erected by the word. . . . Style is a mode of vision as well as a technique. Consequently if we are dealing with an authentic style . . . a structure in the fine arts will normally find its analogy in literature."[5] In accord with this belief, the various stylistic elements of Mannerism should be discernible not only in the visual arts of a period, but in the literature as well. Admittedly, a certain amount of flexibility must be maintained. After all, the visual arts are spatial in form while literature is a temporal art, to cite only one important difference. Nevertheless, even allowing for these dissimilarities, certain interesting analogs can be drawn, demonstrating many affinities between Hamlet and Mannerist painting and architecture, and it will be the purpose of this paper to do so.

In his Principles of Art History, the art historian Heinrich Wölfflin uses a scheme of polarities based on stylistic terms several of which suggest the major characteristics of Mannerist art.[6] First of all, it is "painterly," as opposed to the predominantly linear quality of High Renaissance works. In the latter, the separate parts of the work are clearly and strongly outlined, thus creating a consistent and sharply defined presentation of space. The painterly quality, on the other hand, in its blending and merging of component parts implying a surrender to mere visual experience, an abandoning of tangible design, tends to give the work a limitless aura. The interest here is in "the apprehension of the world as a shifting semblance."[7] Lights and shadows become an independent element. They seek and hold each other from height to height, from depth to depth. "It is obvious that here the immaterial and incorporeal must mean as much as concrete objects."[8]

In Tintoretto's painting The Discovery of the Body of St. Mark the above qualities are displayed. Although the standing and kneeling figures in the foreground seem sculptured, they are rendered primarily as patches of color which suggest the forms rather than model them. The figure of St. Mark, an apparition, seems, strangely enough, more tangible than the "real" figures of the kneeling old man, the searchers. Thus, the difference between appearance and reality is minimized. An air of mystery and tension is heightened by the dark shadows along the vaults in contrast to the deep red of the figures which emerge from the gloom. The arbitrary lighting, not from a natural source, adds to the sense of the supernatural.

In <u>Hamlet</u>, something of this painterly quality is suggested in the sense that Shakespeare too has "blended and merged component parts," ultimately forcing the spectator to re-create the milieu and the characters as in the painting. Is Denmark a princely kingdom where the pomp and ritual of the court with its costly revels and lavish entertainments set the tenor of life, or is it a prison in a world where there are "many confines, wards, and dungeons, Denmark being one o' the worst"? Is Gertrude the rapt and adoring wife that Hamlet's memory would suggest, or is she in reality the weak and concupiscent woman denounced by the ghost as "my most seeming-virtuous queen"? Again, is Polonius a sage whose advice to his son is both ethical and practical? His maxim "This above all, to thine own self be true," has been a moral standard for generations. Or, on the other hand, is he an insufferable old fool, whose prattle so exasperates the queen that she calls impatiently for "More matter, with less art"? Finally, what is the true extent of Hamlet's madness? Surely, at times it seems nothing but "antic disposition," as in the exchanges with Polonius in III.ii. Yet in his apology to Laertes just before the fatal duel, Hamlet declares:

> This presence knows and you must needs have heard
> How I am punished with a sore distraction.
> What I have done,
> That might your nature, honor, and exception
> Roughly awake, I here proclaim was madness.
> (V.ii.232-36)[9]

Here, a different dimension is evident. Hamlet's madness, it seems, is as often reality as it is appearance. Although he himself insists "I am but mad north-north-west, When the wind is southerly I know a hawk from a handsaw," this statement defies a logical, clear-cut interpretation, and thus leaves the whole issue of Hamlet's madness as blurred and puzzling as ever.

Light and shadow, the contrast between them, also play an important role in Hamlet. The murky tones of the scenes of the midnight watch silhouette the tensely expectant figures awaiting the appearance of the ghost against the brilliantly lighted background of the carousing court. Hamlet himself, in his "inky cloak" and "customary suits of solid black," stands out in sharp relief against the garish color and pageantry which represent the sensibility of a court where the remarriage of the bereaved queen took place so soon after the king's untimely death that "the funeral bak'd meats did coldly furnish forth the marriage table." In Hamlet too, as in the Tintoretto painting, the immaterial and incorporeal, the ghost, seems at times more real than the concrete, the actual. The presence of the ghost is continually felt. It, too, seems to direct the action, as the figure of St. Mark does in the painting. It is the ghost with his demands to be avenged who triggers the conflict within Hamlet's soul and exhorts him on when he procrastinates.

A second characteristic of Mannerist art suggested by Wölfflin is that of recession, as opposed to the plane employed by High Renaissance artists. In the latter style, objects are arranged on one fixed plane of vision, where they seem to hold the surface. In the former, however, there is no fixed plane of vision. Instead, "the eye relates objects essentially in the direction of forwards and backwards."[10]

The "Sprecher" is a feature of many Mannerist paintings. This mysterious figure, who is not only detached from the action himself but actually violates the "aesthetic distance" by drawing the spectator into the world of the painting, takes the form of a small boy standing among the mourners in El Greco's Burial of Count Orgaz and yet engaged in direct eye contact with the viewer. The work itself, found in the Church of Santo Tomé in Toledo, seems to encompass at least three different levels of space. In the center foreground is the grave, which is positioned directly over the vault in the church wall where the Count was actually interred. Surrounding the grave is the artist's depiction of the burial, the horizontal rhythms accentuated by the line of white ruffs of the Spanish grandees. The mourners seem remote, indifferent. They stare into the world of the beholder. Above them is portrayed the ascent of the Count's soul, a mystical vision featuring strong vertical rhythms. The intense commitment of the heavenly host is in marked contrast to the detachment of its earthly counterpart.

The multi-dimensional effect presented in the Burial of Count Orgaz is strongly sensed in Hamlet in the scene of the play-within-the-play. There are three dimensions discernible in this tour-de-force designed by Hamlet to "catch the conscience of the king": that of the actors of the play-within-the-play, that of the royal audience attending this entertainment, and that of the actual audience in the theatre itself. The total impression conveyed in this theatrical interlude is almost that of a "trompe l'oeil." As Harry Levin sums it up: "When Hamlet hits upon his ingenious plot, it projects him in two directions at once: back to the plane of intradramatic theatricals, and forward to the plane of his audience. A spectator of the players, he has his own spectators, who turn out to be ourselves, to whom he is actually an ACTOR. . . . Here we stand in relation to him . . . where he stands in relation to the players."[11] Quite clearly, Hamlet functions here as a Sprecher, drawing the spectator directly into the royal audience awaiting the entertainment by the company of players while, at the same time, the spectator is an observer of a greater whole--the course of Hamlet's own tragedy.

Closely related to the recessional characteristic of Mannerist art is the sense of revolving planes of vision. In Parmigianino's Madonna of the Long Neck, one senses a continually changing angle of vision from the lack of consistent proportion exhibited throughout. The Madonna, though she has the legs and thighs of a giantess, has a very small elongated neck and head. The baby in her lap is disproportionately enormous, and in addition, is placed at a most precarious angle. The figure of a prophet, although it seems to stand in the immediate background, is small enough in relationship to the other figures to be a hundred light years away. These anomalies mark a real departure from the observance of a regular canon of proportions by High Renaissance artists in order to achieve an "idealized and normative objectivization."[12] Perhaps, then, the strangeness in the proportion of the figures in Parmigianino's painting can be ascribed at least partially to the Mannerist artist's desire to escape the tyranny of conforming to a normative standard in order to express his own inner vision.

Perhaps the revolving point of view is best exemplified in <u>Hamlet</u> by the problem of determining what Hamlet's "true" nature really is, and it is here especially that an important difference between the media must be acknowledged. In the painting, the revolving point of view functions in a spatial context. Through the eyes of imaginary beholders viewing the scene simultaneously, all of the various angles are visible at once. In the play, on the other hand, the various perspectives are conveyed through the words and deeds of the characters themselves, and are revealed only as the action unfolds in time. Nevertheless, both the painting and play are justifiable as examples of the revolving point of view because in each case no objective norm is evident, only a series of subjective impressions. Polonius sees Hamlet as a man whose vows are:

> But mere implorators of unholy suits
> Breathing like sanctified and pious bawds,
> The better to beguile.
> (I.iii.129-31)

Claudius declares: "Like the hectic in my blood he rages." Ophelia sees him, from another angle, as "The glass of fashion and the mould of form," but this impression is almost immediately usurped by a vision of "That unmatch'd form and feature of blown youth/ Blasted with ecstasy."

Developing even further the sense of revolving vision are Hamlet's own mercurial moods. In the closet scene he reprimands Gertrude with passionate frenzy, yet a few moments later, he speaks with cool detachment of the murdered Polonius.

Finally, there is Hamlet's unpredictable metamorphosis from the warm school companion who greets Guildenstern and Rosencrantz as "my excellent good friends" to the dispassionate schemer who coolly dispatches them to their deaths, declaring "They are not near my conscience."

Thus, the viewpoint for observing Hamlet revolves and revolves and never comes to rest, not even at his death--for even the nobility and tragedy of the ending is marred by the reportage of the cruel and gratuitous killing of Rosencrantz and Guildenstern, and by Horatio's coupling of Hamlet's "accidental judgments" (the killing of Polonius) and "casual slaughters" (the consigning of his unlucky schoolmates to their deaths) with the "carnal, bloody, and unnatural acts" of Claudius--implying that all acts are of the same magnitude in a world where the only point of view is a revolving one.

A third characteristic of Mannerist art suggested by Wölfflin is that of open form. This is opposed to the closed form characteristic of High Renaissance art. In the latter, the work is self-contained in its frame, tectonic. The proportions are balanced and ordered, and the effect is that of harmony and unity. Open form, by contrast, is atectonic. There is a relaxing of the rules of self-containment. "The filling has lost touch with the frame,"[13] and everything is done to avoid the impression that a particular composition was invented for a particular surface. "Treatment of space in mannerist architecture and painting shows this change from the 'closed' renaissance world order to the 'open,' 'loose,' and deviating notions in the mannerist universe."[14]

Michelangelo's Laurentian Library manifests a sense of insecurity and irrationality in its restless, curving lines substituted for the High Renaissance sense of equilibrium. The steps are insecure, liquid in their fluidity. Columns strain like prisoners to be free of their wall niches. The windows are false, and the only light comes from the top. The interior of the library has been likened to a wind tunnel, and the vestibule to a mine shaft: both images suggesting a bottomless, endless abyss rather than any self-containment of structure. The total effect is one of tension, insecurity, instability, with much irrationality manifested in the "functionless" function of the columns which are given nothing to hold up and the windows which are unable to admit any light.

Mannerist painting, too, is characterized by this open form, this straining against the limits imposed by the frame. In The Discovery of the Body of St. Mark, although the space is partially enclosed at the further end of the vault, a small opening is left, allowing the observer to look beyond it and wonder. In the Last Judgment, considered to be Michelangelo's most Mannerist work, the spiralling, overlapping masses of human bodies seem, in their tortuous vertical rhythms, to strain unbearably against the "arbitrary" frame imposed upon them.

This tension, this sense of straining against limits, is also felt in Hamlet, in the breaking of the smooth, regular poetic line by dramatic exclamations, stacatto effects, and jerky rhythms. The best verbal analogs for open form are Hamlet's great soliloquies. Note the beginning of the first of these:

> O that this too too solid flesh would melt,
> Thaw and resolve itself into a dew!
> O that the everlasting had not fix'd
> His canon 'gainst self-slaughter! O God!
>   O God!
> How weary, stale, flat, and unprofitable
> Seem to me all the uses of this world.
> Fie on't! Ah, fie...
>   (I.ii.129-35)

These lines, as well as exhibiting a sense of straining in their enjambment and violent punctuation, reveal an interesting pattern in their repetition of key words and phrases--a pattern which Henry Levin finds consistently employed throughout the play in various forms. "The texture of the verse is characterized by a tendency to double and redouble words and phrases. From the very first scene, the speeches abound in hendiadys: 'gross and scope,' 'law and heraldry.' Sometimes the paired nouns are redundant synonyms: 'food and diet,' 'pith and moment'. . . . These figures are doubtless more ornamental than functional; yet they charge the air with overtones of wavering and indecision."[15]

Again, the famous "to be or not to be" soliloquy engenders the same feeling as the abyss-like appearance of the Laurentian Library, the treatment of space as a coulisse in The Discovery of the Body of St. Mark. If to die were to end:

> The heart-ache and the thousand natural
>   shocks
> That flesh is heir to: 'Tis a consummation
> Devoutly to be wish'd. To die: to sleep.
>   (III.i.62-64)

However, as in the painting, a small opening is left, allowing the observer to look beyond and wonder...

> To sleep? perchance to dream. Aye, there's
>   the rub;
> For in that sleep of death what dreams may
>   come,
> When we have shuffled off this mortal coil,
> May give us pause.
>   (III.i.65-68)

Thus, there is no concept of "limit," even in death--just a never-ending abyss of ills.

A final characteristic suggested by Wölfflin is that of relative clarity of subject, as opposed to the absolute clarity featured in High Renaissance art. In the latter, all elements such as color and light are employed exclusively to define distinctly the objects represented. In Mannerist art, by contrast, the clear explication of the subject is no longer the sole purpose of the presentation. The artist is more interested in the working of his own mind--of his own creative consciousness upon the matter presented. As a result, "the pictorial appearance no longer coincides with the maximum of objective clearness, but evades it."16

This emphasis, this stress on "disegno interno," is found in many Mannerist portraits. Gone are the ideal types found in High Renaissance art. Taking their place in works by Pontormo, Parmigianino, and El Greco, is a series of tense, strained, anxious figures who, steeped in melancholic introspection, seem to avoid ever coming into contact with objective reality. One of the most inscrutable of these, Parmigianino's <u>Self-Portrait</u>, records what the artist saw as he gazed at <u>his reflec</u>tion in a specially prepared convex mirror. What was there so fascinating about this view in which, although his head seems to be of normal proportion, his hand is disproportionally enlarged? "Did he perhaps want to demonstrate that there is no such thing as a single, 'correct' reality, that distortion is as natural as the normal appearance of things?"[17]

Surely there is much evidence of "disegno interno" in Hamlet, as well. The fact alone that there are seven important soliloquies indicates that Shakespeare is concerned here with the workings of a particular mind--with Hamlet's introspective activity. All objective issues are deflected towards this inward focus. Hamlet, too, seems paralyzed by excessive introspection. Much self-examination has made clear to him his weakness; and yet, somehow, he is unable to act. Again, like Parmigianino, Hamlet too seems fascinated with mirrors. In the closet scene he threatens Gertrude: "You go not till I set you up a glass/ Where you may see the inmost part of you." Yet as Harley Granville-Barker remarks: "It is his own disposition that prompts this image. He is always looking at himself in the glass of his conscience."[18] And, as Parmigianino does, Hamlet also finds distortion, for the eye of the mind can no more reflect objective reality than can a deliberately chosen convex mirror.

So much, then, for the stylistic aspects of Mannerism. Going one step further, there are interesting ideational parallels as well between Hamlet and Mannerist art.

The world envisaged by the Mannerists is a world where the Renaissance concept of man as a superior creature who occupied the center of the universe has been despoiled and discarded in much the same way that the magnificent sculptorly figures of the early Michelangelo have given way to the attenuated and anguished creations of his old age. In the Rome Pietà of 1488-99, the anatomical perfection of the figures portrays their humanity; yet the classical restraint, perfect calmness, and sobriety even in the midst of grief give a divine aura to the work. Only a self-confident artist, working at the peak of his creative power, could have rendered this vision with such sublimity. As he grew older, however, Michelangelo became not only more pessimistic about man's place in the scheme of things, but also about his own power as an artist to release the spirit from the stone.[19] Hence the radical change manifested in the Rondanini Pietà, created a half century later. Here the distorted, almost Gothic forms rise up restlessly, but are never completely liberated from the rough-textured marble. The artist seems to be groping for new means of expression, as if his previous work had become meaningless to him--and indeed, he died while still in the process of trying to formulate this new vision. These two works, then, viewed together, suggest a fundamental dualism in man's nature--a basic conflict between man's greatness and his wretchedness--between the grandeur and misery of the human condition.

In <u>Hamlet</u>, too, there is the same dualism evident in Hamlet's vision of man as a creature "crawling between earth and heaven," at the same time "the beauty of the world" and a "quintessence of dust." This denigration of man leads to a condemnation of man's bodily needs, with especial revulsion toward his sexuality, evoked in a series of loathsome images:

>...lust, though to a radiant angel link'd,
>will sate itself in a celestial bed,
>and prey on garbage.
> (III.viii.32-34)

>   Nay, but to live
>in the rank sweat of an enseamed bed,
>Stew'd in corruption, honeying and making love
>Over the nasty sty...
> (III.iv.92-95)

>Not this, by no means, that I bid you do:
>Let the bloat king tempt you again to bed,
>Pinch wanton on your cheek, call you his
>   mouse;
>And let him, for a pair of reechy kisses,
>Or paddling in your neck with his damn'd
>   fingers,
>Make you to ravel all this matter out.
> (III.iv.181-86)

This unwholesome depiction of sex is analogous to a disturbing note of eroticism found in many Mannerist paintings. Bronzino's <u>Venus Disarming Cupid</u> is a prime example. Although ostensibly a playful encounter, the scene offends the sensibilities. The lascivious expressions and posturings of the figures, their nakedness emphasized by the cold colors the artist has used to depict them, suggest that sex is ugly, gross, distasteful. The text could well be taken from the above images in <u>Hamlet</u>.

In the Mannerist world, where the High Renaissance concepts of order, balance, and limit have been replaced by chaos, excess, and change, there is only one certainty left--the certainty of death. Is it any wonder, then, that death plays such an important part in Mannerist painting? The figures of El Greco, especially, are emblematic of death in their extreme attenuation, their ghostly pallor. They seem little more than skeletal forms, uncannily imaging forth Hamlet's wish "that this too too solid flesh would melt,/ Thaw and resolve itself into a dew!"

As in Mannerist painting, the concern with death pervades <u>Hamlet</u>. A death motivates the action and many deaths culminate the action. Throughout the play death is seen in many diverse forms ranging from "casual slaughters" to "deaths put on by cunning and forc'd cause." The reminder of death is constantly with the living. Hamlet's "inky Cloak" casts a perpetual shadow over the feverish gaiety of the Danish court. The scene that is most Mannerist, however, in its treatment of death and perhaps in every other way, stylistic and ideological--so much so that it epitomizes all that is Mannerist in the play--is the graveyard scene, a scene which surely finds its analog in Holbein's series of forty-one woodcuts known as the <u>Dance of Death</u>. In these vignettes depicting death as the ultimate fate of all men regardless of their earthly status, the grimness of the subject is supposed to keep the pious in line. Yet in its execution, this grimness is undercut by the lively and egalitarian skeleton, always playing his part with ironic gallantry.

The same irony, the same controversion of the notion of "degree," is found in the graveyard scene, in Hamlet's <u>sic transit</u> meditation on the relics of the pompous and the powerful, now consigned to rubble. Perhaps most significant is his conjecture on the end of man: "To what base uses we may return, Horatio! Why may not imagination trace the noble dust of Alexander till 'a find it stopping a bunghole?"

>Alexander died, Alexander was buried, Alexander returneth to dust; the dust is earth. Of earth we make loam, and why of that loam, whereto he was converted, might they not stop a beer-barrel?
>Imperious Caesar, dead and turn'd to clay, Might stop a hole to keep the wind away.

> O that that earth, which kept the world
>   in awe,
> Should patch a wall t'expel the winter's
>   flaw!
>
> (V.i.213-22)

Is this, then, a fitting end for a creature "noble in reason," "infinite in faculties," "the beauty of the world"? Here, in the deceptively casual cynicism of this "curious" speculation, Hamlet strikes the chill chord of anxiety which sounds at the very heart of the play, the same anxiety which motivates the straining and striving toward God, the restless vertical rhythms of the figures of Michelangelo and El Greco--the haunting anxiety that cannot be resolved--the ever-gnawing fear that all of the lofty philosophizing, all of the measured meditation on "the undiscover'd country from whose bourn no traveller returns," all of the concern with the ritual of burial and the proper moment for revenge--all this is gratuitous claptrap. The only reality--stark and grim--is the "quintessence of dust."

In summary, the use of this interdisciplinary approach, through which literature and art can be seen as sharing the same stylistic and ideological qualities, serves to corroborate the principle so important to the conception of history that every era has its own particular spirit which pervades all its activities: its art, its philosophy, its science, its religion, even its hopes and its illusions. Furthermore, this approach suggests that we can visualize, through the work of the artist, the most perceptive representative of this spirit, the "index to the structure of contemporary consciousness."[20]

Thus, by approaching _Hamlet_ as a Mannerist work, one can gain not only an _insight_ into the stylistic methods Shakespeare has employed in this great drama, but also an inkling of the contemporary consciousness that shaped the ideas with which he has dealt.

NOTES

[1] "Hamlet and his Problems," in *Discussions of Hamlet*, ed. J.C. Levenson (Boston: D.C. Heath and Company, 1960), p. 48.

[2] "*Prince Hamlet*," in Levenson, p. 82.

[3] "Hamlet: The Prince or the Poem," in *Shakespeare's Tragedies: An Anthology of Modern Criticism*, ed. Laurence Lerner (London: Penguin Books Ltd., 1963), pp. 71-72.

[4] "Hamlet and the Nature of Reality," in *Hamlet*, ed. Cyrus Hoy Norton Critical Edition (New York: W.W. Norton & Company, 1963), p. 214.

[5] *Four Stages of Renaissance Style* (Garden City: Doubleday & Company, Inc., 1955), pp. 17, 30.

[6] New York: Dover Publications, Inc., 1932. Although Wölfflin's dominant concern in this work and most of his other writings was to establish the validity of the Baroque era as a distinctive period in its own right, many of the qualities he defined seem to apply even better to Mannerist art.

[7] Wölfflin, p. 14.

[8] Wölfflin, p. 20.

[9] William Shakespeare, *Hamlet*, ed. Tucker Brooke & Jack Randall Crawford (New Haven: Yale University Press, 1971). All subsequent references are to this edition.

[10] Wölfflin, p. 15.

[11] "An Explication of the Player's Speech," *Hamlet*, ed. Cyrus Hoy (New York: W.W. Norton & Company, 1963), p. 236.

[12] Walter Friedlaender, *Mannerism and Anti-Mannerism in Italian Painting* (New York: Columbia University Press, 1957), p. 1.

[13] Wölfflin, p. 125.

[14] Sypher, p. 134.

[15] The Question of Hamlet (New York: The Viking Press, 1961), p. 49.

[16] Wölfflin, p. 196.

[17] H.W. Janson, History of Art (Englewood Cliffs: Prentice-Hall, Inc., 1962), p. 375.

[18] Prefaces to Shakespeare, I (London: B.T. Batsford Ltd., 1963), 290.

[19] Janson, p. 369.

[20] Sypher, p. 21.

THE ICONOGRAPHY OF ILLUSION AND TRUTH IN THE WINTER'S TALE

Clifford Davidson

The spectacle of Shakespeare's drama on stage in his own time made use of scenes which carefully balanced meanings and mirrored human actions or frailties in a theater which was, as Glynne Wickham has suggested, "emblematic" rather than illusionistic in the sense of "seeming to stimulate actuality."[1] To be sure, the term emblematic as used here perhaps needs careful definition, since stage actions are not always to be identified with either the precise form or function of the emblem in the Renaissance emblem book. The latter is often reductive in its interpretation of visual details; as Francis Bacon defined the genre, "Emblems reduce [italics mine] intellectual conceptions to sensible images, and that which is sensible more forcibly strikes the memory and is more easily imprinted on it than that which is intellectual."[2] On stage, however, such a reductive approach to the nature of the scene would perhaps only be applicable in plays of overtly didactic content (e.g., John Bale's King John or Sackville and Norton's Gorboduc), while the emblematic element instead normally functions to provide a broader meaning than would seem superficially to be present. The emblematic scene on stage thus would be consistent with E.N.S. Thompson's broader definition of the emblem as "any figure . . . or, in fact, any picture signifying more than is actually delineated."[3]

The absence of painted scene or realistic backdrop against which a drama might be played focused attention on such elements as gesture and the tableaux formed by the actors appearing on the stage before the audience. Characterization is also given added weight, especially by the use of symbolic costume and disguise--elements especially underlined for us by the fact of doubling by the actors, each of whom would often play more than one role in a play.[4] Of course, from the perspective of the twentieth century, the visual side of the performance of drama in the Renaissance may seem to be a very ephemeral aspect of play performance; nevertheless, that which was seen needs to be recognized to have been highly significant--as significant for study, surely, as the bare text of the play itself. Much as we might wish to limit ourselves to the tangible words of the text and perhaps also to that which is presented to "the mind's eye" through imagery, we do need to know that from a scholarly standpoint we are shirking our critical responsibility unless we attempt to come to grips with at least those iconographic elements in the spectacle which are accessible to us.[5]

The urgency of such a task is surely underlined for us by recent studies in cognition which demonstrate how the <u>visual</u> level functions in learning, which cannot be restricted to what is known through <u>language</u> alone.[6] We are reminded that, though Renaissance humanism tended to devalue pictorial knowledge,[7] Shakespeare's age still inherited from the Middle Ages a real sense of the importance of the function of sight. As Samuel Daniel wrote, "<u>to represent unto the sence of sight the forme or figure of any thing, is more natural in act, and more common to al creatures then is hearing, and thereupon sayth Aristotle, that we love the sence of seeing, for that by it we are taught and made to learne more then by any other of our senses</u>. . . ."[8]

An iconographic approach to The Winter's Tale therefore needs to be more than a mere imagery study, but rather it must take up in a systematic way the handling of visual motifs as set forth through the spectacle of drama itself on stage. We need to understand precisely through our study how the iconographic material is utilized and for what purpose. In this regard, we will surely note from the outset that the function and purpose of the visual display in The Winter's Tale are distinctly different from what we would encounter, for example, in the ritual forms of the liturgical drama in which the action is principally designed (if we may use Heideggerian terminology) to achieve the direct and immediate deconcealment of Being through an iconic dramaturgy.[9] In The Winter's Tale, the ritual of the earlier drama plays no part, and hence we find a dramaturgy that represents actuality without the aid of either the theology of the religious image--an essential ingredient in the iconic drama of the twelfth century--or strict verisimilitude and scenic illusion.

In <u>The Winter's Tale</u>, the framework is indeed not liturgy or ritual but <u>play</u> (it would almost be tempting to use the word <u>game</u>, a term also associated with drama as _play_ in medieval criticism).[10] _Play_ hence acts to mirror the activity of the world by reflecting its rules and by aping its motions. As the Puritan critics of the stage constantly remind us, what we see before us as members of the audience is not literally true but is a rearrangement of reality; stage players are "hypocrites," for their outward seeming is not consistent with their inner persons. A stage player, as Hamlet reminds us, is one who "But in a fiction, in a dream of passion,/ Could force his soul so to his own conceit/ That from her working all the visage wann'd,/ Tears in his eyes, distraction in his aspect,/ A broken voice, an' his whole function suiting/ With forms to his conceit? And all for nothing. . ." (_Hamlet_ II.ii.557-62).[11] The art of play, even more than _art_ of a work of the visual arts, is _seeming_, _insubstantial_, _shadowy_ when compared to the substance of actual life. A play such as _The Winter's Tale_ is perhaps more dependent upon such insubstantial elements than, for example, one of Shakespeare's histories or tragedies, for this late romance takes as its source a prose narrative that is as improbable as any source to which he turned his dramatizing pen. Though transformed into a _play_, the title and text of _The Winter's Tale_ still seem to maintain that it is a "tale" in form and substance. As such, it has frequently been called an ill-made play, broken in its center by a "gap" of sixteen years that is bridged only by the emblematic figure of Time, intruding to gloss over the alleged mismanagement of plot and action.[12]

    In spite of its seeming flaws, however, _The Winter's Tale_ illustrates in the _playing_ of its action how the mirroring of man's imperfect seeing (for Leontes' jealousy is perhaps above all itself a failure of _sight_) becomes convincing in its own terms, and by the end of the play we see events which we believe are actually somehow able to reveal _truth_.[13] As the Pygmalion story which helps to inform Shakespeare's play suggests, art may be able to come alive when its beauty is impelled by love toward transcendental experience. The clue is perhaps to be found, as Inga-Stina Ewbank suggested in an article published in 1964, on the title page of Shakespeare's principal source, Robert Greene's _Pandosto_, where the story is presented as an example of "The Triumph of Time" and the motto chosen for the narrative is "_Tempora filia veritas_."[14] The motto, as Professor Ewbank demonstrates, is of very great importance for our understanding of the iconography of the play; through the function of Time (the figure that appears allegorically at the beginning of Act IV), Truth is brought to light at the moment of the deconcealment of Hermione--a surprise intended for audience as well as for the characters on the stage. At the deepest level, therefore, it might be relevant to note that the conventional illustration of Tempora filia veritas shows Time bringing his daughter Truth out of a cave in a manner reminiscent of the Harrowing of Hell, when Christ on Saturday of Holy Week grasps the forearm of Adam as he steps forth from darkness following the soteriological work on the cross which has made triumph over time's bondage possible.[15] (Fig. 1) The recovery of truth in The Winter's Tale, like the release of Adam, brings with it a vindication of the value of penitence extended over a period of years (though, to be sure, Leontes' period of penitence is nothing like the 4000 winters during which Adam lay bound in limbo), and likewise it shows the role of love in the triumph of that which is transcendentally true.

But when Time appears as a character on stage at the beginning of Act IV, he represents not the figure of Tempora filia veritas but rather the figure of the visual spectacle of the Triumph, the equivalent on stage of the popular literary triumphs of Petrarch.[16] The scene is a simple one, with Time pointing out his familiar attributes--his wings and his hour glass. Like the Triumph of Time as it appears in the visual arts--e.g., in Brueghel's engraving of Time's triumph[17] --Shakespeare's character has the power to bring to life and to destroy--"in one self-born hour/ To plant and o'erwhelm custom" (IV.i.8-9). (Fig. 2) That which Time has brought into being, he will also terminate--a fact of life illustrated in the engraving by Brueghel by the detail of his infant which he is devouring. In The Winter's Tale, Time's glass abrogates the laws of nature and, proclaiming a "wide gap" of sixteen years, sets in motion the final portion of the play, which will focus upon providential events that will conclude in a scene marked by wonder. As a triumphal figure, Time as chorus indeed (in Nevill Coghill's words) "stands at the turn of tide of mood, from tragedy to comedy, and makes a kind of pause at the play's centre."[19] But because in the play the normal order of the triumph is reversed-- destructive forces are presented in the first three acts, and the creative ones are illustrated in Acts IV-V--the theme of the play becomes renewal, as a closer examination of the iconographic tableaux of the drama will demonstrate.

Donald Stauffer's Shakespeare's World of Images insists that The Winter's Tale "proceeds in its pictures: the court of justice, the reading of the oracle, the swooning of Hermione, the dancing on the shepherd's green, the unveiling of the statue with Leontes silently weeping."[20] From the standpoint of the play's spectacle, these scenes are all ones with iconographic meaning. The play opens with two scenes that visually underline the friendship of two princes, whose association dates back to childhood innocence when "there rooted betwixt them then such an affection which cannot choose but branch now" (I.i.23-24). Leontes and Polixenes participate in that classical sharing of friendship of which Cicero's De Amicitia had provided the precepts.[21] With the passage of time, the friendship has endured, almost surpassing for them their loyalty to the nations which they lead. As their friendship is "rooted" in their childhood, so it will be seen as necessarily sustained by the truthfulness of their relationship. It is no accident also that Cesare Ripa in his Iconologia personified Friendship in terms of "a fair young blonde woman, simply draped in the white color of truth, upon which friendship is based. She points to her bosom, the seat of the heart."[22] (Fig. 3). Without forcing Ripa's allegory onto the play, it is nevertheless curious that this drama should in its second scene focus the audience's attention upon the two friends, one of whom wishes the other to extend his visit, and upon the queen of the host. That queen, Hermione, will, of course, take her place in the revelation of truth in the last scene of the play. Yet it is enough to see the iconography of this scene in terms of a visual exposition of friendship and of Hermione's chaste devotion to her husband's wishes.

The growth of the friendship between man and man will, however, be cut off all too quickly. The friendship tableau will be replaced by another kind of emblematic scene--an illustration of jealousy that bears comparison with Othello. Leontes, watching but not hearing his wife and friend talking--she is attempting to convince Polixenes to stay longer in Sicily in order to please her husband--suddenly is struck by a kind of insanity that pierces him to the heart. The effect has been compared to the mental transformation of Macbeth (described in <u>Macbeth</u> I.iii.130-42);[23] it is as if Leontes, like Macbeth, has suddenly been bewitched and cut off from even good sense. The mutation occurs in his mind and transforms him into a monster, with his new hatred being expressed in both face and gesture in spite of his efforts to hide what is within his heart. Leontes' sight has failed him: this dangerously deceitful sense, which is so strongly involved in male sexual fantasies and which hence is often deeply responsible for consequent feelings of guilt, here paradoxically traps him into believing more than would literally have been possible in the given situation--i.e., that his pregnant queen had been made with child by his friend very, very early in his nine-months' visit. Leontes' unwilling (for jealousy is not something that he chose freely) suspension of belief turns him into a tyrant, whose actions now will serve as the spring for the tragic action up to his conversion in Act III, when he finally is made to <u>see</u> the truth about his self-deception. At last in Act III he knows that he has been <u>blinded</u> by his passion, which has severed him from the <u>devotion</u> to truth that is so necessary for a ruler, husband, and friend.

In the interim between his blinding and the moment when, figuratively speaking, he receives his sight again, Leontes' inward rage and outward malice both display themselves. Fortunately, Camillo, whom he attempts to solicit to murder Polixenes, instead tells the guest of his danger--a danger that is grounded in the "sickness" that as a healthy man he has ironically communicated to his host. Camillo explains that the Sicilian king has become convinced "as he had seen't" that his guest has "touch'd his queen/ Forbiddenly" (I.ii.415-17). The first act then ends with the establishment of a plan of escape for Polixenes and Camillo, whose new loyalties are based on his integrity and truthfulness. For the "rare" Hermione, however, there is no such easy escape. Act II shows Leontes as calumniator, convinced of her faithlessness now that Polixenes has slipped away. Accusing Camillo and calling him a go-between who must have served the guest in his affair with the queen, he expresses the fears of a paranoid person no longer capable of friendship of love:

> There is a plot against my life, my crown;
> All's true that is mistrusted. . . .
>
> (II.i.47-48)

The words are ironic in their context, for indeed he is mistrusting all that is true. And his distrust makes him a dangerous man indeed. In contrast to Leontes' distraught demeanor, the queen, however, is the model of patience. The charges, of course, are totally beyond credibility.

Leontes, unable to rest either by night or day, is closely related to Shakespeare's other stage tyrants. Like Macbeth, he feels that through the unjust taking of life he can make himself whole and healthy of mind once more, and in the meantime he is unable to sleep. Not even the new-born Perdita can affect him in a natural or healthy way, and he orders her death, which is commuted to exposure in "some remote and desert place" (II.iii.175). The scene on stage is frightening. A king who thus destroys his own child is as guilty of crime as Herod, the archetypal child-murderer whose role in the slaying of Innocents was often graphically illustrated, as in a painted glass of c.1500 from Fairford, Gloucestershire.[24] It is hard to see how Leontes, possessed as he is of the irrational belief that his queen is "disloyal," can insure the "just and open trial" that he promises at the conclusion of the second act. "While she lives/ My heart will be a burden to me," he comments (II.iii.204-05).

The central scene of Act III will present "this sessions" in which Leontes will expect to "be clear'd/ of being tyrannous" (III.ii.1-5). The tableau we see on stage is a symbolic court of law with the king as prosecutor and judge. Hermione, in the dock, protests her innocence with dignity, while Leontes presents a caricature of the tyrannical husband and king whose insane dreams have become the basis of his wild actions. Ultimately, in the context of this mad court of law wherein the law is being violated so grossly, she must call on the oracle of Apollo, the pagan source of truth which is appropriate to the romance form that lies beneath the structure of The Winter's Tale. Where all else fails, she will appeal to the divine revelation which the oracle will provide. And, contrary to Leontes' expectation, the oracle gives quite different testimony than the king had expected or desired:

> Hermione is chaste; Polixenes blameless;
> Camillo a true subject; Leontes a jealous
> tyrant; his innocent babe truly begotten; and

> the king shall live without an heir, if that
> which is lost be not found. (III.ii.132-36)

Blasphemously, the tyrant Leontes charges the oracle with untruth--"There is no truth at all i' th' oracle" (III.ii.140)--and insists against reason that the "sessions shall proceed; this is mere falsehood" (III.ii.141). Providential retribution seems quick, however: a messenger with stunning immediacy reports that the prince and heir to the throne has died, and the queen first faints and then apparently quickly dies. Leontes' conversion to reason has not come soon enough to prevent disaster; the forces he has set in motion in this emblematic trial scene will seem to bear ill fruit.

Fully as emblematic in its structure is the next scene in the play in which Perdita is exposed on the desert shore of Bohemia. Not surprisingly, the heavens show their anger, and the storm that breaks upon the scene is symbolic of the terrible destruction that has been loosed by the ill-tuned music of Leontes' mad jealousy and tyrannical malice. The audience now is being confronted with what William Blissett has called "the hungry center of The Winter's Tale"[25] since Antigonus with his small burden is literally caught between shipwreck and a wild beast--a bear intruding on the stage. The tempest, as Blissett explains, illustrates time gone awry and demonstrating its most destructive aspect.[26] But we are not quite at the play's center after all, for Perdita, that "Blossom" whom Antigonus has placed on the ground (III.iii.46), will in fact be spared and rescued by shepherds on a day that they will regard as "lucky" (III.iii.136). The true center of the drama, as previously noted, will only come at the beginning of Act IV when the audience sees Time turning his glass and reversing the fortunes of those in need of renewal.

As a source of renewal, Shakespeare turns to the ground on which Perdita has been exposed, to nature, and to a scene remarkably different from the treacheries of the court that have been exposed in Acts I-III of the play. As Adam's ultimate redemption was tied up with his working of the soil and his husbandry (see, for example, his penitent figure with spade in hand in the glass of Canterbury Cathedral),[27] so also from the earth will come the renewal that will bring a successful conclusion at the close of The Winter's Tale. Quite appropriately, Soji Iwasaki has called attention to the printer's mark of John Knoblouch of Strassburg, which shows Truth emerging from the earth like a flower in a graphic illustration of Psalm 85:11.[28] Perdita, Nature's child, is as closely associated with truth as her mother. Furthermore, as a daughter she is emblematic of renewal and growth--elements that are reflected in the linking of Perdita with Flora, the classical goddess of flowers who is often associated with Venus and the season of spring.[29]

    In her dual role as queen of the sheep-shearing feast and as Flora, Perdita is a hostess who gives flowers to those in her presence, and in so doing she provides a traditional function associated with the flower goddess.[30] Her perfect grace and natural royalty, of course, are what captivate Florizel, whose name indicates that he is an appropriate husband for Perdita in her aspect as Flora.[31] Everything that is falsely artificial has been purged from her character, and she herself without question "shares/ with great creating nature" (IV.iv.86-87). In the play, art is mended by Nature.[32]

    For the careful scholar, it may therefore be disconcerting to turn to what the Renaissance mythographers have to say about Flora, who was, according to Abraham Fraunce, originally a "strumpet" of ancient Rome who left her wealth to the city and was for this reason made "a goddes of flowres."[33] Such a view of Flora was widely held in Shakespeare's time, and this explanation of her origin continued up to Dr. William King's <u>An Historical Account of the Heathen Gods and Heroes</u> (1710). In the visual arts, Flora as a courtesan thus is not surprisingly a fairly common subject.[34] In a popular Elizabethan form, the text of John Wilbye's madrigal "Flora gave me fairest flowers" echoes the libertine tradition as it was united with pastoralism: "Smiling meadows seem to say: Come, ye wantons, here to play."[35] No ironic undercurrents seem present in Shakespeare's presentation of Perdita-Flora, however, and it would hence appear that the playwright intended a straightforward portrait of the young woman in a manner that would compare favorably with Spenser's lovely Pastorella in <u>The Faerie Queene</u>.

    Very influential in Shakespeare's time was the account of Flora in Ovid's <u>Fasti</u>, V.183ff. Here Flora is depicted as one whose "lips breathed vernal roses."[36]

She is the wife of Zephyr, and formerly was called (in Greek) by the name of Chloris. "I enjoy perpetual spring," she explains. She is shown in the same scene with the three Graces, as in Botticelli's famous Primavera, a painting which may be recognized as illuminating some aspects of the Whitsun pastorals celebrated in Shakespeare's The Winter's Tale. Of course, it is not possible to suggest that Shakespeare had ever seen Botticelli's painting, but in certain ways the pattern of renewal traced forth by the painter is also the pattern of the play. Storm and destruction in the play are followed by spring with its festivities and its flowers. There are dances which suggest the integrative function of the festival in The Winter's Tales--dances which pattern themselves rudely after and also perhaps parody the perfection of the dance of the Graces. In Botticelli's painting, if Edgar Wind is correct, Flora is seen at the right separating herself from Chloris, who is behind her.[37] At the left, the Graces inscribe the neo-Platonic pattern of descent, rapture, and return--precisely the pattern of renewal which will fill things and persons with renewed life--while Venus holds up her hand in blessing. So in the play the burned-out world of Sicilia with its heirless and grieving king is countered by the green countryside of Bohemia, where Nature re-activates human lives and brings them into proper focus through the power of love. Even when the old world of the court intrudes into the tableau to attempt to divorce Perdita and Florizel, the young lovers nevertheless will be able to overcome all potential barriers to a richer and fuller life in which the audience seems invited to participate imaginatively. Like Prosperpina, who is mentioned in The Winter's Tale IV.iv.116, Perdita illustrates the rebirth of the green world within the context of the season of spring--a context which is echoed in the characters of the play. In her presence, even the roguish Autolycus is forced to reform.

The final tableau of the play is, of course, its most famous. Here, as we have seen, the revelation of Hermione's statue and of its true nature is to be regarded as reflecting Tempora filia veritas. There are, as we would expect, some problems with any simplistic application of this iconography, since Hermione is in fact the appearance of a standing polychrome statue (and not, therefore, the expected piece of funerary sculpture)[38] placed on a pedestal or base.

And here Time does not take her by the forearm, but rather the statue herself steps down and takes Leontes by the hand. This is done to the accompaniment of music, which provides the harmony against which the achievement of harmony in the royal family of Sicily in its relationship with the royal family of Bohemia will be concluded. Because the lost Perdita has been found, the prediction of the oracle now can be fulfilled: Hermione can be restored to her husband in a scene which is designed to stir wonder in the audience.[39]

    The tableaux of the play illustrate how family and friends have been "dissevered" for sixteen years--a "wide gap of time" indeed--and now they are once more brought together and united. Reconciliation has, through the marvelous stagecraft of Shakespeare, been effected. In spite of the tragic elements in Acts I-III, the visual display in The Winter's Tale has been ultimately recreative in its function--and the recreative aspect has been health-giving both within the structure of the play and for the audience. However, from another perspective the play has also dealt directly with human experience--with illusion and truth at their deepest levels--in a way that has been more _true_ than any abstract description of such events. Error has been overcome, and truth has been finally established. The spectacle and play performed before and after "this wide gap of time" separating Acts III and IV ultimately dissolve into music and dancing, which confirm what an insubstantial pageant this winter's tale has been made of. But as emblematic drama, it has also signified much more than has been on its surface presented for the audience to see and hear.

Fig. 1 Truth as the Daughter of Time. From Lancelot Andrewes, <u>The Wonderfull Combate betweene Christ and Satan</u> (1592).

Fig. 2 Detail from Brueghel, Triumph of Time.

Fig. 3 Friendship. From Cesare Ripa, *Iconologia* (Venice, 1669). Author's copy.

NOTES

[1] Glynne Wickham, Early English Stages, 1300 to 1660 (London: Routledge and Kegan Paul, 1963), II, Pt. 1, 155. See also my "Death in His Court: Iconography in Shakespeare's Tragedies," Studies in Iconography, 1 (1975), 74-86.

[2] De Augmentis Scientiarum, V, 5, as quoted in E.N.S. Thompson, Literary Bypaths of the Renaissance (New Haven: Yale Univ. Press, 1924), p. 32.

[3] Thompson, p. 33.

[4] See especially David M. Bevington, From Mankind to Marlowe (Cambridge: Harvard Univ. Press, 1962), passim.

[5] See my "Death in His Court," pp. 74-86. Considerable emphasis on the iconography of the Shakespearian play as staged will be found in John Doebler's Shakespeare's Speaking Pictures (Albuquerque: Univ. of New Mexico Press, 1974), which also contains an extended bibliography.

[6] See Gillian Cohen, The Psychology of Cognition (London: Academic Press, 1977), pp. 26-45.

[7] See E.P. Goldschmidt, The Printed Book in the Renaissance (Cambridge: Cambridge Univ. Press, 1950), p. 37. Quite typical is Ben Jonson's strong preference for text over the visual side of dramatic production-- i.e., for what he regarded as the "soul" of the play over its "body."

[8] Samuel Daniel, The Complete Works in Verse and Prose, ed. Alexander B. Grosart (1896; rpt. New York: Russell and Russell, 1963), IV, 16.

[9] On liturgical drama, see my "On the Uses of Iconographic Study: The Example of the Sponsus from St. Martial of Limoges," Comparative Drama, 13 (1979-80), 300-19.

[10] See the study by V.A. Kolve, The Play Called Corpus Christi (Stanford: Stanford Univ. Press, 1966), pp. 8-32, and my edition of A Tretise of Miraclis

Pleyinge (A Middle English Treatise on the Playing of Miracles) (Washington, D.C.: University Press of America, 1981).

[11] Except for The Winter's Tale for which I quote from the Arden edition (ed. J.H.P. Pafford [London: Methuen, 1963]), references to Shakespeare's plays are to the Riverside Shakespeare, ed. G.B. Evans et al. (Boston: Houghton Mifflin, 1974).

[12] See, for example, S.L. Bethell's otherwise very perceptive The Winter's Tale: A Study (London: Staples Press, n.d.), p. 89. The significance of Time as Chorus is defended by Nevill Coghill, "Six Points of Stage-craft in The Winter's Tale," Shakespeare Survey, 11 (1958) 35-36. See also the perceptive note by Raymond J. Rundus, "Time and His Glass in The Winter's Tale," Shakespeare Quarterly, 25 (1974), 123-25.

[13] The phenomenological groundwork for my discussion is to be found in Hans-Georg Gadamer, Truth and Method (New York: Seabury, 1975), pp. 91-119.

[14] Inga-Stina Ewbank, "The Triumph of Time in The Winter's Tale," Review of English Literature, 5 (1964), 83-100.

[15] The connection of an English woodcut showing Tempora filia veritas with the Harrowing is suggested by Fritz Saxl, "Veritas filia temporis," in Philosophy and History: Essays Presented to Ernst Cassirer, ed. Raymond Klibansky and H.J. Paton (1936, rpt. New York: Harper and Row, 1963), p. 204.

[16] See also the woodcuts by Hans Burgkmair et al., The Triumph of Maximilian I, ed. Stanley Appelbaum (New York: Dover, 1964).

[17] Graphic Worlds of Peter Bruegel the Elder, ed. H. Arthur Klein (New York: Dover, 1963), p. 177.

[18] This detail apparently owes its origin to confusion between Chronos and Kronos-Saturn. See Erwin Panofsky, Studies in Iconology (1939; rpt. New York: Harper and Row, 1962), pp. 73-74.

[19] Coghill, p. 36.

[20] Donald Stauffer, Shakespeare's World of Images (New York: Norton, 1949), p. 296.

[21] Cicero's treatise was translated anonymously in *Foure Severall Treatises: Conteyninge Discourses of Frendshippe, Old Age, Paradoxes and Scipio His Dreame* (London, 1577). See also Laurens J. Mills, *One Soul in Bodies Twain: Friendship in Tudor Literature and Stuart Drama* (Bloomington, 1937).

[22] Cesare Ripa, *Baroque and Rococo Pictorial Imagery: The 1758-60 Hertel Edition of Ripa's 'Iconologia'*, ed. Edward Maser (New York: Dover, 1971), No. 52; the text cites the 1603 edition in translation.

[23] Hallett Smith, "Leontes' *Affectio*," *Shakespeare Quarterly*, 14 (1963), 163-64.

[24] Herod holds a child in his left hand, and a sword in his right hand (Oscar Farmer, *Fairford Church and Its Stained Glass Windows* [Bath, n.d.], p. 38).

[25] William Blissett, "This Wide Gap of Time: The *Winter's Tale*," *English Literary Renaissance*, 1 (1971), 59.

[26] Blissett, pp. 58-59.

[27] Madeline Harrison Caviness, *The Early Stained Glass of Canterbury Cathedral* (Princeton: Princeton Univ. Press, 1977), fig. 6.

[28] Soji Iwasaki, "*Veritas Filia Temporis* and Shakespeare," *English Literary Renaissance*, 3 (1973), 261; Saxl, pp. 202-03, fig. 3.

[29] Julius S. Held, "Flora, Goddess and Courtesan," in *Essays in Honor of Erwin Panofsky* (New York: New York Univ. Press, 1961), I, 203.

[30] Held, I, 201-02.

[31] Edward William Tayler, *Nature and Art in Renaissance Literature* (New York: Columbia Univ. Press, 1964), pp. 129-30.

[32] See the classic essay on *The Winter's Tale* by G. Wilson Knight in *The Crown of Life* (Oxford: Oxford Univ. Press, 1947).

[33] Abraham Fraunce, *The Third Part of the Countesse of Pembrokes Yvychurch* (London, 1592), fol. 27r.

[34] Held, I, 213-17; II, 73-74.

[35] Edmund H. Fellowes, *English Madrigal Verse, 1588-1632*, revised and enlarged by F. Sternfeld and D. Greer (Oxford: Clarendon Press, 1967), p. 308.

[36] Ovid, *Fasti*, trans. James George Frazer (Cambridge: Harvard Univ. Press, 1931), p. 275.

[37] Edgar Wind, *Pagan Mysteries in the Renaissance*, revised ed. (New York: Norton, 1968), p. 115.

[38] Cf. Glynne Wickham, *Shakespeare's Dramatic Heritage* (London: Routledge and Kegan Paul, 1969), pp. 264-65. See also David M. Bergeron, "The Restoration of Hermione in *The Winter's Tale*," in *Shakespeare's Romances Reconsidered*, ed. Carol McGinnis Kay and Henry E. Jacobs (Lincoln: Univ. of Nebraska Press, 1978), pp. 125-33, for the suggestion that the final scene of Shakespeare's play may have had some connection with Anthony Munday's *Chruso-thriambos: The Triumphes of Golde*, a civic pageant presented 29 October 1611. The reference to Julio Romano as the painter of the statue is discussed sensibly by Richard Studing, "'That rare Italian Master'--Shakespeare's Julio Romano," *Humanities Association Bulletin*, 23 (1971), 22-26, and see also the same author's "Spectacle and Masque in '*The Winter's Tale*'," *English Miscellany*, 21 (1970), 55-80.

[39] See Rosalie L. Colie, *Shakespeare's Living Art* (Princeton: Princeton Univ. Press, 1974), especially pp. 280-83. In spite of the emphasis on the marvelous in the last act, however, time is not reversed: Hermione has all the wrinkles that she has developed in the sixteen years since the trial scene. See Martin Mueller, "Hermione's Wrinkles, or, Ovid Transformed: An Essay on *The Winter's Tale*," *Comparative Drama*, 5 (1971), 226-39.

PART TWO

SHAKESPEARE AND PERFORMANCE

Patricia K. Meszaros' article on <u>Pericles</u> showed that a consideration of speculative music could lead to the practical consideration of what sort of music (if any) should actually be performed during a stage production. Similarly, Lois Ziegelman's discussion of <u>Hamlet</u> as a mannerist work provides background for Peter B. Young's analysis in this section of what sort of set designs enhance a play defined as mannerist. Furthermore, just as a knowledge of the "language" of iconography, mannerism, speculative music and masque enrich our understanding and have practical implications for productions, so the theatrical tradition formed by centuries of productions can lead not only to an awareness of what "works" in the theatre, but also to greater comprehension of the structure and meaning of the plays. Too often have scholars and directors been isolated from each other. Ellen J. O'Brien's paper on the stage tradition of Ophelia's mad scene provides a map to direct them to mutual enrichment.

While the tradition of Shakespearean stage production has grown for centuries, the television tradition is barely decades old. The papers presented here, among the few written thus far on this developing medium, constitute an important exchange on the intrinsic possibilities of presenting Shakespeare on television. These three papers relate to other articles as well. Whereas Ellen J. O'Brien commented negatively on the Ophelia scenes in the BBC <u>Hamlet</u>, H.R. Coursen uses this version of the play to come to grips with what can and cannot be done in the "cool" medium. Bernice Kliman addresses the same question in her analysis of Maurice Evans' early television productions. And Susan Willis discusses the BBC <u>All's Well</u> with special attention to the use made of contemporary art in the designs for the set. However, Dutch interiors, rather than mannerist paintings, were the basic for the design of this production.

Finally, giving some historical perspective to the entire question of Shakespeare and performance, Jane L. Donawerth looks for clues to Shakespeare's relationship to acting theory in the Renaissance. The tradition of performance--from the "Wooden O" to the television screen--makes another dialect in the language of the plays.

CWC

MANNERISM IN HAMLET SCENE DESIGNS

Peter B. Young

Several scholars have noted ways in which Shakespeare's Hamlet exhibits Mannerist elements,[1] while in a quite different area of work, producers and their scene, costume, and lighting designers have been making their own statements about the visual styles considered appropriate to the play. What seems to be all too often lacking in the mass of Hamlet criticism is a means of joining the insights of theatrical production to those of traditional scholarship. As a tentative step towards drawing these two worlds closer together, I would like to examine the appropriateness of a few scene designs for past productions of Hamlet.

Useful analogies can be made between certain styles in the visual arts and corresponding aspects of dramatic construction. The result is that we need no longer be limited by the merely verbal pictures arising from studies of imagery, valuable as these are for all of us, but we can now also literally see what we mean when we describe the complexities and ambiguities of a Hamlet or any other play. We can create in our mind's eyes analogous visual understandings of the texts themselves, as well as incorporate them into production designs.

Before examining the scene designs, we must briefly define Mannerism. The task is not easy, for there is scholarly disagreement on what the term means when used to describe a style.

Mannerism in art developed in Italy after the High Renaissance and spread to much of the rest of Europe soon after. The term was long used in a rather narrow and derogatory way, though as Janson points out in his History of Art, "More recently, the cold and rather barren formalism of their work has been recognized as a special form of a wider movement that placed 'inner vision,' however subjective or fantastic, above the twin authority of nature and the ancients. . . . Here is what amounts to a revolt against the classical balance of High Renaissance art; a profoundly disquieting, willful, visionary style that indicates a deep-seated inner anxiety."[2]

John Shearman,[3] investigating the period in more detail, sees Mannerism as the "stylish style," exhibiting refinement, sophistication, artificiality, elegance, polish, accomplishment, and savoir-faire. On the other hand, there are scholars such as Arnold Hauser[4] who see Mannerism as a style embodying tension, ambiguity, strain, and discord. I find myself aligned with Henri Zerner,[5] who expresses rather well the view many of us have that there is something of value in both the Shearman and Hauser approaches.

Hamlet can be called a Mannerist play, for it certainly exhibits many characteristics analogous in dramatic terms to aspects of the style called Mannerism in the visual arts. Zerner, after stating that Shearman's description of the "stylish style" has much that is useful to offer us, returns to a statement that might have been stimulated as much by considering Hamlet as by studying the visual arts: "In the end, it still seems profitable to envisage sixteenth-century art in terms of a crisis and collapse of humanistic ideals of the High Renaissance."[6]

The assigning of a description of Hamlet as a Mannerist work is not meant to imply that the play can be thereby explained. Hamlet is far too rich in subtleties and complexities of character, plot, motivation, and use of language, to ever allow for a pat explanation of the work. Far from explaining Hamlet, the description of it as Mannerist, in fact, leads us into a realm that seems to defy a rational explanation by discursive means. We may profitably talk about Hamlet, of course, provided such talk always returns us to the play with renewed appreciation of the richness and uniqueness that precludes its translation into any form other than its theatrical one. In a similar way we may, without explaining either painting, say valuable things about El Greco's View of Toledo and Tintoretto's Last Supper. It is precisely because works such as these paintings and the play Hamlet have so rich and profound an effect upon us and yet are full of troubled, dark, and sometimes frightening or unexplainable elements that we describe them as Mannerist to begin with.

Just as the term Mannerism does not explain Hamlet, neither should it mean that all who produce the play must be restricted to that particular period in seeking sources for settings and costumes. I do suggest, however, that the term can be useful as an indication of the play's particular kind of appeal to us, and further that whatever period or form for the visual elements is chosen by producers should have that decision based on the fact that the design source in question either exhibits Mannerist characteristics already, or at the very least lends itself to being presented and used in a fashion altered so as to reflect Mannerist elements.

As a way of illustrating the usefulness of considering visual approaches to the study of Hamlet, let us now turn to considering a few examples of scene and costume designs for the play, most of which were done for the Royal Shakespeare Company at their theatre in Stratford-upon-Avon.[7] The RSC production best incorporating a Mannerist style is that of 1961, for which Leslie Hurry designed both the sets and costumes (Fig. 1). Mr. Hurry based his set on the tracery and statuary of Gothic architecture, but interpreted his Gothic elements with the hands of a Mannerist.

The reviews of the 1961 production often fault much of the acting, including that of Ian Bannen in the title role, but they give no hint that the setting was anything but appropriate. Excerpts from two reviews will give us an idea of how the set was perceived in the theatre:

> Mr. Leslie Hurry's sets, with their vast pillars, autumnal curtains and flaming candelabra, were hauntingly evocative. The production got off to an impressive start with the platform before the castle at Elsinore shrouded in the impenetrable black of midnight which gives way, after a few moments, to a small light glinting on the helmet of a soldier, all very hauntingly--eerily tense.[8]

And the second review:

> It is a night of flickering torches, lanterns, and candles, which serve both to throw Hamlet's half-lit mind into relief and add a certain realism to Leslie Hurry's Elizabethan costumes.
> ....a richness in gold, blue, and

> old-rose, against great joints of masonry
> and heavy curtains--fluid before a back-
> drop of gauzed arches which have the musti-
> ness of an ecclesiastical hayloft--never
> intruding and always heightening the
> essential mood.[9]

These and other descriptions suggest aspects of Mannerism, and a close study of the production photographs reveals that many elements of the set did indeed exhibit Mannerist characteristics.

James Bailey had also designed a Gothic setting for the earlier 1948 RSC Hamlet, but one distinctly different from Hurry's design. This version is balanced and ordered in a way quite alien to the tone of Mannerism and the play. It is a nostalgic and comfortable Gothic world, the kind of place where we feel people would play at being medieval without having to endure any of the discomforts or pain of the age itself. The director of the 1948 production, Michael Bentham, in a press interview, confirms a visual reading of the set as owing far more to the nineteenth-century romanticism of a Victorian Gothic Revival than to more appropriate images:

> In Elizabethan costume, much of Hamlet's
> essential realism can, I feel, be lost.
> At Stratford, I sincerely aimed at pre-
> senting it in a mid-nineteenth-century
> setting, brought to everyone's mind by
> memories of our grandparents.
> The play is staged in Gothic scenery
> with all the elegant, colorful crinolines
> and uniforms associated with the atmosphere
> of a mid-European court. In this way I
> hope to have retained the magic of the
> theatre without destroying the play's
> vital contemporary relevance.[10]

Most reviewers of this production wrote that what they had received were pleasant images of the Prince Consort and other likable figures of the previous century, images they quite rightly found to work against the text.

In looking at the two designs more closely, we find that the gothic arch set-pieces of Hurry's Mannerist design were never complete forms as in the 1948 set of

Bailey (Fig. 2), but were always broken and partial, suggesting both that here was more than met the eye, and that Elsinore was not at all a closed, comfortable, or well-ordered place. All of the set-pieces--the large flown units, the tracery hung with draperies, the large column with spiral fluting, the bed for the closet scene, and the asymmetrical piece with twisted statuary figures that resembled a series of late-Michelangelo Pietas transferred to the portal niches of an early Gothic cathedral--had a monumentality both in scale and in their rough, stony texture that gave the stage a powerfully disturbing quality and yet never seemed to overwhelm the action. Massive and solid looking, these set-pieces had a distinctly severe quality given them by their deeply incised grooves and their hard edges.

The large stone set-pieces appeared as brown and grey masses occasionally shot with glancing beams of amber and dull blue-lavender lights from high above the playing area. Motivating light was provided by three large candelabra and a single large chandelier. The rest of the stage was quite shadowy, giving the scene an atmosphere, a mood, a tone very like Tintoretto's Last Supper, and which brings to mind the reviewer's words, "It is a night of flickering torches, lanterns, and candles."

In the Closet Scene, two huge draperies hung from fragmentary Gothic arch units, and a large bed gave the scene a size and tone appropriate to its violent, active, and climactic character. The drapes were covered with a very busy, swirling design that was as thoroughly Mannerist as the pattern Bronzino paints on the dress of his Eleanor of Toledo in the well-known portrait. The curtains were of an old gold color at the bottom, but lighting changed their upper halves to a tarnished green that resembled the effect intense heat or chemical corrosion has on certain metals. A final cold, blue highlight at the very top of each curtain unit created a tension between it and the stage picture by pulling our eye upwards and then re-directing it back down once it had been caught.

The thrones for Claudius and Gertrude were completely Mannerist in their hard, severe lines that also suggested their Gothic source. Mr. Hurry did not imitate Gothic chairs, however, but created virtuoso variations, quite Mannerist in style, with frighteningly toothed backs that threatened to devour anyone who sat in them. In contrast, Mr. Bailey's thrones were amusing Rococo-Victorian designs that had nothing at all disturbing about them.

Hurry's costumes were as appropriately designed as his scenery. They were late Elizabethan in silhouette, and definitely Mannerist in the way they distorted the natural outline of the human body. Hips were greatly enlarged by bulbous pumpkin hose for the men and by farthingales for the women. Shoulders were also unnaturally enlarged by puff sleeves, and wings and cresents. Sexuality was both denied by severely flattening the female breasts and then flaunted by codpieces on the male costumes. All of the designs used a great number of puffs and slashes, which augmented their Mannerist character by unnaturally cutting the outer garment into panes so that fabric of what was worn underneath could be allowed periodic bits of escape as it was deliberately teased and pulled through the slits in the covering fabric. Trim on many of the costumes was restricted to narrow bands, but within those areas it was very busy, crowded, twisted, entwined or even tortured in look and seemed to be seeking release from its confining boundaries. These costumes were both gorgeous and frightening at the same time.

In 1965 the RSC again produced <u>Hamlet</u>, this time with rather modern, though timeless, scenery by John Bury and modified Elizabethan costumes by Anne Curtis. Although not set at all in the period Art Historians label Mannerist, Bury's design nevertheless exhibited certain Mannerist qualities. Tony Church, who played Polonius in the production, described the scenery thus: "John Bury's design was enclosed and impervious--a huge black funnel--like the Establishment."[11] The set was comprised of monolithic walls that looked like huge blocks of black stone. Two huge doors opened at the rear, or could remain closed, and two large panels in each side wall could also be opened to reveal other units for certain scenes. The floor was largely covered with very shiny, reflective and hard-surfaced black masonite, set off by a recti-linear pattern in a lighter-colored material. The black floor was itself a Mannerist accommodation of opposites, for while it was hard-surfaced and reflected back everything that hit it, it also gave the impression of infinite depth lying beneath its surface. This Denmark was made to seem a prison indeed.

For some of the scenes this basic set was altered to give it a more active, expressive look. For both II.ii and IV.v, the four side panels were opened to reveal large paintings of nude figures distorted in a manner suggesting both Picasso and Parmagianino. Similar paintings were seen through the up-center doors. For the closet scene in III.iv, a large bed was placed downstage and a huge arras flown in that completely hid the basic set upstage of it. The arras was covered with a large design full of rather tortured twists and swirls. For the graveyard scene in V.i, two of the side stone panels changed to partially destroyed monuments based on the type seen in the walls of many older English churches. The up-center doors stood open to reveal a grave monument. All three items were asymmetrical and disturbing in design. The two thrones used in this production were original creations that exhibited severe, hard lines and were built with slightly distorted angles to their sides that gave them an effectively strange, unbalanced look.

Anne Curtis's costumes had a contemporary feel, like the sets, yet achieved a non-specific period look by using a greatly simplified Henry VIII silhouette. Under those broad-shouldered coats, however, most of the court characters wore a pinstripe fabric which achieved, in modern terms, much the same effect as the tightly controlled but busy bands of trim on Hurry's 1961 Elizabethan costumes.

In 1976 Bury designed the sets for another Hamlet, this one produced by Peter Hall at the National Theatre in London. The basic set consisted of a semi-circular patterned floor whose curved outline was given emphasis by radiating lines that marked off pie-shaped wedges of hard-surfaced paving. At the back of the set was a monolithic wall, heavily textured like stucco, that ran across the stage from one wing to the other. In the central portion of this wall was placed a large pediment surmounting a narrower, though also large, base of nearly flat pilasters and other framed mouldings. This upstage center unit could be used for entrances or closed off with a neutral backing, as in the play scene of Act III. All molding elements of this dominating central unit were quite dark compared to the middle value of the wall itself, making the effect not unlike that of Michelangelo's design for the vestibule of the Laurentian Library. Although symmetrical and placed center on the wall, this unit nevertheless had a disturbing, unbalanced quality because the top pediment was too heavy, visually, for its base. The effect was as though the English designer, Robert Adam, had suddenly gone mad and designed a Mannerist overmantel for a huge fireplace and then had left it sitting on the floor upstage center.

The play scene was staged with Claudius and Gertrude seated downstage center, backs to the audience, with the players performing on a large tilted table top placed upstage against the pediment. Two huge wheel candelabra stood at either side of the scene. The overall placement of courtiers and props was balanced but so treated in either proportion or detail that the scene had a disturbing feeling. This production provides an excellent example of how a set can still be Mannerist in feeling even though it is basically symmetrical.

No other <u>Hamlet</u> productions of the RSC exhibit Mannerist qualities as clearly in their visual elements as do the 1961 and 1965 versions. Michael Northen's set for the 1956 <u>Hamlet</u>, for example, was an extremely simple design. It consisted of a large octagonal platform surrounded by black velour drapes that read like black space. This acting platform was approached by a ramp sloping downwards from the wings upstage-right. A large blue drape hung in place throughout the play. The only change or addition made to the set was to put down a large piece of red carpet for the play scene in Act III. The costumes of Desmond Heeley were appropriately somber but lacking in Mannerist line or trim. The best we can say of this production is that is seems to have had a slight harmony with Mannerist tendencies but was really more neutral than active in this respect.

The RSC's <u>Hamlet</u> of 1958 reverses the situation of 1956. Motley's costumes were definitely Mannerist and were based upon Albrecht Dürer and Urs Graf as design sources. Most involved a profusion of puffs and slashes and tight, violently patterned trim, both often set in diagonal accents. The scene design was also by Motley, though almost certainly by a different member of this team of three women. Only one minor aspect of the set owed anything to a Mannerist style: the finishing of the six major pillars in a shiny black material with gilt accents on the vertical ribs. The placement of these columns, however, as well as the steps and platform levels comprising the basic set was completely symmetrical and balanced. The columns and steps also provided a strong horizontal-vertical dominance that communicated order and stability rather than Mannerist unrest and tension. The colors of the red and blue backcloths used in some scenes were too vibrant and pure, belonging more to a sunnier Renaissance world than to a dark Mannerist one.

What has emerged from our brief scrutiny of these several Hamlet productions? Certainly no formulaic approach to a design solution for Hamlet is discernible, though hopefully a sense of the appropriateness of Mannerist qualities in designs for the play has been conveyed. Further, I hope the reader has gained a sense of the value of using visual material from productions to illustrate what we mean when we call Hamlet a Mannerist play. This approach is not meant to substitute for more traditional and detailed studies of imagery, character, plot construction, and so on, but to supplement them. By studying one or more appropriate design solutions to Hamlet, or to other plays, we can gain a feel for the overall tone and mood of the play at hand much more accurately than words alone can convey. Such designs can be used to give students an introduction to the play's style or to provide established scholars a background companion to further study.

Fig. 1 Hamlet, 1961, Royal Shakespeare Company. Leslie Hurry, designer. Permission of Thos. F. Holte Photographers, Ltd.

Fig. 2 Hamlet, 1948, Royal Shakespeare Company. James Bailey, designer. Permission of Shakespeare Centre Library, Stratford-upon-Avon.

NOTES

[1] Una Ellis-Fermor, *The Jacobean Drama: An Interpretation*, 5th ed. (London: Methuen, 1965), Cyrus Hoy, "Jacobean Tragedy and the Mannerist Style," *Shakespeare Survey*, 26 (1973), 49-67; Andrew Kennedy, "Natural, Mannered, and Parodic Dialogue," *Yearbook of English Studies*, 9 (1979), 28-54; Clifford Leech, *Shakespeare's Tragedies and Other Studies in Seventeenth-Century Drama* (London: Chatto and Windus, 1950).

[2] H.W. Janson, *History of Art* (Englewood Cliffs, N.J.: Prentice-Hall, 1962), p. 374.

[3] *Mannerism*, Style and Civilization, (Baltimore: Penguin, 1967).

[4] *Mannerism: The Crisis of the Renaissance and the Origin of Modern Art* (London: Routledge, 1965).

[5] "Observations on the Use of the Concept of Mannerism," in *The Meaning of Mannerism*, ed. Franklin W. Robinson and Stephen G. Nichols, Jr. (Hanover, N.H.: University Press of New England, 1972), pp. 105-121.

[6] Zerner, p. 118.

[7] I would like to acknowledge the assistance of the National Endowment for the Humanities and its Summer Seminars for College Teachers, as it was participation in one of those programs during 1980 in Stratford-upon-Avon that gave me access to much of the material used in preparation of this paper.

[8] *Bristol Evening Post*, 15 Apr. 1961.

[9] *Stratford-Upon-Avon Herald*, 14 Apr. 1961.

[10] *Birmingham Sunday Mercury*, 28 Mar. 1948.

[11] Personal interview with the actor in Stratford-upon-Avon, July, 1980.

OPHELIA'S MAD SCENE AND THE STAGE TRADITION

Ellen J. O'Brien

In John Barton's *Hamlet* of July 1980, Gertrude saw the ghost--a startling moment, and one which epitomizes for me the fruits of a summer in Stratford-upon-Avon.[1] I began the summer working with the plays and critical texts as I always have, but Stratford offered other resources as well--theatre history at the Shakespeare Centre, performance at the Royal Shakespeare Theatre, and interviews with Royal Shakespeare actors and directors--all of which combined to change my perspective on the critical uses of performance and stage history quite significantly. Not surprisingly, I learned a great deal about Shakespeare in Stratford, but I learned even more about my own stance as a scholar and as an audience--and most particularly about the intersection of the two. Prior to this experience, I had responded to productions of Shakespeare primarily by measuring the performance against my own understanding of the play--a useful practice, if a bit egotistical, and one I have no intention of abandoning. Yet I have now learned the value of complementing this approach with its mirror-image: measuring my understanding of the play against the performance. The practice is hardly unprecedented; indeed, I suppose we all respond this way to the production which exudes the aura of "the definitive." However, it is one which deserves wider exercise, particularly among those of us who work habitually with Shakespeare as literary text.

Individual productions (definitive or not) may produce flashes of illumination, as Barton's *Hamlet* did in confronting us with a Gertrude who could see the ghost and then repress what she had seen. Yet we have even more to learn from the accumulated wisdom of performance which is found in enduring stage traditions, a fact recognized by Brander Matthews as early as 1916.

> We need to have in black and white the whole body of stage tradition. . . . It may be admitted frankly that some of these traditions are incongruous excrescences, occasionally foolish and sometimes offensive, handed down from a time when the essential quality of Shakespeare was less highly appreciated

than it is to-day.
. . . These may be dismissed as unwarrantable obtrusions to be discarded unhesitatingly; but to admit this is not to discredit the utility of the traditions in general. They are to be received as precious heirlooms . . . a store of accumulated devices always to be cast aside only after mature consideration.[2]

Arthur Colby Sprague responded to Matthews' appeal with his valuable <u>Shakespeare and the Actors</u>, though wisely proceeding with a more critical attitude toward "the precious heirlooms." His caveats are well taken, for he reminds us that "the force of tradition in the nineteenth century is hard to overestimate" and that for the mediocre actor of the time, compassing the role often meant knowing "the business" rather than infusing it with meaning. Nevertheless, he asserts that "Shakespeare's plays were written for performance, and surely, through performance, light has been shed on many dark places in them--often, it is my belief, by means of stage-business."[3] My experience in Stratford bears out Sprague's assumption.

If a piece of stage-business rings true, it is apt to be repeated and, eventually, to become traditional. Admittedly, there are stage traditions which are absurd --usually, as Matthews' "incongruous excrescenses" would suggest, because they are rooted in elements external to the play. Happily, the shift away from abject reverence for tradition at the turn of the century destroyed many of these; the survivors, having met the needs of two very different ages of theater, deserve our attention. The ultimate test, of course, is the text itself; if the business can be grounded there, it is difficult to rule illegitimate. Though we cannot accept every tradition as insightful, the testimony of actors and directors supports the assumption that traditions are largely shaped by the play itself; the text has an implicit logic which will not be violated without resistance. John Barton, for instance, reported that his original intention to abandon the tradition of a Hamlet who returns to Denmark a changed man was thwarted by the logic of the play in rehearsal. Although Barton found few words in the text to prove Hamlet's change, the shape of the dramatic experience worked inexorably toward that result. Traditions like this one grow very directly out of the

essentials of the play, and from these we may derive
both new critical insights and corroborations of our
own interpretations of the text.

We have the foundations of a mode of criticism
which actively incorporates performance in the work of
Sprague and Carol Jones Carlisle. Attempting to define
the particular role of such a criticism, Alexander
Leggatt argues that performance can be especially helpful in revealing implicit connections between widely
separated scenes, thus establishing continuity and
context.[4] This takes us one step beyond the flash of
illumination. I would argue for one further step:
examining stage tradition for structural principles
which give shape and form to scenes which are often
perceived as chaotic. Perhaps we have done so much with
the larger structure of Shakespeare's drama that stage
tradition would teach us little that is new about most
plays; yet there are bits of plays whose structures
continue to puzzle us. Here the tradition may be a
source of new insight. Ophelia's mad scene provides
a case in point. Complicated in shape by its densely
allusive nature, the scene functions like a poem, or,
if we take Ophelia's point of view, a nightmare, drawing
together in symbolic form all the horror that has gone
before and foreshadowing the calamity to come. Critical
attention has focused principally on explication of the
songs and flower language, and stage-business, too, has
attempted to articulate those allusions, providing the
kind of continuity with other scenes discussed in
Leggatt's study. Yet actresses and directors are forced
to consider continuity within the scene as well, for
they must incorporate those songs in a complete dramatic
context, giving shape and structure to the scene in
performance which we in the study may choose to slight--
and which our students often fail to perceive altogether.
The actress must find a way to weave the meaningful
nonsense of the songs into a coherent fabric. Hence,
examining the stage history of the scene also helps us
perceive its implicit structure.

Nevertheless, we must approach stage history with
wariness, taking into account the prejudices of each age
and the consequent alterations to the text. Ophelia's
case is particularly slippery. To the eighteenth
century, the role was of little consequence. Indeed,
according to Sir Theodore Martin, until his wife, Helena
Faucit, agreed to play Ophelia with Macready in Paris

in 1844, the part was one "which no English manager would ever have dreamed of asking a leading actress to play, it having been for years thought only good enough for the singing lady of the theatre."[5] There is some husbandly hyperbole here, but Faucit's fascination with Ophelia was important to the gradual change in attitude toward the role; Macready told her after her first performance that she "had thrown a new light on the part and that he had never seen the mad scenes even approached before."[6] Although it is not quite true that Faucit was the first major English actress to undertake the role, the commentaries on her notable predecessors are revealing. Mrs. Cibber, "charming in every role. . . . but identified with Ophelia," was praised for "her features, figure and singing" which made her "the best Ophelia that ever appeared."[7] Often, the mad scene was treated as a kind of musical interlude, to be judged on the quality of the singing rather than the coherence of the scene. Even in 1852, Henry Morley complained that Fraulein Schafer, by speaking the songs rather than singing them, "acted well in vain."[8] The attitude of the time is summed up in the comments on Mrs. Smith (like Cibber, one of Garrick's Ophelias):

> . . . a young woman and a good singer, who is admirably suited to the part (although she has not the vivacity for several others that she takes) . . . her whole demeanor in her madness was as gentle as the passion which caused it. The songs, which she sang charmingly, were fraught with such plaintive and tender melancholy that I fancied that I could hear them far into the night. . . . Shakespeare makes this whole scene so moving as to cause one actual pain and leave a sore place in the heart, which goes on throbbing until one could wish never to have seen poor unhappy Ophelia.[9]

The early Ophelias are almost unredeemedly pathetic, preserving "favor and prettiness" at all cost. Of course, this kind of pathos was to be had only at the expense of Ophelia's bawdy lines, cuts which remained standard in the promptbooks until the 1940's. Moreover, although the mad scene was greatly admired for its realism, there is no evidence that early actresses concerned themselves with the roots of that madness. Instead, the scene seems to have been done as a kind of set-piece. Sarah Siddons was reportedly the only actress before Faucit to bring anything more to the role, and, according to James Boaden, her performance was

> caviare to the multitude; too long accustomed to receive a dishevelled <u>singer</u> as the true and perfect image of Oph<u>eli</u>a, all the fine essence of such a being, breathing through Siddons herself, hardly moved their wonder; though . . . her distraction was the truest delineation that was ever made from a "ruined piece of nature!" But methinks I hear some very inquisitive reader exclaim, "What! Mrs. Siddons <u>sing</u>!" No, Sir, it was Ophelia who sang, or <u>rather</u> the <u>melancholy</u> of the poet Collins.[10]

The reference to Collins may give us pause, but there are other testimonies to the power and coherence of Mrs. Siddons' mad scene. Indeed, tradition has it that the actress playing Gertrude was so stunned by Mrs. Siddons' depiction of the mad Ophelia that she forgot her own lines.

Helena Faucit may have been the first to seriously examine the shocks which lead to Ophelia's madness (I can find no evidence for Mrs. Siddons), but she was followed by a number of actresses and critics who wrote at length on Ophelia, complaining that the role had been appallingly under-rated.[11] By 1864, a number of observers (including medical doctors) had come to see the madness as the result of a series of psychological blows, beginning with the disturbing advice of Laertes and Polonius in I.iii and continuing through each of Ophelia's scenes: in Hamlet's strange and abusive behavior, the death of her father, and so on.[12] Ophelia's madness then gradually came to be seen as drama rather than set-piece. Thus, from the nineteenth century on, we can begin to look for meaningful stage traditions, remembering that until the 1940's the most sexually suggestive of Hamlet's lines to Ophelia were regularly cut along with the songs, crippling any attempt at a full exploration of the roots of her madness.

Textually, the songs are the substance of the scene, and there is much to be exploited here: interpreters have found persuasive evidence of references to Claudius, Gertrude, Polonius and Hamlet--often in the same lines.[13] The critic may be content with identifying the allusions, but the actress must somehow convey their significance to an audience which has little time to ponder riddles and symbols. Guiding us through her nightmare vision, she must take us back to its sources. Much of the traditional stage business has been directed to this end, particularly to underscoring the King's guilt. Ophelia's actions often hint at what she has no direct knowledge of; in the words of a promptbook of 1900, "her spirit recognizes an evil spirit" in the King.[14] The recognition has been evinced in two ways, sometimes both within the same production. Ophelia often avoids the king, shrinking away at his question "How do you, pretty lady?" In a Sothern production, Ophelia offered fennel to the King "distrustfully"; as the King reached out to take it, she dropped the fennel, "withdrawing [her] hand quickly." The Queen's rue, by contrast, was offered with sympathy.[15] Alternatively, Ophelia might behave quite aggressively toward the King: directing "It is the false steward that stole his master's daughter" to him (either in fear or in angry accusation); shouting "My brother shall know of it" as a warning; or advancing toward the King as she sings her dirges. By 1884, these suggestions of the King's guilt in the murder of old Hamlet and, indirectly, of Polonius, had been supplemented by business which evokes his sexual guilt. Ellen Terry not only singled out the King as "the false steward," but "imitated a crude seducer "with becking nods and wreathed smiles."[16] An aggressive, sensual embrace of the King is not unusual today; Harriet Walters went further in a 1980 Hamlet with Jonathan Pryce. Dancing Claudius about at the end of the Saint Valentine song, she then began fondling him, first touching his chest, then moving her hands lower and lower until she was "fumbling with his belt" at "By Cock, they are to blame." Finally, she joined his hand to Gertrude's, "like a priest." As Miriam Gilbert observed, this made the song a "reference to their sexuality rather than hers."[17]

Although interplay between Ophelia and the Queen has generally been more sympathetic, (perhaps because the extent of Gertrude's guilt is less clear), Ophelia sometimes shows fear of the Queen as well. "Where is the beauteous majesty of Denmark" is often addressed to Gertrude by an Ophelia who does not recognize her, suggesting that her deeds have stripped her of beauty and majesty. (The line may also refer to Hamlet, literally packed off to England and figuratively obliterated by his unbeauteous deed, but multiple reference is the norm in the mad scene.) The suggestion that Gertrude should wear her rue "with a difference" is perhaps the most frequent locus of business. One Ophelia, taking the Queen's hand, looked hard at her wedding ring, then at her own ringless hand.[18] Other Ophelias have made the line an accusation. Curiously, I have found no record of locket play in the scene, though an extension of the comparison of locket portraits of old Hamlet and Claudius, traditional in the closet scene, seems natural here. Ophelia might thrust her locket toward Gertrude as she sings "How should I your true love know, from another one," unconsciously but effectively recalling Hamlet's violent comparison of Gertrude's two loves. Following on the heels of Hamlet's accusations, both this song and the Saint Valentine song may seem to Gertrude to refer to her condition.

Even as the actress reinforces these individual allusions, she must keep us always aware of the pervasive references to a lost love and a dead father. What is important is not to determine which is which, but to see that the two strands are interwoven--at times indistinguishable--and that together they create an informing structure for the scene. Although both Hamlet and Polonius haunt the two separate segments of the mad scene, the songs do suggest differing emphases in each part: the first songs, of true love and betrayed love, point most obviously to Hamlet; the dirges of Ophelia's second entrance, while applicable to a Hamlet dead to Ophelia through the murder of her father, seem a more immediate allusion to Polonius. Stage traditions evince tacit recognition of this division, and, to some degree, this shifting emphasis has been allowed to shape the scene, providing a method to Ophelia's madness: a symbolic structure which makes the mad scene more than a collection of suggestive songs. It is here that performance can teach us most, for we are no longer dealing simply with reinforcement of verbal allusions but with the embodiment of structural principles.

The second half of the scene has been more fully defined by this process than the first, probably because it has been less radically cut in most productions. As early as 1826, its funeral motif was recognized and began to mold a stage tradition. Wearing a scarf which had already become traditional for the scene, Miss Glover removed the scarf and used it to form a shroud; she then laid herself down beside it, an action which "excited loud and earnest applause."[19] This mock burial soon became a regular piece of business and by mid-century was established firmly enough to be included in the printed stage-directions of at least one of the standard acting editions of the play. Many other editions printed instructions for Ophelia to kneel for the dirge. Prompter's notes were sometimes more extensive: "Kneeling . . . laying scarf on the ground for grave with wreath for headstone. Sinking on her hands and face upon the ground with a heavy heart. Broken Sigh." Ophelia was then directed to exit with "her eyes fixed mournfully on the imaginary grave and scattering flowers and repeating verse."[20] Similar exits appear in other promptbooks, making the grave the central symbol of the scene. The business was sometimes extended to include formation of a cross of flowers and symbolic performance of the funeral rites which had been so abridged for Polonius. At least one Ophelia completed the action with a momentary return to sanity which led her to fail "fainting over the cross."[21]

More recent Ophelias have worn Polonius' robe in the scene, using this rather than the scarf as a shroud, and costuming has been used to express the funeral motif of the scene in other ways as well. Ophelia's traditional white, though it may have originated in the seventeenth-century mourning color, had lost its meaning by the nineteenth century. In a Forbes Robertson production of the 1890's, Mrs. Patrick Campbell "introduced . . . a note of mourning" by draping a black veil over her white dress. When the production toured in 1900, Gertrude Elliott appeared all in black as the mad Ophelia, apparently the first to do so. Ellen Terry's desire to wear black had been squelched by Henry Irving, who capped his assertion that white was the proper mourning color for the Elizabethans by declaring that "there must be only one black figure in this play, and that's Hamlet!"[22] Despite Irving's conviction, black became commonplace for Ophelia, and an actress who described the role in 1914 went beyond the change to mourning costume to produce an Ophelia distinctly nun-like in appearance, thus weaving into the funeral an ironic echo of the nunnery scene. Around her neck, she wore "as a rosary" a chain with Hamlet's picture, in the links of which she had woven purple daisies. In her

hands, she carried other flowers.[23] The mock funeral
and Ophelia's final prayer for all Christian souls were
given particular poignancy through this image; in
recalling Hamlet's advice on the nunnery, the image also
gave visual representation to one aspect of the scene's
pervasive sense of ironic reversal. Again and again,
the mad scene invites Ophelia to embody the words of
earlier scenes which have contributed to her psychological destruction.

In a variety of forms, the funeral structure has
persisted into our own time, suggesting that it is
deeply rooted in the play. Directors like John Gielgud
and actresses like Barbara Leigh-Hunt have stressed the
importance of Polonius' "huggermugger" burial to the
scene. Hunt also insists that Ophelia should be in
mourning, recalling Hamlet's appearance at the opening
of the play:[24] now Ophelia is the bereaved child of a
murdered father. Like most of the scene's allusions,
the funeral motif has multiple referents, pointing not
only backward to Polonius and Hamlet but forward to
Ophelia's own "maimed rites"--and, of course, to the
multiple deaths which close the play. The importance of
this shaping structure is reflected in Richard David's
comparison of two 1975-76 Hamlets, one with Yvonne
Nicholson as Ophelia and the other with Susan Fleetwood.
Nicholson's mad scene centered on an "obsessive composing and recomposing, a mock laying-out, of the red
dressing gown in which her father had died"; Fleetwood's
version--more "realistic" but less "fluent"--developed
no central ritual and was consequently reduced to "a
thing of shreds and patches, lacking altogether the
singleminded drive that made the Nicholson version such
an exciting experience."[25]

Nothing comparable to the funeral motif has emerged
out of either the critical or the stage tradition to
shape the first segment of the mad scene, though the
funeral business has occasionally been transferred to it.
(Given the cuts traditionally made in the scene, the
transposition is not surprising, for the references to
death which mingle with the mourning of a lost love
become central in the reduced scene.) However, two
secondary motifs have emerged, each embodying one of the
ironic echoes noted above. The first is the motif of
repressed sexuality evident in the St. Valentine song.
This motif is relatively new to the acting tradition,
not because it is a twentieth-century idea but because

the material from which it grows (including the third verse of the Saint Valentine song) was cut from most productions until quite recently. Even in 1969, Robert Speaight would note that "no part in Shakespeare had suffered more from the sentimental evasion of sexuality" than Ophelia's.[26] Nevertheless, the pervasive sexuality of the scene gave rise to suggestions of the motif in stage business long before the critical lines were restored to performance. Ellen Terry's late nineteenth-century Ophelia is reported to have emphasized "budding voluptuousness".[27] In the Barrymore production of 1924, Rosaline Fuller developed the motif in the second half of the scene (again, a reasonable transposition given the cuts in the first half). She entered "ogling, and smiling at Laertes" and throughout his speech gazed at him, smiling and ogling him "in a coquettish manner."[28] Ophelia's seductive behavior toward the King in more recent productions is only a fuller development of the same impulse. Since the restoration of the complete Valentine song, the sexuality of the scene has rapidly become almost inescapable. Directing Hamlet in the 1960's, John Gielgud initially complained of the "wild indecency" of the scene in recent productions, with Ophelia "tearing off her clothes and clutching all the gentlemen," yet he, too, finally succumbed to the demands of the text, asking Linda Marsh to do the scene in only a brassiere and skirt. When she protested, he settled for an open blouse, admitting that she might look like "the Playboy Bunny of Elsinore" if it were omitted altogether.[29] Rosemary Harris' mad scene in 1963 "showed the fury of sexual frustration working on a nature too delicate to sustain the double shock of her father's death and Hamlet's repudiation.[30]

The other secondary motif, although less firmly established, moves us closer to an implicit structure and may have paved the way for a breakthrough in Barton's *Hamlet*. This is the motif of performance: the sense that Ophelia's songs are not isolated bursts of madness but part of a felt whole. On one level, this is a song recital: not the eighteenth-century actress' musical interlude but a structure created by Ophelia in an effort to restore some sense of order to her shattered world. Even in the nineteenth century, an attitude of self-conscious performance was conveyed by a number of actresses who shouted the repeated demand, "pray you, mark," as though to silence an unruly audience. Reviewing Helen Mirren's Ophelia in 1970,

Peter Lewis characterized the scene as a song recital "to which all else is an interruption. She shuts up the King and Queen and dishes out the rosemary and rue with fierce matter-of-factness which is truly disturbing."[31] Moreover, the recital also functions as a kind of sermon which echoes the lectures on sexuality thrust upon Ophelia by her father and brother in I.iii and by Hamlet in III.i. Clearly, Ophelia has something to say and "will make an end on it" whether or not her listeners wish to hear. Incorporating the motif of sexuality, the motif of performance begins to shape the first half of the scene as the mock-funeral shapes the second.

Yet the performance motif has had less effect than the funeral on stage tradition and critical interpretation--probably in part because it is more difficult to embody. It was therefore particularly exciting to see this implied structure crystallize into a form which deserves to become a part of the tradition in Barton's Hamlet; there the idea of performance was made structural by creating an ironic reversal of Ophelia's last appearance (and, we should note, her final step toward madness)--the play scene.

Preparation for this began in the play scene itself, in a break with the traditional staging which places Hamlet at Ophelia's feet for a private exchange. In this context, Hamlet's remarks are distressing but well below the pitch of the nunnery scene. Barton's production, however, maintained a steady crescendo to Ophelia's distress by making these words anything but private. Rather than joining Ophelia after calling attention to her with "here's metal more attractive," Hamlet placed himself in the Player King's throne, at center stage, and virtually shouted his insults at Ophelia, to the embarrassment of a suddenly silenced court unable to ignore his noisy performance. The degradation of Ophelia by her lover thus became inescapably public. As in the nunnery scene, she was made the object of observation, again to be assailed with words which overturned her understanding of herself; her audience this time not just her father and the king, but the assembled court-- in effect, her entire world. No longer simply a painful post-script to the nunnery, the scene became an experience even more devasting than what had preceded it.

At the close of the play scene, Ophelia remained frozen in her place as the others exited, lost in her confusion and horrified by the inexplicable disruption of the court entertainment. Only when Hamlet hurled one of his antic rhymes directly at her, did she break into the wail which had been building within and run wildly off-stage--in a direction no one else had taken. This graphic representation of her isolation and horror made it easy to accept the madness which soon follows. Lest we doubt the connection, Ophelia staged an inverted reprise of the play scene in her madness, simultaneously affirming the cause-effect relationship between the two scenes and giving the mad scene architectural coherence. She began the process by seizing the chair which had been the Player King's throne and placing it back at center stage, thus reconstructing the set of the play-within-the-play. Flinging herself into the chair, she sang her songs to an accompaniment of broad sexual gestures, thus taking Hamlet's place as the performer of a bawdy entertainment. Once again the court was ranged about in embarrassed silence to hear Ophelia's reputation sullied by implication--but this time through her own words. As Ophelia thrust upon the court the exposure from which she had earlier shrunk, the play scene was brought forcefully to mind and Ophelia's madness took on newly meaningful form. The violent energies of this performance electrified the familiar funeral motif of the second segment, allowing Ophelia to turn "all to favor and to prettiness" there without defusing the impact of the whole. As the reprise of the play scene recalled Hamlet's inexplicable brutality to Ophelia, so her spreading of Polonius' robe at center stage evoked the shocking loss of her father. This framework, without depriving the scene of its essential chaos, created a shape which set off the elements of that chaos to devastating effect. I have never experienced a more powerful--or comprehensible--mad scene.

What do we see then, when we return to the text of the mad scene with the insights of performance and stage tradition? The images of chaos and nonsense are now, as in a nightmare, informed by a highly meaningful and deeply grounded structure. This implicit framework is one of careful architectural balance: the mock-performance which inverts the final incident in Ophelia's inexplicable alienation from her lover is succeeded by a mock-funeral for her lost father; here there is no need to search for the roots of Ophelia's madness. The importance of some such structure is articulated in the Saturday Review's comments on Ellen Terry's 1878 Ophelia, which praised her "natural . . . consistency of . . . conception" and the "perfect expression given to her idea."

> These qualities are especially remarkable in the mad scene. Here, instead of the incoherent outpouring of imbecile unconnected phrases which has too often passed for Shakespeare's representation of Ophelia's madness, Miss Terry shows us an intelligible, and . . . consistent state of dementia. That is, her power of facial expression, her action, and her intonation, combine to show us the origin in her disordered state of mind of each wild and whirling word that she utters. Every broken phrase and strange image is suggested by some recollection of the time before she was distraught.[32]

In the absence of carefully-shaped stage-business, the mad scene too easily falls back into the old "incoherent outpouring of imbecile unconnected phrases." Regrettably, such mad scenes have by no means disappeared. For an example, we need only turn to the recent BBC Hamlet (in many respects quite good) where the mad scene did lack form--more than a little--and hence achieved only pathos. Although it was disturbing to watch Ophelia wrap herself suggestively around Claudius as she sang the Saint Valentine Song, the absence of any informing structure left the moment isolated and unexplained. It showed us Ophelia's madness without defining its shape. Yet Ophelia's mad world is not formless, but a precise inversion of the forms of the court world--the forms of her destruction.

Lest I be accused of abandoning the critical process to the actors, I will hasten to acknowledge that such insights are not the sole province of performance. Francis Fergusson's characterization of the mad scene as a combination of mock-marriage and mock-funeral offers just one example of parallel discoveries from other critical approaches--though it does leave the ritual of performance unexplored.[33] Indeed, if these structures were not to some degree accessible within the texts themselves, I would hesitate to argue their intrinsicality. Yet is is worth noting that the actresses discovered Ophelia's rituals at least a century ahead of the myth critics.

More important than who is first, however, is the

fact that the route between the theater and the study is--happily--a two-way street. As my vision of Ophelia's mad scenes was being reshaped by research into stage history, current performance and discussion with members of the Royal Shakespeare Company, it was satisfying to note that performers learn from scholars just as we learn from them. An inescapable example in John Barton's <u>Hamlet</u> was the influence of Ann Righter Barton's <u>Shakespeare and the Idea of the Play</u>, evident in the sense of self-conscious performance which informed the production and confirmed in the program notes--written by Ann Righter Barton. It may be helpful to marry a director, of course, but in the long run such cross-fertilization promises to breed new and vital fruits in both criticism and theater--for all of us.

NOTES

[1] I am indebted to the National Endowment for the Humanities for sponsorship of the 1980 Summer Seminar which made my work possible: "Shakespeare, Poet and Playwright," directed by Marvin Rosenberg.

[2] Brander Matthews, "Shaksperian Stage Traditions," in Shaksperian Studies (New York: Columbia University Press, 1916), p. 12.

[3] Arthur Colby Sprague, Shakespeare and the Actors: The Stage Business in his Plays (Cambridge, Mass.: Harvard Univ. Press, 1944), pp. xviii, xix, xxv.

[4] Alexander Leggatt, "The Extra Dimension: Shakespeare in Performance," in Mosaic 13 (Spring 1977), Shakespeare Today, ed. Ralph Berry (Winnipeg: University of Manitoba Press, 1977), p. 38.

[5] Sir Theodore Martin, Helena Faucit (Lady Martin) (London: William Blackwood and Sons, 1900), p. 131.

[6] Martin, p. 135.

[7] Charles E. Wingate, Shakespeare's Heroines on the Stage (New York: Thomas Y. Crowell and Co., 1895), p. 288.

[8] Henry Morley, The Journal of a London Playgoer from 1851-1866, (London: George Routledge and Sons, 1866), p. 50.

[9] Gamini Salgado, Eyewitnesses of Shakespeare: First-Hand Accounts of Performances 1590-1890 (London: Cox and Wyman Ltd., 1975), p. 239.

[10] James Boaden, Memoirs of Mrs. Siddons (London: Henry Colburn, 1827), II, 208.

[11] See, for example: Jesse Dorynne (pseud.), The True Ophelia and Other Studies (London, 1913); Grace Latham, O Poor Ophelia! (n.p.: n.p., 1884); Ellen Terry, Four Lectures on Shakespeare's Characters (London: Hopkinson, 1932). Ethel Barrymore, for whom the role was a favorite, complained that the part was usually relegated to "little flibbertigibbets, chosen apparently for both their youth and imbecility, so that when

Ophelia does go mad, the shock which Shakespeare meant the audience to feel is no shock at all." Quoted in Carol Jones Carlisle, Shakespeare from the Green Room: Actors' Criticisms of Four Major Tragedies (Chapel Hill: University of North Carolina Press, 1969), p. 138.

[12] See, for example: Carroll Camden, "On Ophelia's Madness," Shakespeare Quarterly, 15.2 (1964), 247-255; A.O. Kellogg, M.D., Shakespeare's Psychological Delineations: Ophelia (Utica, N.Y.: n.p., 1864.)

[13] A comprehensive discussion of the allusions in Ophelia's songs can be found in Peter J. Seng's The Vocal Songs in the Plays of Shakespeare (Cambridge, Mass.: Harvard University Press, 1967), pp. 131-156.

[14] Shakespeare Centre Library Promptbook 72.907 CHA.

[15] Folger Library Promptbook, Hamlet #32.

[16] Alan Hughes, Henry Irving, Shakespearean (Cambridge: Cambridge University Press, 1981), p. 69.

[17] Having missed this production, I am indebted to Miriam Gilbert for the use of her extensive unpublished notes on the performance. Although this Hamlet was unabashedly eccentric in many respects, Ophelia's action here is only an extension of a well-developed tradition.

[18] Folger Library Promptbook, Hamlet Fo4 v.1.

[19] Sprague, p. 172.

[20] Folger Library Promptbook, Hamlet #29.

[21] Shakespeare Centre Library Promptbook 72.907 CHA.

[22] R. Mander and J. Mitchenson, Hamlet Through the Ages: A Pictorial Record from 1709, ed. Herbert Marshall (London: Rockliff, 1952), p. 181.

[23] Dorynne, p. 49.

[24] Richard Sterne, John Gielgud Directs Richard Burton in Hamlet (London: Heinemann, 1967), p. 109; Barbara Leigh-Hunt, discussion with NEH Summer Seminar, Stratford-upon-Avon, July 16, 1980.

[25] Richard David, "The Problem of Hamlet," in Shakespeare in the Theatre (Cambridge: Cambridge University Press, 1978), pp. 75 & 83.

[26] J.C. Trewin, Peter Brook: A Biography (London: Macdonald, 1971), p. 92.

[27] Carlisle, p. 145.

[28] Folger Library Promptbook, Hamlet #31.

[29] Sterne, pp. 20 & 109.

[30] Carlisle, p. 147.

[31] Peter Lewis, "Hamlet Goes Strangely and Excitingly Mad," Daily Mail, 6 June 1970.

[32] As quoted in Austin Brereton, The Lyceum Theatre and Henry Irving (London: Lawrence and Bullen, Ltd., 1903), p. 213.

[33] Francis Fergusson, The Idea of a Theater: A Study of Ten Plays Princeton, N.J.: Princeton University Press, 1968), p. 115.

SHAKESPEARE AND TELEVISION: THE BBC-TV HAMLET

H.R. Coursen

I begin with the no doubt banal assertion that no film can be "true to Shakespeare." Film can give us Agincourt, as Olivier did so magnificently, but as Shakespeare claims he cannot in the opening Chorus of Henry V. Film must create a visual equivalent for language. A visual medium can give us little of the language per se. We might agree, however, that language is the basic stuff of Shakespearean drama. I suggest, with comparable banality, that television is not film. While TV can give us more language than film, its image is not larger than life, but smaller, except when extreme close-ups are employed. TV's basic reduction of the image can make the camera even more of a dictator than it is on the wide screen, where depth can be evoked, sky, vista and detail incorporated within an amplitude that the picture tube cannot embrace. I suggest further that a really good production of Shakespeare on television is akin to the "event" that is theater. Discussions of the conventions and techniques of television--so different than those of the theater--are vital and often fascinating, but their focus is upon the way the performance is presented. The best TV productions gradually erase our concentration on technique and draw us into that attentiveness similar to what happens to us in the theater. The question becomes, what are the actors and their director doing with the script? I believe that the greatest compliment can be paid to a television version of a Shakespeare play when the production allows us to deal with it in the vocabulary of the theater, not just of the tube.

The problems of producing Shakespeare for television become more obvious as the hasty and under-budgeted BBC-TV productions continue to emerge. A "cool" medium like television may be inappropriate to the fiery energies of living theater, particularly of Shakespearean drama. If Shakespeare called for a "muse of fire" to ignite the imaginations of an audience staring at a "wooden O," he might, if confronting many of the recent renditions, have shrugged with Bardolph and said, "Well, the fuel is gone that maintained that fire."

Unlike the tube, Shakespeare elevated mass expectation to create, among other things, the greatest audience that ever existed--the Elizabethan-Jacobean audience of the two-decade blaze of his genius. It was a living audience within the space where the words and actions were being heard and seen for the first time. That audience sought entrance to the Globe, not merely escape from this world. Nowadays, surrounded by thermostats, refrigerators full of beverages, and other creature comforts, we turn the television on to turn ourselves off. If Shakespeare transcends, the tube diminishes, and the mating of the two represents a kind of generic mid-air collision. The conflict between the commitment of going to the theater and the passivity of flicking on a switch, between living <u>mimesis</u> and canned imitation, is probably irresolvable.

    Still, Shakespeare should work on television! Television evolved from radio, with its reliance on voice and sound. TV demands language to augment the size of its image. Television should be a better medium for Shakespeare than film, which has evolved from the imagery of the silent screen. Can we imagine a made-for-cinema film that incorporated a laugh-track? I'm sure that what we recall of the great Shakespeare films <u>is</u> the image--the Capulet Ball and the sweaty duel from Zeffirelli's <u>Romeo</u>, all those arrows pin-cushioning Kurosawa's Macbeth-figure, all those arrows quivering off like miniature Spitfires towards the French armor in Oliver's <u>Henry V</u>, and the documentary effect projected into the monumental scenes structured by Kosintsev in his virtually silent versions of <u>Hamlet</u> and <u>King Lear</u>.

    The BBC version of <u>Hamlet</u> was one of the better productions of the series, and looks even better in retrospect, after the abysmal versions of <u>Shrew</u> and <u>Antony and Cleopatra</u> of recent bad memory. (One wishes memory were worse, could become oblivion!). Since all productions of <u>Hamlet</u> represent inevitable reductions of the vast possibilities of the script, television's inevitable reduction of a stage play into a tiny and mechanical frame was not overly oppressive. The major problem with this <u>Hamlet</u>, as with so many of the BBC-TV versions of the plays, was that this was too obviously a studio production. Such productions can work well with the one-on-one confrontations and psychologically intense "super soap" of <u>Measure for Measure</u>. But this <u>Hamlet</u> kept calling attention to limitations of time and money, to problems behind the production which the most brilliant acting or direction could never overcome.

This studio-bound _Hamlet_ created the feeling of Oliver's film of _Othello_. The latter was a recording of a great performance, as Bowsley Crowther suggested when the "film" was nominated for an Academy Award. While watching that _Othello_, I yearned for a view of Venice, or for a glimpse of the rack dislimning over Cyprus Harbor--for what _film_ can do. While _Hamlet_ may be a "claustrophobic" _play_ in many ways, the world of Elsinore does have flowers, streams, and graveyards, an out-of-doors that Masterpiece Theater productions like _Our Mutual Friend_ and _Pride and Prejudice_ often brought brilliantly to the tube. A graveyard scene shot at Holy Trinity Church at Stratford--a consummation devoutly to be desired. The BBC-TV Shakespeare series has surrendered too often and too readily to the dimensions of its diminished medium.

The BBC-TV _Hamlet_, however, did what the best of the Masterpiece Theater productions do. It focused on individual performance, primarily _via_ closeups, where facial nuances and subtle vocal qualities could be captured--_if_ the acting is "pulled back" to the kind of understated performances the medium demands. With this focus on acting, other technical aspects became, for me, gradually more insignificant. I felt myself being allowed to respond _past_ the medium, as if it had become an invisible window into the play as play. Let me frame that comment between two examples. In _Shrew_, in the Padua scenes, a single camera squatted over the town well. Jonathan Miller's actors gathered around the camera to butcher their lines. We were made aware not only of remarkably inarticulate acting, but of direction that did not know enough even to employ the three-camera format of, say, "All in the Family," or "Barney Miller." On the other extreme was the Deposition Scene in _Richard II_. After Carlisle had delivered his denunciation of Bolingbroke, the camera trucked back to pursue Northumberland's removal of the Bishop. Into the frame came Charles Grey's York, staring open-mouthed at the courageous Carlisle, as if to say, "That's what I should have said, much earlier!" There, David Giles created a marvelous moment of integration, linking two characters who have no overt contact with each other in the play within a shared emotional context.

The camera in the BBC-TV _Hamlet_ was so subtle that I found myself responding to the production as if it were _theater_. And it is with that vocabulary--_Hamlet_ as play--that I wish to respond to Derek Jacobi's version of The Prince.

Jacobi's strength lay in his recognition that Hamlet is characterized as "inconsistent." The would-be perpetual graduate student is shattered by external events. His behavior becomes, to put it mildly, erratic. He "swings," as Jacobi says, "into suddenly intensely traumatic states" (WNET Dial, No., 1980, 28). As Hamlet's introverted thinking is charged with that psychic pressure known as emotion, feeling lashes out in flashes of impetuosity, and in radically negative judgements--of Claudius, of Gertrude, and of himself. Jacobi captured this sudden shifting better than any Hamlet I have seen, with the possible exceptions of stage performances by Richard Burton and Sam Tsoutsouvas. By allowing his Hamlet to ebb and flow between fruitless introspection and frantic activity, Jacobi articulated a large sector of the characterization. It may be, of course, that the very quality of his performance allowed me to forget that all of this was happening inside a bright square surrounded by thin metal and thick plastic.

Jacobi's finest moments occurred during the climactic play-within-the-play scene. Here, theatricality was nicely accommodated to the tube. Jacobi borrowed from his Old Vic stage performance and donned a skull-mask as emblem of his "idleness." "How fares [pause] our cousin, Hamlet?" Claudius asked with sour amusement. The skull-mask anticipated the Graveyard Scene, and reminded us that, among other roles, Hamlet plays that of jester, the function vacated by Yorick over two decades before. The court of Claudius is characterized accurately by Michael Long in The Unnatural Scene (London: Methuen, 1976) as "manipulative, expeditious and politic, a matter of espionage and the political use of man by man against man," a place that holds "psychic energy [in] contempt" (pp. 127, 144). Some of Hamlet's engery must flow towards the role of "fool," alter ego, "foil," and Jungian "shadow." Claudius can afford no jester, yet it is precisely the purpose of the play-within-the-play to activate the alter ego in Claudius, signalled by his earlier tortured aside: "How smart a lash that speech doth give my conscience!"

Jacobi extended his Yorick into the "Gonzago" sequence, upstaging the actors, who were discomfited by Hamlet's invasion of their space. Having introduced the play <u>via</u> his jester, Hamlet allowed his manic energy to go too <u>far</u>. Had he allowed his fool to rest and watch the play? Well, it is a question this production raised. As it was, Jacobi's Hamlet destroyed the great potential of "Gonzago," and allowed Claudius to evade the trap without giving anyone a glimpse of his guilt--except Hamlet, who saw what he wished to see.

The skull-mask that Jacobi plucked from the Players' prop-chest linked "Gonzago" with ancient drama. While "Gonzago" is more modern than is the Player's speech, which reports, <u>à la</u> Greek drama, rather than imitates action, "Gonzago" is an "old" play. It is cast in sententious couplets, held firmly within its melodramatic generic premises, and solidly embraced by the so-called "unities." It stands as anti-type to the sprawl of the play surrounding it. The outer play represents the "reality" in which Prince Hamlet lives. But the inner play, for all its antique formalism, might have had the power to translate the outer play into something other than a tragedy. Hamlet, the university student who knows what is "caviare to the general," would disapprove of the play <u>he</u> is in. Here, as elsewhere, Shakespeare's characterization of Hamlet is profoundly ironic. Jacobi is the only actor I have seen equal to the irony I describe. Hamlet, the critic of theater and dramaturgy, rejects his own standards, as the character is delineated by Shakespeare. The intellectual, of course, tends to repress the feeling level. Jacobi showed feeling exploding through the rational surface, as Hamlet merged with Lucianus, "nephew to the <u>king</u>!" and destroyed his potential masterpiece, a play that might have forced a guilty creature to proclaim his malefactions. Jacobi's Hamlet became a character Hamlet would scorn (as he does, at times) within a play of which Hamlet would also disapprove. Jacobi's Hamlet became, among other good things, the tragedy of the "detached" literary critic ambushed by his own psyche.

The richness of Jacobi's performance suggests the value of a "stage history" behind a television production. The Royal Shakespeare Company made this point in objecting to the BBC-TV Series when it was announced. R.S.C. produced Trevor Nunn's studio version of <u>Macbeth</u> (with Ian McKellan and Judi Dench) as a proof of <u>its</u> premise. Further proof was provided in the <u>Hamlet</u> by Patrick Stewart's Claudius, either under-rehearsed or badly-directed. Hardly a "mighty opposite," this

Claudius seemed merely amused by Hamlet's little entertainment. This interpretation made nonsense out of Claudius's earlier guilty aside and of his attempt to pray after the breakup of "Gonzago." Stewart showed by default how vital the role of Claudius is in the script, and, in contrast to Jacobi, how important the mastery of the role on stage might have been. A fully realized Claudius, having worked out the nuances of his interplay with the actor playing Hamlet, might have made this a "Hamlet for our times," a truly successful translation of the stage play to television. Jacobi came close to doing so singlehandedly, but no Hamlet can really succeed without the substance and complexity of a fully-characterized Claudius. The vocabulary of the theater is, I am convinced, necessary to an understanding of why this very good production was not even better.

If we are, as McLuhan argues, a "global village," a tiny planet linked in simultaneously via satellite, then the BBC-TV series is tremendously significant. Perhaps the single universal the world does share is Shakespeare. As Bradley Pearson, the eccentric protagonist of Iris Murdoch's The Black Prince, says of Hamlet, "it is the best known work of literature in the world. Indian peasants, Australian lumberjacks, Argentine ranchers, Norwegian sailors, members of the Red Army, Americans, all the most remote and brutish specimens of mankind have heard of Hamlet."

Whether the BBC-TV productions, often bland, sometimes banal, will communicate Shakespeare's universality to our global village is doubtful. BBC seems to have pulled Shakespeare down into the dimensions of a diminished medium, where the cramped studio corresponds to the tiny screen, and too often to have cooled Shakespeare to the tonality of a tube designed to deflect emotional response. But perhaps television is a product of our own expectations. We should, then, insist on at least good television productions. We are getting some-- Measure for Measure, most of the Second Henriad (I found Jon Finch much too histrionic as Henry IV), Twelfth Night, and Hamlet. BBC-TV could turn a generation on to Shakespeare, as did the Olivier films for my generation, or BBC could cool a generation into a permanent chill-- as productions like the vapid Romeo and Juliet, the dull As You Like It (where the out-of-doors was ill-used), the drab Tempest, and Miller's indescribably awful Shrew and Antony and Cleopatra are likely to do.

Television would seem to be the diminished medium of a global village. Perhaps it provides a shallow equivalent for the unexamined modern psyche, a substitute for our inability to confront our deeper, inner energies. Could Shakespeare deepen, expand, transcend our need for emotional baby-sitting? If the tube serves as alter ego for our souls, a great production of Shakespeare might mousetrap us into a meeting with the deeper faces of the self. It has happened during moments within these productions. Such moments--for me--included the close-ups of Alec McCowan's Malvolio duping himself via Maria's letter, David Gwillim's dispatch of the Cambridge Conspiracy in Henry V, Kate Nelligan's scornful response to Claudio's plea for life in Measure for Measure, John Tordoff's brilliant cameo as Cinna the Poet, and, of course, the skull-mask sequence in Hamlet.

But such moments seem to be pearls without a string. And it may be the lack of stage history behind most of the productions that denies a mechanical, already-taped production its opportunity to create that great, final release known as catharsis. Catharsis can occur after comedy as well as tragedy, I submit. That the actors have not worked together in ensemble is too obvious in these productions. That the actors are learning their characterizations as they go along is also clear, as in the recent Winter's Tale, which developed uncertainly towards a fine final scene. A television studio is more like a stage, I suggest, than is a film set. The development of television's technique towards the experience of theater should be the goal of BBC-TV. But these rush jobs, too often lacking the depth of development of, for example, Jacobi's Hamlet, too seldom allow us to approach the plays as plays. When and if that fulfillment occurs in this series, BBC-TV will have translated a medium that insists upon our passivity into a Shakespearean production that will emerge from his age into our time. Shakespeare, I feel confident, is equal to the challenge. But is BBC-TV? So far, only now and then, but seldom with the consistency of rhythm and depth of characterization that we expect from the best stage productions of these plays.

THE SETTING IN EARLY TELEVISION
MAURICE EVANS' SHAKESPEARE PRODUCTIONS

Bernice W. Kliman

In the heyday of live television, Joyce C. Hall, daring President of the Hallmark Card Company, sponsor of the Hallmark Hall of Fame, agreed to an innovative experiment: live Shakespeare in a two-hour production, not only the first "complete" Shakespeare on American television, but also the first dramatic production of that length in the medium.[1] To accommodate the experiment, NBC delayed other scheduled broadcasts. It was 1953, and one of the principal Shakespearean actors was Maurice Evans, who, only a few years before, had produced and acted in the successful G.I. Hamlet, performed in the Pacific theater for American soliders during World War II, with George Schaefer, a young sergeant, as director. The soldiers had responded to a Hamlet living in a state of siege, where every man wore a uniform, where the sense of imminent disaster was palpable. It was all familiar to them. This Hamlet, produced on Broadway shortly after the war, in 1946, was the basis for the Hallmark production.[2]

Reviewers, hopeful about what the experiment boded, were ecstatic.[3] As late as 1975, Cecil Smith, columnist for the Los Angeles Times, said that the two-hour Hamlet "made Hallmark a television standard for the rest of the industry" (22 Oct., Sec. 4, p. 20). This production was followed by many others starring Evans. These early live broadcasts, fortunately saved by the kinescope process,[4] offer valuable insights into television during its "golden age," give those too young to have seen him a sense of Maurice Evans as an actor, and form the basis for the whole interesting topic of Shakespeare on television in that they offer an opportunity for an experiment in criticism. Normally, the number of variables among productions makes almost foolhardy an attempt to evaluate the important factors--concept, acting, setting--as they are shaped by the medium. To take the analogy of film: can one compare Olivier's Hamlet to Kozintsev's to find out what the film medium can do when the goal of each is so different, the one to write an essay on Hamlet for the millions, the other to shape an Aesopian political message? Can one meaningfully compare a 1936 quintessentially Hollywood Romeo and Juliet with the robust Zeffirelli film of 1968? But the four television productions I am concerned with--<u>Hamlet</u>, <u>Richard II</u>, <u>Macbeth</u>, <u>Taming of the Shrew</u>--were all directed by Schaefer, starred Maurice Evans, and were produced live during a three-year period in the fifties.[5] With so many significant constants, perhaps one can decide what makes Shakespeare on television successful. These four indicate, by demonstrating the range of television possibilities, that Shakespeare on television works best when producers do not try to imitate the illusion we expect of movie space, but opt for a semi-illusionist setting like that of the proscenium-arch stage, or for the even more suggestive and imaginative bare television setting.[6]

First, <u>Hamlet</u> (26 April 1953): The opening shot of King Hamlet's tombstone (1830-1890) tells us it is the nineteenth century. In a dissolve, we move to I.ii, the first court scene, to see a fussy interior. Nothing could be further from Olivier's moody set in his 1948 filmed <u>Hamlet</u> than the Victorian clutter.[7] Having once settled on a definite time, however, the producers are committed to a specific kind of space. In drawing rooms and sitting rooms, we see urns, crystal, candlesticks, statues, couches, portraits, china, inkstands, cushions, chests, pilasters, clocks, bric-a-brac of all kinds, all over. These environmental trivia are not only distracting but also contrast ironically with the elemental passions of the play--either that or they swamp any passions entirely.[8] The setting opposes the atmosphere that the uniforms were to help create.

The producers seem to be aiming for the measure of illusion movie sets afford. But the set, not large enough to represent convincingly a castle interior, inevitably clashes with the solid weight of so many objects. The spatial relations of one part of the set to another are studio-like, that is, unrealistically close to each other, while in any one shot, realism dominates the frame. This combination is similar to Olivier's successful design for <u>Richard III</u> (1955), a film partly financed by arrangements to show it on television coincident with its theatrical release, and thus filmed with television in mind. But its set was much larger and more sparsely furnished. Another difference may be that the time of <u>Richard III</u> allows for a medieval-renaissance grandeur while the time of Evans' <u>Hamlet</u> diminishes mystery with distance as it places us

in our Victorian grandmothers' living rooms. In any
case, the set designer's mix of artifice (in connections
between parts of the set representing different areas
of the castle) and reality (within each part) is not
quite right, though it is difficult to pinpoint the
specific errors of judgment and taste. That such a mix
can work is clear not only from Olivier's nearly contemporary work but also from the more recent BBC-TV
Shakespeare Plays, such as <u>Measure for Measure</u> and <u>All's
Well That Ends Well</u>.

The nunnery and prayer scenes take place in the
set's most believable section, which has few distracting
objects. A wrought iron doorway allows for some attractive shots, especially of Hamlet peering through at the
praying Claudius. Also workable is "The Mousetrap"
setting which, like the nunnery setting, provides
opportunities for scenes in mid- to long-shot with at
least two planes of action.

Even when some of the cluttered areas of the set
are used, creative camera work sometimes minimizes the
oppressive effect. For example, when Horatio confronts
Hamlet for the first time (I.ii.159),[9] the camera shoots
from outside a window looking in on Hamlet, who is
framed by the window, with Horatio dimly behind him.
Since the resolution of the television picture is not
sharp enough to present scenes with much depth of field,
Horatio, behind Hamlet, is almost a blur. In effect,
Hamlet, isolated, concentrates our attention. The
director also controls response with tight shots. While
these do avoid the set for a time, inevitably it intrudes again. (Richardson, who filmed his <u>Hamlet</u> for
television in 1970, solved the problem of the set and
shallow depth of field by shooting virtually the whole
play in close-up.)

This is not to say that had the <u>mise-en-scene</u> been
different, Evans' would have been a great <u>Hamlet</u>.
Several funny bloopers interfere with the audience's
attempt to set aside its understanding that the characters are not real.[10] The most amusing is the stagehand
who tiptoes upstage across the set after Hamlet, downstage, says, "Now I am alone" (II.ii.515); also distracting are microphones and wires in full view. An unlucky
shot catches (and he realizes it) a groom who is carrying
the poisoned cup from Gertrude's side around the whole
set to get to Claudius in time for Hamlet to make the

King drink. This constitutes not only a blooper but also an error in concept. Why would the groom do anything with the poison but remove it or leave it where it was?

More seriously, we sense no informing intelligence desperate to communicate with a receptive yet agonistic audience (to use George Steiner's formulation). There seems to be no overall interpretation.[11] We do not grasp motivations, relationships and their connectedness to the whole. It is "Let's run through <u>Hamlet</u>, Gang," with interpretations only within scenes. Is Claudius friendly or not? Gertrude does not let Claudius finish his pompous lecture on mourning (I.ii.87-106), yet Claudius motions her to persuade Hamlet to stay at Elsinore (in the pause between lines 117 and 118). The courtiers do not react to the news that Hamlet is heir. Is it therefore an empty promise in this version? Or were the supernumeraries not rehearsed? Later, Ophelia and Laertes exchange a knowing look--"Oh, no, not again"--when Polonius advises Laertes (I.iii.58-81). This is a mistake, because Ophelia and Laertes must respect as well as love their father, however he may appear to others, or their subsequent behavior is inexplicable. For the sake of an easy laugh here, the producers rip the web of connections. Similarly, in the same scene, Ophelia shakes her head, objecting to Polonius' aspersions against Hamlet, but then she says, "I shall obey" without being pressed. The two responses are at odds. Hamlet, in his scene with Ophelia, shows his love for her, making unintelligible Claudius' cruel declaration, "Love! His affections do not <u>that</u> way tend" (pointing at her). From behind the wrought iron doors, Claudius and Polonius have presumably seen that Hamlet becomes bitter only after Ophelia reveals the spying by looking towards them. Since in this production she realized fully, with deep chagrin, that she has given herself away, her last speech of the scene, "Heavenly powers, restore him!" (III.i.138), is incongruous; she knows very well how to account for Hamlet's agitation.

Such inconsistencies continue throughout the production. The producers unfortunately place Ophelia's mad scene at her bed, with a doctor and nurse in attendance, making it difficult to understand how she gets away to drown herself. (On the other hand, the rag doll she cradles in her arms is effective.) And since

Laertes does not jump into the grave (there is none; the scene takes place inside at the altar where Claudius was praying and near the spot where Ophelia and Hamlet had their last "private" talk), Hamlet's passionate outburst seems unmotivated.

Other choices, while not creating inconsistencies, are timid or obvious. Hamlet, for example, does not speak his "What a piece of work is a man" to Rosencrantz and Guildenstern but almost to himself as he turns away from them and looks out a window (II.ii.292-97). Thus Schaefer loses the opportunity, grasped by some other productions, to show that Hamlet tests them with these lines, tentatively revealing some of his inner pain to them--but their callous response, laughter, persuades him they are no longer his friends. Instead, Schaefer chooses the banal ploy of having them, early in the scene, try to steal a letter from Hamlet's book when he turns away.

These courtiers are suitably sycophantic but many of the actors are less than adequate or sadly miscast. Sarah Churchill is too forthright and steady a soul to go mad. In close-up, Evans, at 52, seems old for the part, older than Claudius, played by Joseph Schildkraut (58). Gertrude, perforce, has to be too old to consider seriously as a sensuous woman, and Ruth Chatterton (59), who plays her, forgets some lines. Her smile is grotesque, a false-looking grimace that flashes on and off. Our last view of her is indeed strange. As she sings (literally) "poisoned," those around her spirit her off the set before she falls. Hamlet says no "adieu" to her.

Some viewers may have an aversion to Evans' mannered and rhetorical acting style, with quaver in voice and quiver on lips, "Shakespearean" in a somewhat exaggerated way. His technique, however, illustrates the historical development of Shakespearean acting. Clearly, Evans' method was in fashion in the '30s, '40s, and even the '50s in a way it cannot be today. George Jean Nathan (1882-1958), in praising Evans' stage performance, cites particularly his naturalness, yet this is precisely the quality that modern audiences might miss in Evans' television performance.[12]

Although bloopers, failures of conception, downright poor acting by some of the supporting cast and old-fashioned acting by Evans hinder this production, the sets finally spoil it because by imposing, with those artifacts, an artificial kind of realism on the play, they highlight all the other defects, which in essence are failures of verisimilitude.

Richard II and Macbeth (from Hallmark's third and fourth seasons, respectively) are superior to Hamlet because the settings, which the producers did not update, serve both concepts and acting styles. Richard (24 January 1954), an intelligent and well-conceived production, uses a variety of sets. The interiors are illusionistic while the exteriors are quite obviously studio shot. Filmed shots of Queen Elizabeth II's coronation introduced the television production. Such spectacles demonstrate that television can capture the pomp and ceremony of grand scenes, even if heads in some shots must be seen as pinpoints. The large-scale prologue lends plausibility to the public scene that follows in the play,[13] which opens in a large, medieval interior.[14] Gothic windows and soaring clusters of slender, engaged columns banded by shaft rings recall features of Westminster Abbey (where Queen Elizabeth II's coronation had taken place). The only inauthentic touch in this room is a multi-cusped doorway arch that looks like something out of Dr. Caligari. The smaller room where Gaunt confronts Richard is a well-realized, intimate medieval setting, with casement windows, fireplace, and a few, well-chosen artifacts. In a room filled with natural-looking light, low camera angles provide good views of the room's beamed ceiling. In other interiors, a brazier lights the tent where York and Bolingbroke contend (II.iii), and the prison at Pomfret, a cavernous setting, has bone-chilling stone walls, weak candle light and barred windows. Throughout these interiors, the illusion of reality holds.

The outdoor scenes, with their flat studio floors for ground, artificial leaves and paper maché stones, include the approach to Gaunt's room; the orchard where most of Isabel's scenes take place (including, rather strangely, II.iii, for when York says, "Come, cousin, I'll dispose of you," it is rather a shock to find her still there in III.iv); the dock where Bolingbroke embarks and disembarks; the coast of Wales and the exterior of Flint Castle. The set designer, Richard Sylbert, who also designed Hamlet and Macbeth, merely nods toward illusion for these, fully half the scenes of the play.

In sum, Sylbert compromises between illusion and stage convention. We are not able to forget for long that this is a play (not a real-life event like the coronation that proceeds it), yet the settings of the opening scenes of the first two acts place Richard in his own milieu of medieval splendor (I.i) or intimacy (II.i).[15] Perhaps Sylbert attempted illusion throughout, for the producers were evidently very proud of the 40-foot structure they built for the Flint Castle scene. Still, sighting it as we do from the vantage point of Northumberland's horse, it seems too dwarfish to fool anyone's eye.[16]

Just as the set is part illusionistic and part not, so too is the acting. Evans' natural geniality and urbanity serve him well in the early scenes of this production. Quavering utterances are often completely absent, and when there seem to fit Richard's self-pity better than they did Hamlet's introspection. He pauses within verse lines more infrequently than he did in Hamlet, especially in the first part when his whole demeanor breathes confidence and competence. Yet when the camera catches Richard's entry not in mid-act but in a frozen tableau, we are not seeing an imitation of reality.[17]

But if setting and acting are sometimes contradictory in the effects they evoke, the interpretation is unified and coherent. Evans spans the character's full emotional breadth. We see a king boyishly well pleased with his ability to manipulate those around him, a spoiled playboy who has never had anyone say "nay" to him. His arrogant entrance with two wolfhounds characterizes him well. Although this production eliminates I.ii. and thus Gaunt's implication of Richard in Gloucester's death, Richard implicates himself by the look he exchanges with his friends when Bolingbroke accuses Mowbray. Immediately plunged into the ambiguity of the play, we are forced to feel ambivalent about the antagonists, the present and the future kings. Richard later becomes a pitiable spectacle as he recognizes his own vulnerability, but when he confronts Bolingbroke at the deposition, he achieves a grandeur and a stature that had eluded him at first. Richard, a deeply flawed king who nevertheless does not deserve his fate, reaches tragic dimensions through self-recognition.

There are several brilliant scenes, including York's capitulation to Bolingbroke; partly he is convinced, partly bullied into acquiescing. York is truly touched when Bolingbroke calls him "father" (II.iii.116-17), and he recognizes the validity of Bolingbroke's claim, but he is also ringed by hostile noblemen who dare him to resist. Bolingbroke suggests his own probity as his cohorts expose their malevolence. The claustrophobic tent setting embodies York's difficult moral position, sympathetic as he is to both Richard and Henry.

Throughout, the camera is handled with skill and tact, deftly varying point of view to focus audience attention. A high angle shot of the swearing scene from I.iii, for example, makes God a witness to Bolingbroke's and Mowbray's oaths. Later, because the camera keeps him at the foreground, Northumberland dominates the scene with Ross and Willoughby after Gaunt's death (II.i). In the wrenching scene when Richard takes blow after blow, rallying after each one until the last, York's defection, the frame varies from wide long shots to five-shots, three-shots and one-shots of Richard (III.ii). This camera flexibility keeps Richard at the center of our interest but frequently, as Shakespeare intended, shows the reactions of the others as well. Similarly, long shots of the deposition scene allow us to feel fully the public spectacle of Richard's fall. We see all the players in the drama: silent, frozen Henry; embarrassed, sunken York; peremptory Northumberland; passive bystanders. Contrasting close-ups of Richard explore the dynamics of pain. The settings provide the kinds of space that allow this variety in camera technique.

While they make the production something different from Shakespeare's play, cuts and transpositions not only keep set changes to a minimum but also emphasize the struggles between Richard and Bolingbroke. With no women beside Isabel and her ladies, the Duchess of Gloucester and the Duchess of York are gone and so therefore is the Aumerle plot. With no tournament, Richard decisively banishes Mowbray and Bolingbroke immediately--and apparently meant to do so even before they came forward, for he had the bills of banishment prepared in advance. The gardener's scene (III.iv), which follows the deposition, merges with Richard's and Isabel's farewell (V.i). Instead of being a preparation, then, for the deposition, the gardener's speech about weeds is an ex post facto rationalization. For

142

the most part, the changes are intelligent, and though we may miss the balance of characterization or the sweep of history afforded by the missing scenes (including the one that mentions the truant Hal), given the producers' need to reduce the play to one-and-three-quarter hours (fifteen minutes for commercials), the cuts are unobjectionable.

Pleasing transitions, with metaphoric content, connect disparate scenes and settings, supplying the connective thread missed in Hamlet. A close-up of cups raised by Bushy, Bagot and Green in I.iv dissolves to a close-up of Gaunt's cup of medicine in II.i, aptly pointing the contrast. Near the end of II.i, as the King, Queen and others, after Gaunt's death, leave the medieval room, the camera frames them as they walk outside past the casement window. After they have gone by, the camera tracks up to the window to show the rebels, Northumberland, Ross and Willoughby, looking out at the departing royal party. Then, with a cut to the inside, the scene is completed. Later, the fire in the prison scene (V.v) dissolves to the fire in the grating of Gaunt's room for the Exton-Bolingbroke scene and then back to the prison again. The break in this scene, much like the dissolves in the 1978 BBC production, suggests that Richard's musings cover a span of time. The fire, used here to underline, also harks back to its use analogically in II.i when, just as he opens the grating, Gaunt says "His rash fierce blaze of riot cannot last, For violent fires soon burn out themselves" (lines 33-34). Because the Exon-Bolingbroke conversation takes place in the same room, by the same fire, Gaunt, as it were, not only describes Richard but prophesies about Henry.

The connection is emphasized by one profound change from Shakespeare's text. In a scene derived from Marlowe's Edward II (V.iv), King Henry talks personally to Exton, instead of Exton talking to his servant as in Act V, scene iv in Shakespeare.[18] Speaking Lightborn's part, Exton reveals himself as totally evil, an assassin who is proud of the several ways he has disposed of victims for clients. Henry, taking Mortimer's role, gives him a bag of money and tells him never to return unless he eliminates Richard. This is far from the hesitant, questioning Exton of Shakespeare's play or from the repentant Exton from Holinshed. Correspondingly, Hallmark's Exton kills Richard treacherously:

after Richard rushes out, Exton stabs him in the back. He expressed no regret. Plotting directly with Exton blackens Henry's character considerably, especially since no mercy scene with Aumerle mitigates his crime. This Henry is less the enigmatic politician, more the ambitious hypocrite, especially when he repudiates Exton in V.vi. Though we cannot altogether blame him for the usurpation, for we recognize that Richard, through misrule, has abrogated his right to the crown, pity for Richard grows through the textual change. Ironically, too, the scene takes place in the same setting where Richard, by his callous indifference to Gaunt, most alienated our sympathy.

For _Macbeth_ (28 November 1954), the producers chose a set that seems much smaller than the one used for _Richard II_.[19] We see for most of the play a primitive castle interior with bare flagstone floors, stone walls, arched windows and doorways, stone balconies, with pools of light created by torches. Jack Gould, in his _New York Times_ review of this performance, deplored its realistic sets because he felt they distracted the viewer.[20] But to a viewer of today--more obviously than for _Hamlet_ or for _Richard II_--these interiors do not create the illusion of reality. The producers here seem to be aiming for the level of realism possible on film but instead fortuitously achieve the level possible on the proscenium-arch stage. We are to imagine the imposing entrance hall of a castle in a cramped studio space. The drawbridge is a squat little thing. Stairways sweep upwards about ten feet. High angle shots used to attempt a sense of spaciousness and to place the audience in position of judge cannot overcome the set's fortunate limitations in terms of realism. Welles's insistent wide-angle lens in his filmed _Macbeth_, 1948, succeeded in creating the illusion of deep space in a small set because the film medium responds better to such tricks. Exteriors of Evans' _Macbeth_, as in _Richard II_, are frankly studio shot.

Whether by intention or not, the stagey contrivance of the set is an asset in the Hallmark performance because Judith Anderson's Lady Macbeth and Maurice Evans' tremolo Macbeth, both larger than life, need the artifice of a stage background to be acceptable. Setting, objects and acting do not clash.

Television's shallow depth of field, which accounts for the difference between what Welles and Schaefer can do with limited space, does not allow for great variety in blocking, but some good moments stand out. One occurs when Ross and Angus arrive to tell Macbeth about his promotion to Thane of Cawdor (I.iii). Macbeth stands downstage; Banquo, just a foot or so behind him, faces Ross and Angus at the rear, talking to them (line 143) as Macbeth broods about the witches (lines 127-43; 146-47). Banquo then pivots toward Macbeth to say "Worthy Macbeth, we stay upon your leisure" (line 148). In a very small space, with the slightly high-angle shot, the director gives the impression of two planes of action rather than one. Again, when King Duncan arrives, Macbeth eavesdrops from behind an arch downstage while upstage Lady Macbeth greets the entourage. And this same device is used when Malcolm and Donalbain decide to leave: we see them in the background as Macbeth in the foreground listens from behind an arch. Blocking also emphasizes the stylized, formal court of Macbeth contrasted to the loose informality of Duncan's court. Finally, in the last scene, in a tour de force on live television, Evans fools the eye when fighting with Macduff; with swords in action all the while, the frame cuts Evans out for a second of two, allowing him to be replaced by a stand-in who falls down the stairs, dead. Few will detect the substitution.

As in <u>Hamlet</u>, however, no strong overall concept unifies the work. Banquo should not be suspicious of Macbeth from the start, for that does not match Evans' portrayal of him as a good man who disintegrates. More importantly, this production suffers, in spite of its effective touches, because Evans' depiction of Macbeth falls short of the variety of his Richard portrayal. He lacks the driving force of evil; a weariness at his center saps the play's energy. Evans amplifies the effect of his persona by transposing the announcement of Malcolm as heir from I.iv.35-42 to just before scene vii. In the text, the earlier announcement stirs Macbeth's murderous ambition, but then Duncan's geniality reactivates Macbeth's conscience. In Evans' version his conscience awakens on the heels of the announcement. Like the <u>Hamlet</u>, this production is sometimes too obvious, as when Macbeth points to crown and scepter as he says the words,

> Upon my head they placed a fruitless crown
> And put a barren scepter in my gripe.
> (III.i.61-62)

When Hallmark decided to repeat Macbeth in 1960--still directed by Schaefer, with Evans and Anderson as principals--off they went to Scotland to film the drama in color on location.[21] Live television was dead by 1960. This is a film rather than a television drama.[22]

Virtually anything can be filmed, but not everything filmed is a film. Television, like film, can accommodate many formats, many kinds of content: lectures, lessons, advertisements, serials, drama, "magazines"--the range is almost limitless. Television, however, is most itself, at least today, when a videocamera is pointed at someone in the street who has witnessed a robbery, who has an opinion, whose house has just burned down. It is the real and now, Queen Elizabeth II's coronation or Charles' and Diana's wedding. Shakespeare, obviously, is not real and now in the same way. But when a television production repudiates the real, cuts its easy connection to the mundane by avoiding illusionist settings, it liberates us from the conventionality of the everyday that undermines what Shakespeare is--an assault on the audience's intellect, emotion and sensibility, a subversion of our usual white-noise existence. What can startle in the real after we have seen presidents and popes shot? Onstage, too, for present sensibilities, Shakespeare seems to respond best to the barest stage, allowing for quick exits and entrances and the creation of space in the audience's mind by Shakespeare's words.

Taming of the Shrew, broadcast 18 March 1956, with Evans, Schaefer as director, and a charming Lilli Palmer as Katherine, cuts those connections to the real. The set, created by Roubben Ter-Arutunian, is a large, almost empty space with clowns carrying on props as needed in this commedia dell'arte production.[23] Though twenty-five years old, it stands up very well. One might say that Shrew, after all, is a comedy and thus has a better chance at success than the tragedies; but this is unlikely, because Maurice Evans is better known for his tragic than for his comic characterizations, and because Shrew is so full of vexing questions of male-female relationships that it could be difficult to present a widely-acclaimed version. Shakespeare, of course, deflects criticism by treating it as a play within a play, framed by the "real" play of one Christopher Sly. Although the Hallmark production omits Christopher Sly (along with Gremio, the widow and other subsidiary characters), the non-illusionistic setting constantly informs us that these hi-jinks are not all that serious and those who dislike the play's politics are making earnest out of game. In spite of the artifice of the setting, however, the audience can accept the characters and their dilemmas as real enough to empathize with because the emotional states of the actors are realistic.[24]

As a distancing effect, a pair of adagio dancers dressed like Kate and Petruchio recreate as part of the wedding entertainment the wooing, wedding and taming of Kate, whip and all--except this Kate makes the last move, breaking a paper hoop over her husband's head. (The male looks like Douglas Fairbanks, perhaps an allusion to the 1929 Taming of the Shrew with Fairbanks and Mary Pickford; also like Fairbanks, Evans wears a ring in one ear.)

The medium is used throughout to good effect, with unexpected camera angles, wipes from right and left (an anti-illusionary transitional device), and traveling camera. Baptista's house is a raised scaffold between two enclosed boxes that represent the interior. The scaffold quickly becomes a boxing ring for Petruchio's and Kate's first encounter, with bells, handlers, and ringside audience to complete the conceit. When Petruchio and Baptista walk in the arbor, the arches that represent it suddenly appear in the frame, held by white-clad clowns, as the two walk towards the camera, which tracks back with them. Petruchio's horse is a man in a horse costume, the church a two-dimensional facade. Petruchio's home walled with hanging furs expresses his uncouthness.

All is light, bright and joyful--and not a little of the effect is owing to the creative bareness of the set that allows space for infectiously exuberant acting. Suddenly Evans, who in 1953 looked too old to be a credible Hamlet, in 1956 at fifty-five is as youthful a Petruchio as one would want, illustrating that perception is based on style rather than form.[25]

The interpretation is clear and unexceptionable but unified and satisfying. Petruchio's boasting, with its bombastic excess, is stretched to the edge of the ridiculous through the camera angle (very low), the music (parodic) and the reactions of his auditors (delighted). He is having fun. In this same spirit he

woos Kate, and since he loves her and is immediately
drawn to her energy, neither his words nor actions
offend. Kate, too, responds to him. She rises in our
estimation through comparison to her sister, whose
characterization comments on those men who prefer coy
passivity to forthrightness. Much worse than Shakespeare's character, this Bianca is depicted as mercenary, choosing her lover solely on the basis of riches, and as shrewish, for she has the widow's part at the banquet. At the end, then, she and Kate each occupy the original position of the other, but with more truth. Petruchio tames Kate, first by physical force (he literally pins her down, withholds food and rest) and second by showing two mirrors to her: the mirrow of what she truly is, by describing her as sweet and loving, and the mirror of how she is acting, by behaving as shrewishly as possible himself. Kate can change because she _is_ curst for policy. What else can she do with a simpering blonde sister? She is not innately an angry person, for our first view of her shows her smiling at a bird.[26] She is tamed when she joins the fun.[27] Setting gives physical dimension to the concept and helps to determine the acting. The process is dialectical: the shaping energy of the text flows outward to the setting, that of the setting inward to the text.

    Probably no one way of televising Shakespeare will work at all times for all plays. Since television does not yet have the depth of field of film, to attempt a cinematic kind of realism seems to be a mistake. Live television performances, moreover, with no opportunity for reshooting defective moments, for moving from one to another space readily, are inherently more likely to be nonrealistic than film treatments, more likely, in fact, to be akin to stage performances than to film. Illusionist and non-illusionist elements must co-exist in delicate balance. In emulating theater, television has two choices, something equivalent to the proscenium arch, with its own version of realism, or the bare set, with actors alone providing the illusion of reality. A survey of television productions preserved on kinescope, tape and film could tell us which methods or combinations of methods have been most successful. The example of the four live Shakespeare productions, however, seems clear: the bare set is best. Next is the overtly theatrical semi-illusionist set. Either of these complements the artifice of the plays. Either gives Shakespeare the last word.

NOTES

[1] *TV Guide: The First 25 Years*, comp. and ed. Jay S. Harris, in assoc. with the editors of *TV Guide* magazine (New York: Simon & Schuster, 1978), pp. 203-5. Two-hour productions were not, however, to become a television norm for some years. Hallmark sponsored only a few such productions in the '50s.

[2] See Maurice Evans' *GI Production of Hamlet by William Shakespeare: Acting Edition, with a Preface by Maurice Evans* (Garden City, N.Y.: Doubleday, 1947). Stage directions reveal this as similar in concept to the television production. Photographs and sketches, however, show that the stage setting was non-illusionistic.

[3] See, for example, Jack Gould, "Television in Review," *New York Times*, 27 April 1953, p. 29, and Philip Hamburger, "The Dane," *The New Yorker*, 9 May 1953, pp. 67-68.

[4] Kinescopes may be seen at the University Film Study Center, M.I.T.; ATAS/UCLA Television Archives, Los Angeles; Museum of Broadcasting, New York City. I am grateful for a S.U.N.Y. Faculty Research Grant (1981) for affording me the opportunity to view these productions.

[5] According to a letter he sent me, for *Hamlet* Schaefer "cast and directed the actors" but did not work with the camera, the responsibility of Executive Producer and Director Albert McCleery.

Because television, like film, is a group enterprise, praise or blame cannot easily be assigned: McCleery certainly played a strong role while television novices Schaefer, Evans, and producer Mildred Freed Alberg were learning the ropes until, after a disagreement with Evans about mounting R2, he left. Evans, as sometime producer and text adaptor as well as star, certainly had a strong voice. The set designer's independence is not demonstrable. I therefore sometimes ascribe responsibility to one person with the knowledge that I am using synecdoche.

See Ernest Roderick Diehl, "George Schaefer and

the Hallmark Hall of Fame: A Study of the Producer-Director of a Live Television Drama Series," Diss. Ohio State Univ. 1964, pp. 34-68.

[6] I use the work "illusionist" much as John Styan does throughout The Shakespeare Revolution: Criticism and Performance in the Twentieth Century (Cambridge: Cambridge Univ. Press, 1977)--to describe a theater that attempts to create the sense that the audience is looking, as it were, through a window on reality. Styan finds spatial realism to be a distortion of Shakespeare's intention (p. 30). On TV, moreover, because the proscenium arch is absent (it is not the frame around the picture tube), the illusion can be complete. When the setting looks like a studio or stage setting rather than an actual location but with some realistic attributes, then I would call it semi-illusionistic.

[7] Although we expect realism in film, Olivier upsets that convention to provide a poetic setting. See Sheryl W. Gross, "Poetic Realism in Olivier's Hamlet," Hamlet Studies, forthcoming.

[8] Marvin Rosenberg, "Shakespeare on TV: An Optimistic Survey," Film Quarterly, 9 (1954), 166-74, deplores the setting because "background clutter is poison to complex drama." On the other hand, Alice Venesky Griffin, "Shakespeare Through the Camera's Eye--Julius Caesar in Motion Pictures; Hamlet and Othello on Television," Shakespeare Quarterly, 4 (1953), 331-36, says that the 60' x 70' set is "visually helpful and generally uncluttered." Hallmark's setting was lavish compared to those of some other television series, such as Studio One's Julius Caesar (1 May 1949) and Coriolanus (1 June 1951).

An Old Vic production of Hamlet aired on the Dupont Show of the Month in 1959 shows what is possible for early Hamlet on television using uniform and non-time-specific, rather simple yet large, palace settings.

[9] Texts used in this paper are the Norton Critical Edition of Hamlet, ed. Cyrus Hoy (New York: W.W. Norton, 1963), the Arden Richard II, ed. Pater Ure (London: Methuen, 1978), and the Signet Classic editions of Macbeth, ed. Sylvan Barnet (New York: New American Library, 1963), and of Taming of the Shrew, ed. Robert B. Heilman (New York: New American Library, 1966).

[10] For the effect of errors on the audience, see Erving Goffman, *Frame Analysis: An Essay in the Organization of Experience* (Cambridge, Mass.: Harvard Univ. Press, 1974), pp. 136-37. See also, "Alas, Poor Stagehand, We Saw Him Well," *New York Journal American*, 27 April 1953. (When page numbers are omitted in citations, I saw the article at the Lincoln Center Performing Arts Library, where pages are not always noted on clippings.)

[11] Bernard Grebanier, *The Heart of Hamlet: The Play Shakespeare Wrote, with the Text of the Play* (New York: Crowell, 1960), p. 307, says this also of Evans' stage *Hamlet*.

[12] Nathan is quoted by Alan Dent, "Hamlets--Modern and Ancient," in *The Film Hamlet*, ed. Brenda Cross (London: The Saturn Press, 1948), p. 65. The sound track of the film "Enter Hamlet," a 3-minute short distributed by Pyramid, demonstrates a typical speech by Evans, the "To be or not to be," with its characteristic pauses and quavers. Evans does not act in this "Shakespearean" way in non-Shakespearean roles, for example in Hallmark's "Dial 'M' for Murder," 25 April 1958. He was performing in this play on Broadway in 1953 while he was in rehearsal for *Hamlet* on TV. A contemporary reviewer says that Evans, whom he likes in the modern play, "often struts and 'tears a passion to tatters' when he comes to Avon": *Saturday Review*, 16 May 1953, p. 33.

[13] The Coronation was in June 1953. The strategy of beginning a large play like *R2* with a coronation is much better than the current BBC practice of beginning in a producer's or scholar's study (or facsimile thereof).

[14] It was actually shot in "NBC's huge new Brooklyn studio," according to *Time*, 1 February 1954, p. 59.

[15] Interestingly, Evans' break-through *R2* on Broadway (1937), the first in over 60 years in America, employed a similar mixture of illusion and unfeigned staginess. See Walter Prichard Eaton, "Shakespeare--With a Difference," *Atlantic Monthly*, April 1937, pp. 474-77. Critics praised Evans' portrayal highly.

[16] "Video Rushes in Where Angel's Fear," *Life*, 8 February 1954, pp. 54, 56, has some photos that illustrate this point.

¹⁷ Commercials in the '50s begin just so--in frozen tableaux--and then, as if at a signal, the woman starts mopping her floors, or whatever. Current conventions, however, call for capturing an action in progress.

¹⁸ Thanks to Peter Saccio for identifying the interpolated scene as Marlowe's. Evans' Broadway version did not make this substitution, according to the two prompt books at the Lincoln Center Performing Arts Library.

¹⁹ Perhaps they were affected by Jack Gould's criticism of the impersonality of huge sets and long shots in his review of R2: New York Times, 25 January 1954, p. 25. If so, they got small thanks, for Gould criticized the Macbeth for too many close-ups, giving the play a disjointed, episodic feeling: New York Times, 29 November, p. 32.

²⁰ Gould misses the artifice of the proscenium arch, but to me this production comes as close as a television production can to the ambience of the proscenium-arch stage, without the arch itself. This is a semi-illusionist setting, effected by the studio look. The fact that Gould finds this set too realistic for his taste tellingly demonstrates that willingness to accept a given performance as realistic varies with time and technology.

This Macbeth won five Emmy awards, including one for best direction.

²¹ The earlier version had been broadcast both in black and white and in color, but apparently color technology was not at a high level then. At least Jack Gould criticized the garish color. Cue, 11 Dec. 1954, says only a few thousand color sets existed at the time. I have seen only the black and white versions of all four productions.

²² In The Tempest, a taped production of the 1959 season, Shaefer preserves an aura of spontaneity by taping in sequence and avoiding retakes. See the press release, "NBC Color Television News," 19 Oct. 1959.

²³ Jack Gould's review, New York Times, 19 March 1956, p. 63, called it "infectiously inventive." On 23 April the Times, p. 23, announced that Evans got an American Shakespeare Theatre and Academy Award for the production. Olivier was one of the other recipients, for his production of R3.

²⁴ In the ACT production broadcast on 23 April 1976 over Public Television, the setting was similarly bare and non-illusionistic, but in addition the acting was farcical to such a degree that realism disappeared altogether. See "A Video Taming of the Shrew," Shakespeare on Film Newsletter, 1 (Dec. 1976), 1.

²⁵ This idea is supported by thirty-six-year-old Norma Shearer's film performance of Juliet (directed by Cukor, 1936); she acted the girl and then was better able than any other actress I have seen in this role to demonstrate the character's growth.

²⁶ In contrast, Meryl Streep's Kate grounds out a flower and growls on first view in Joseph Papp's production in Central Park, 1978.

Gould objects that Palmer is not spitfire enough at the beginning, but he misses the point. Her Kate is only playing the role of termagant because until Petruchio arrives she has no other choice.

²⁷ For an illuminating discussion of the text, which shows that rather than being tamed Kate joins the fun, see Irene Dash, Wooing, Wedding, and Power: Women in Shakespeare's Plays (New York: Columbia Univ. Press, 1981), pp. 57-61.

MAKING ALL'S WELL THAT ENDS WELL:
THE ARTS OF TELEVISED DRAMA AT THE BBC

Susan Willis

All's Well That Ends Well is one Shakespearean play Sir Laurence Olivier never made into a film, nor is it ever likely to receive such treatment. Not a great tragedy, a rollicking romantic comedy, or an important history, All's Well is frequently considered a problem in Shakespeare's canon--a dark comedy or tragicomedy, a puzzlement, overshadowed in that category by its more popular cousin Measure for Measure and by the later romances. Although it has a very playable comic role in the pompous boor Parolles and an apparently virtuous, clear-headed heroine--who, like Portia, Rosalind, or Viola, finally gets her man after much maneuvering and anxious waiting--the play is rarely remembered for its compelling action or captivating characters. It is not the play one instantly chooses to produce when given the chance to do Shakespeare. But the British Broadcasting Corporation is in the process of taping all of Shakespeare's plays, greater and lesser, over the span of six years, and among the 1980-81 season's six scheduled broadcasts is All's Well, taped in July, 1980. One might wonder how well even the BBC can do All's Well, but one need not wonder long, for--as this observer will testify--a production of All's Well can end very well indeed when Shakespeare's art is combined with an art-historical sense of the period and with the arts of studio production, the sophisticated camera techniques, solid acting, and careful interpretation that yield a successful television production.

One element production adds to the text of a play is a visual context for the action: a reader sees words; a theatre or television audience sees a definitely delineated space. Shakespeare's stage, of course, was mostly an empty space, a platform backed by a several-storied playhouse and surrounded by a "wooden O." Lit only by the sun, with few props and virtually no set other than the playhouse itself, and with actors in contemporary garb, the details of Shakespeare's dramatic "space" were largely defined by his blank verse. Since Shakespeare's time productions have variously attempted to capture and convey the essence of that Shakespearean dramatic space. One way of recreating it is to reconstruct the effect of his stage; consequently, in theatre

155

open staging has been one of the foremost production techniques of the past several decades. Television can and does borrow this theatrical technique; a modified open staging is used for the BBC's <u>Hamlet</u> and <u>Winter's Tale</u> in the 1980-81 season. Yet Dr. Jonathan Miller, the current producer of the BBC Shakespeare series, believes that the use of open staging has run its course, that we have seen it enough that its fresh perspective no longer automatically startles and excites, and that the time has come to recreate another sense of Renaissance "space." In the BBC productions he favors giving a strong and detailed visual sense of the period, as synchronous with Shakespeare as possible; therefore, for setting and atmosphere he turns to the art of painting in the late 16th and early 17th centuries in addition to the dramatic art of that period.

Miller's concern for the Renaissance "look" of the productions is shared by Elijah Moshinsky, director of the BBC <u>All's Well</u>, who obviously thinks the television camera can frame a picture worthy of an Old Master. In the plays he directs, Miller will occasionally copy a painting exactly, as he did Vermeer's "Young Lady and Gentleman at the Virginals" during the first wooing scene of <u>Taming of the Shrew</u>. But rather than copy art, Moshinsky more often wants the <u>All's Well</u> sets and costumes to suggest the paintings of Rembrandt, Hals, and Vermeer, and the engravings of Abraham Bosse. Moshinsky sometimes has definite paintings in mind for costumes, such as Rembrandt's portrait of Margaretha de Geer for the Countess or Rembrandt's "Jewish Bride" for Helena at the end of the play;[1] the sets, on the other hand, are not intended as direct copies. Instead, the realistic interiors with their dark wooden furniture, richly colored tapestries, pewter pitchers, and seemingly natural window lighting are reminiscent of many Dutch Renaissance paintings. This sense is enhanced by the fact that in many of the scenes the camera will capture main action in the foreground and through a doorway also show secondary action in a room beyond. Such a device gives visual depth, a quality characteristic of Renaissance painting and also valuable in television, given its proclivity for close-ups and the absence of panorama. Thus the "space" in such a BBC production of Shakespeare refers to the look of the age's art, not just its stage.

Part of what makes Renaissance "space" recognizable in art is the artist's use of light, especially the

chiaroscuro--that is, the blend or contrast of light
and dark used to model and define shapes--so striking
in Renaissance painting. In creating the Renaissance
"space" in All's Well Moshinsky consequently paid great
attention to the lighting in his production; for him
chiaroscuro became a primary visual and thematic effect
in the BBC's All's Well. The night scenes are dark by
normal television standards; the entire set is not visible since most of it falls deep in shadow, reminding us
how the world looked in the ages before the uniform
glare of electric light. Firelight plays on Helena and
the Countess as Helena confesses her love for Bertram,
the warmth and light of the fire matching the emotions
discussed, the flickering much like the uncertainty of
the social situation. A fire also blazes in the background as Bertram arranges his supposed assignation
with Diana. And in the dinner scene when the Widow and
Diana agree to help Helena, their faces are lit by the
glow of a single candle, just as if Georges de la Tour
had arranged the scene. Not only are these effects
lovely, but also technically challenging, to the great
joy of the production's lighting designer, John Summers,
who relished the chance to provide something other than
the standard portrait lighting traditionally used for
television.

   While the visual element may turn the screen into
a living work of art, the director and producer are also
vitally concerned with telling a story, with giving life
to the words and implicit actions of Shakespeare's play.
The play must be interpreted for television even as for
the stage--production is a series of choices, a vital-
izing in particular forms. In his interpretation of
All's Well, Moshinsky applied the Renaissance principle
of chiaroscuro metaphorically; it appears not only in
the lighting but throughout his production choices,
especially through contrasts of character. He con-
sciously cast actors of radically different ages and
styles for the two generations represented in the play.
And, as he points out, this idea also underscores the
spirit of the play's remark, "The web of our life is of
a mingled yarn," a remark which shaped his interpretation. By combining veteran traditional actors as
Countess, King, and Lafew with young naturalistic actors
for Bertram and Helena, Moshinsky had a nearly explosive
mix in rehearsal due to the actors' different methods
of approaching character and developing scenes, but one
that finally blends quite well in performance, as

actors' styles complement the nature of the characters for the viewer.

Most of the storytelling decisions for television involve recognizing and refining the script's suggestions.[2] A major alteration the BBC made in telling the story of All's Well concerns Shakespeare's scene structure, especially his big scenes. Shakespeare's All's Well has 23 scenes in all; the BBC version, even after cutting the two small scenes with the Duke of Florence, has 32. The expansion most often results from breaking up scenes, especially the big scenes, into several smaller ones to indicate a brief passage of time in the action. The notes of the script editor in the BBC text suggest that scene shifts merely indicate a change of location, but the more significant shift for interpreting the play is the implicit time lapse attendant on such a change, as in Shakespeare's II.iii, a scene in which the King, cured of his fistula, enters with Helena and offers her, as promised, her choice of bachelors, whereupon she chooses Bertram. The King overrules his ward's protests and hustles the couple off to be wed while Lafew and Parolles remain behind to comment on the match and to greet the bridegroom upon his return; Parolles ends the scene by convincing him to fly to the wars in Italy. This continuous rush of action in Shakespeare becomes four separate scenes in the BBC's camera script--the King's entrance and the choosing of Bertram being a single daytime scene, the conversation between Lafew and Parolles taking place that evening before the wedding banquet, and the discussion between the pouting Bertram and Parolles occurring later that night, after the banquet. Thus in the BBC version Bertram does not seem like a rebellious child exploding from the chapel to reject his bride; the effect grants him the dignity to suffer the ceremonies of wedding and feast, and afterward, alone, to bang his head against the wall in frustration. By allowing the passage of some hours with this scene division, the BBC gains a bit of suspense about Bertram's response and also gives him a deeper sense of adolescent agony at being shamed by union with a social inferior and at being reined in before he had ever gotten to run wild.

Another major instance in which scene division enhances character as well as passes the time is in the scenes of Helena's soliloquies, I.i and III.ii. In Shakespeare's play her soliloquized resolves to act--

first by following Bertram to court, later by leaving his home if her presence there will keep him in exile--appear abrupt, even scheming. In the BBC's portrayal, however, the meditation, separated as it is from the preceding action, seems more nearly an actual process of thought. She discovers what she will do in the course of her reflections instead of immediately stating her intentions.

Naturally, a number of such effects and decisions result from the very necessity of producing the play, whether for stage or 21-inch television screen. As in any production, the text provides clues for action and characterization. For example, in II.ii where the Countess sends Lavache, her servant and the play's clown, to court, the dialogue and jests make frequent mention of food amid the clown's satiric account of courtly manners; therefore, the BBC sets the scene at breakfast, with Lavache shoveling down his porridge as he banters with the Countess. This setting not only provides an ironic comment on Lavache's own boorish table manners as he praises his courtly facility, but opens the production to interpret his response to the Countess's "You understand me?" more straightforwardly than the usual sexual innuendo conjectured by editors. He says, "Most fruitfully," and taking the napkin from his collar with one hand he reaches with the other across the table for several nearby apples, pausing to wipe his mouth and grab an additional apple before he hastens out. Such felicities are the stuff good productions are made on.

Yet television as a production art form offers some advantages the stage does not. As Henry Fenwick, author of the production notes for the BBC scripts, observed, "Everyone knew that in the TV plays the little scenes would gain," because with stronger actors and close-ups they would not get lost as they too often do on stage. The BBC <u>All's Well</u> proves Fenwick's point, for the little scenes gain not only significance but beauty. The shortest scene in the BBC production (21 lines) is V.i, in which Helena hopes to see the King only to discover he has gone to Rousillon the previous night. The BBC shifts the site from Shakespeare's Marseilles to the corridor of the King's palace in Paris, thus necessitating a far longer hypothetical journey for the women coming from Florence but thereby avoiding the need for an extra set. Helena and her party proceed down the hall, which is lit by shafts of the late

afternoon sun, an effect like sfumato or haze in a
Renaissance painting. The deep, resonant voice of the
Astringer, played by Valentine Dyal, famous in Britain
for his radio broadcasts during World War II, echoes
down the corridor to open the scene, "What's your will?"
Helena receives the disappointing news of the King's
departure, returns to console her group, walks back
through the motes of dust tumbling in the sunlight (a
fog carefully blown in just before taping began) to
beseech the Astringer's aid, then moves her group away.
The quiet, empty hall, the contrast between voices, and
the pattern of sunlight all combine to create a striking
effect. As the scene ends, court pages are shuttering
the windows in the corridor, so that when Helena finally
turns away a page places the last shutter in place,
closing the scene by plunging it into darkness. Other
small scenes benefit from similar care and artistry;
consequently, the major scenes in the play do not monop-
olize the visual interest: the entire production is
consistent in its visual beauty and studied, harmonious
effect.

   Telling the story can be a matter of clarifying
movements, motivations, and meanings; it is also a matter
of interpreting, of choosing to emphasize one movement,
motivation, or meaning rather than another, or to provide commentary on the action and actors by repetitive
effect. The long scene mentioned earlier involving
Helena's choice of Bertram at court also contains a rare
exception the BBC's creed of utter fidelity to the text.
In the original conversation between Lafew, Parolles,
and Bertram about the King's miraculous recovery, just
as the King enters with the maid who healed him a
surprised Parolles exclaims, "Mor du vinager! Is not
this Helen?" and Lafew responds "'Fore God, I think so."
But Lafew, as the "Pandarus" who introduced Helena to
the King, is one of the few people at court who know it
is Helena, so his reply cannot be surprise but rather a
jab at the superficial, pompous courtier who had plagued
his preceding comments with "knowing" interruptions. In
the BBC's All's Well the response is not Lafew's but
Bertram's; his surprise at Helena's sudden appearance
and remarkable feat is deeper than Parolles', and his
delivery of the line allows the camera a long close-up
of that astonished face just as the bachelors are
summoned. The change plays so well for television that
Shakespeare himself, that practical man of the theatre,
would undoubtedly approve it.

A more visual interpretive commentary follows that scene. Parolles' vanity and superficiality are easily portrayed by his incessant preening before mirrors, of which the King's palace in Paris, designed as a precursor of Versailles, has an abundance. In II.iii Lafew chastizes Parolles after one such bit of business, and two scenes later as he discusses Parolles with the unsuspicious Bertram, Bertram listens while garbing himself for his escape and carefully examining his appearance in a mirror. Such doubling of props and conversational topics complements the action of the scene, which shows Bertram modeling himself on Parolles' self-seeking injunctions and ignoring Helena's beneficent requests. The presence of the mirrors helps us see the point.

Helena, in that wedding-night farewell, asks Bertram for a kiss. He denies her curtly; no stage direction in Shakespeare indicates a kiss, and none is given in the BBC portrayal. Bertram refuses the union both spiritually and physically. Since Moshinsky stresses the sexual element in All's Well, Bertram's cool, stiff rejection of Helena and the honeymoon stands out amid the bawdy interests and comments of most other characters and his own libidinous interests later in Florence. At the end of the play, however, after Bertram has been publicly betrayed in his amorous double-dealing, Helena returns to redeem him, and at long last he not only calls her his wife and pledges his love, but in the BBC version also kisses her, an affirmation that speaks the louder for his earlier denial of the kiss. Like the ailing King who in the BBC's II.i pledged his faith in Helena's healing powers with a somewhat less that Platonic kiss, Bertram's character and honor are also healed through Helena's powers in the last scene. As a comedy All's Well does not end with the classic dance, feast, or wedding, though it does assert reunion and restoration. The wedding ceremony is behind this couple, but the union is not sealed until the kiss. Despite sixteen more lines of dialogue from other characters, that gesture is the comic conclusion of the play. It tells the story. And the more intimate medium of television can carry it off far better than the broader medium of the stage.

The King's public proclamation of joy at the action's end, his tribute to Diana for her service, these round off the happy ending and the production could flow, as many have, into a grand finale of welcoming the sweet. But the BBC production modulates that closing mood in two distinct ways. As the BBC portrays them, the King's last two lines in V.iii are separated from those preceding by a long pause wherein the family celebrates its reunion in the background while the King moves to stare into the fire with stern brow and brooding visage to render: "All yet seems well, and if it end so meet,/ The bitter past, more welcome is the sweet." Such a delivery keeps the sweet from becoming saccharin and adjusts the mood of the ending to harmonize with the tentative, hopeful, but nonetheless grim moments of this so-called "dark" comedy.

The epilogue, which was taped but excised during editing due to time considerations, would have provided a different sort of adjustment to the play. Stalking majestically before an obviously painted backdrop, the King--in exaggerated make-up--saws the air with his hand to complement his bombastic delivery, for as director Moshinsky commented in rehearsal, "Yes, we want a slightly tacky theatrical ending." He would have achieved one. The sharp contrast between the realistic scene ending at Rousillon and the stagey conclusion of the play would jar the audience to attention and out of its suspended disbelief. It is an effect Sir Laurence Olivier would recognize as similar to that at the close of his film version of Henry V. That may not be enough to make him wish he had made an All's Well himself, but it again demonstrates the sense of tradition--in painting, theatre, and film--evident in the current BBC productions of Shakespeare.

NOTES

[1] All information and quotations about Moshinsky's views on *All's Well* come from Henry Fenwick's production notes for the BBC script of *All's Well That Ends Well* (London: BBC Publications, 1981). Information about Miller's views come from his conversations with the author during the production.

[2] Although scenes are carefully planned in script editing and in rehearsal, sometimes a producer or director may have a sudden, serendipitous recognition of narrative opportunity in the studio. For instance, after watching camera rehearsals of the King's bedroom scene in which Bertram is introduced to the court, Jonathan Miller suggested the addition of a wordless scene to show Bertram's awe upon arriving at the palace. Within minutes the scene was arranged: Ian Charleson, the actor playing Bertram, stood in the set for the hallway outside the King's bedroom, gazed about in amazement at the splendor, then walked slowly between the busy courtiers toward the massive double doors of the royal bedchamber. As a result of this addition, when the King hears a knock at the door in I.ii, the BBC audience would already know the identity of the indistinct figure entering through the shadows. The addition would thus prepare the audience while providing another look at Bertram's youth and inexperience. This particular serendipitous suggestion, however, proved fleeting; it was cut during the editing. Nonetheless, we can appreciate the effort made on television to portray Shakespeare's story to the audience as well as to deliver his lines.

SHAKESPEARE AND ACTING THEORY IN THE ENGLISH RENAISSANCE

Jane L. Donawerth

Throughout Shakespeare's plays, characters describe their own or other's acting: in The Two Gentlemen of Verona, Julia, disguised, relates her acting of "Ariadne passioning/ For Theseus' perjury" (IV.iv.167-8);[1] in Twelfth Night, Feste claims that he "delivers the madman" (V.i.291) when he reads Malvolio's letter; and in The Tempest, Prospero praises Ariel's harpy--"a grace it had, devouring" (III.iii.84). Yet these speakers attribute to acting different characteristics: Julia stresses the portraying and moving of emotions, Feste, the characterizing of Malvolio by means of voice, and Prospero, Ariel's idealized movement. In this paper I wish to show that Shakespeare's conception of acting changed in correspondence with acting theory in the English Renaissance. My purpose thus differs from that of most preceding critics, who treat Elizabethan acting theory as an unchanging whole, and argue that it implies an acting style either as natural as our modern one, or more formal.[2]

Dependence on rhetoric is the main reason to suppose the art of acting the same throughout Shakespeare's career. Preparing Moth to be their prologue, the lords in Love's Labour's Lost teach him the basics of rhetorical delivery: "Action and accent"--"'Thus must thou speak,' and 'thus thy body bear'" (V.ii.99-100). Twenty years later, in 1615, in the Overburian character written perhaps by John Webster, the "excellent Actor" is still compared to "the graue Orator . . . for by a ful and significant action of body, he charmes our attention: sit in a full Theater, and you will thinke you see so many lines drawn from the circumference of so many eares, whiles the Actor is the Center."[3] That rhetorical delivery and acting depend on the same elements of language--voice and gesture--does not mean, however, that they share all other features. On a similar basis, Thomas Heywood and the author of "An excellent Actor" compare acting to painting: both arts speak through the body's language.[4] In accord with theatrical practice and in response to Puritan criticism, the players gradually developed a theory of acting as an art distinct from both its model, rhetorical delivery, and its occasion, dramatic poetry. We may trace three stages in theory, each with a corresponding moral purpose, each borrowing but adapting ideas from rhetoric or poetic: the first emphasizes passion, the second, character, and the last grace.

The earliest Elizabethan notion of acting is decidedly rhetorical: the actor, like the orator delivering his speech, adds voice and action to the words, and so liveliness and passion. In the prologue to Damon and Pithias, in 1571, Richard Edwards assumes that the poet provides character, framing "eche person so,/ That by his common talke, you may his nature rightly know"; the actor merely delivers what is there, so that the "speeches well pronounste, with action liuely framed," will please the audience.[5] In The Faerie Queene, Spenser portrays Ease as the typical actor:

> And to the vulgar beckning with his hand,
> In signe of silence, as to heare a play,
> By liuely actions he gan bewray
> Some argument of matter passioned.[6]

To Spenser, acting is passion expressed through gesture and aimed at the crowd, who understand this universal language better than the reasoned message of words. Spenser thus inculcates many commonplaces from classical and Renaissance rhetorical delivery,[7] yet represents acting as a vulgar art (as is all the art of the House of Busyrane), separated from the reason, and dangerous in its power to express and move the passions.

Even defenders of the art in the 1590's would not have challenged Spenser's basic assumptions about acting, although they granted actors more respect. When Thomas Nashe praises actors in 1592, for example, it is for their ability to move the audience's emotions: "How would it haue ioyed braue Talbot," he asks, ". . . to thinke that after he had lyne two hundred years in his Tombe, hee should . . . haue his bones newe embalmed with the teares of ten thousand spectators?"[8] Dekker, in an actor's prologue in 1612, enthusiastically describes acting as the artful evocation of feelings:

> That Man giue mee; whose Brest fill'd by
>   the Muses,
> With Raptures, Into a second, them infuses:
> Can giue an Actor, Sorrow, Rage, Ioy, Passion,

>   Whilst hee againe (by self-same Agitation)
>   Commands the Hearers, sometimes drawing
>   out Teares,
>   Then smiles, and fills them both with
>   Hopes and Feares.⁹

Like many literary men before him, Dekker borrows a rhetorical commonplace to expound the art of acting. Quintilian had cautioned that the orator moves his audience by combining the natural with the fictional: "excite the appropriate feeling in oneself, . . . form a mental picture of the facts, and . . . exhibit an emotion that cannot be distinguished from the truth"; only then will the voice "produce precisely the same emotion in the judge that we have put into it."¹⁰ In England, Thomas Wilson had echoed Quintilian's warning in his rhetoric, and Thomas Wright, in his treatise on the passions, had even offered a "scientific" explanation: since passion is a physical motion, passing from the heart to external expressions, and so to the eyes and ears of the audience, the force with which it originates determines the response; a feigned emotion, lacking force, will get little response.¹¹ In Dekker's adaptation, the poet's fiction inspires the actor with a true emotion, which he then arouses in the audience: players thus move men by the power of emotions that are fictional and true at once.¹²

   In the plays of the 1590's, Shakespeare's characters also speak of acting as an art of voice and gesture expressing and moving the passions. "Give me a cup of sack to make my eyes look red," demands Falstaff when he acts Henry IV, "that it may be thought I have wept, for I must speak in passion, and I will do it in King Cambyses' vein" (1H4 II.iv.384-7). The disguised Julia claims the utmost success for her presentation of "Ariadne passioning" (TGV IV.iv.167): "Which I so lively acted with my tears/ That my poor mistress, moved therewithal,/ Wept bitterly" (ll.169-71). One may see that this idea encourages melodramatic acting: the actor's craft is his emotional voice and gesture. "Come," demands Hamlet when the players enter, "give us a taste of your quality, come, a passionate speech" (Ham. II.ii. 431-2). And if Shakespeare is modeling the players in Hamlet on an earlier age, it is not too far in the past. "Come," says Richard to Buckingham in Richard III, "canst thou quake and change thy color,/ Murther thy breath in middle of a word,/ . . . As if thou were distraught and mad with terror?" "Tut," replies

Buckingham, "I can counterfeit the deep tragedian" (III.v.1-5).

Part of the impetus for change in acting theory came from Puritan criticism, part from theatrical practice. The Puritans attacked the English stage in the 1570's and 1580's along three important lines: the immoral content of plays, the lewdness of actors and theater-goers, and the obscenely passionate acting. In the 1580's responders defended the morality of poetry in general, and the good character of most actors, but not the passionate acting, for which they had no moral defense.[13] In 1615, the Puritan John Greene is still warning against the same "wanton gestures" used by players, the "lipping and kissing, . . . clipping and culling," the same presentation of "lustfull passions," and the same results:

> Then these goodly Pageants being done, euery one sorteth to his mate . . . then begin they to repeate the lasciuous acts and speeches they haue heard, and thereby infect their minde with wicked passions, so that in their secret conclaues they play the Sodomits, or worse.[14]

But by 1615, the players have a defense.

An early but unsuccessful attempt at such a defense is Henry Chettle's Kind-Heart's Dream, in 1592. Through the mouth of Tarleton's ghost, Chettle satirizes the Puritans' own arguments: "Fie . . . vppon players speeches, their wordes are full of wyles; vppon their gestures, that are altogether wanton. Is it not lamentable, that a man should spend his two pence on them . . . and in liuely gesture see trecherie set out, with which euery man now adaies vseth to intrap his brother?" Chettle wonders how the Puritans can miss the point: we players deliver the viciousness of passion before the audience so that they may feel and know its power. Finally, however, Chettle begs the question: "he that at a play will be delighted in the [vice], and not warned by the [punishment], is like him that reads in a booke the description of sinne, and will not looke ouer the leafe for the reward."[15] The playwright should provide the moral, and the audience should respond to it--ignoring the actor's responsibility, Chettle fails to distinguish between exploiting and moving the passions, and between sentimental and more natural characterizations.

As actors assumed more importance in the theatrical industry, however, their giving "life" to their characters came to mean more than expressing passion with voice and gesture. The old idea was still there, but overlaid with a new one closer to our idea of characterization. In 1600, Jonson's sketch of his character Puntarvolo, a man "resoluing (in despight of publike derision) to sticke to his owne particular fashion, phrase, and gesture,"[16] requires from the actor a physical presentation of Puntarvolo's idiosyncratic habits of mind. Similarly, in the "Induction" to <u>Antonio and Mellida</u>, Marston portrays the players--shown discussing their parts--as independent artists who "personate" the characters. The actor of Matzagente adds "a spruce Attick accent of adulterate Spanish" (with no textual authority) in order to indicate his "corrupt and mungrel'd" ancestry. The actor of Antonio, who disguises himself as an Amazon, frets over playing both sexes: "when use hath taught me action, to hit the right point of a Ladies part, I shall growe ignorant when I must turne young Prince againe." His concern is not rhetorical, but natural movement, not passion, but realistically playing two very different parts. Alberto claims that his role, "impossible to be made perspicuous by any utterance," must be acted out "by signes & tokens"; he then conveys, with a series of gestures, the conflicting aspects of his character.[17] Webster's praise of "the action" of <u>The White Devil</u> in 1612 includes "the true imitation of life, without striving to make nature a monster"; and Chapman later defends playing because "the personal and exact life it gives to any history . . . adds to [it] lustre, spirit, and apprehension."[18] No longer adding merely passion, the actor creates his own imitation: his personation, with its particularity and spirit, gives life to the part that the playwright imagines.

"Life-like" rather than "lively" acting gave rise to a new conception of the moral purpose of acting, best illustrated by Hamlet's advice to the players. Hamlet's instructions (<u>Ham</u>. III.ii.1-45) incorporate many of the commonplaces we have already discussed: the actor's medium is voice and gesture, and a major concern is delivering passion. But Hamlet also defines a moral purpose for the art by distinguishing between good and bad actors and audiences. The bad actor "tear[s] a passion to totters" and "spleet[s] the ears of the groundlings"; he performs for those "who for the most part are capable of nothing but inexplicable dumb shows and noise," those who expect only passionate gesture and voice. The good actor, on the other hand, aims his performance at the "judicious" spectator. He "o'er-step[s] not the modesty of nature," and so assumes a responsibility at once moral and aesthetic, "to show virtue her feature, scorn her own image, and the very age and body of the time his form and pressure."

Hamlet includes special instructions for the clowns, who must "speak no more than is set down for them, for there be of them that will laugh to set on some quantity of barren spectators to laugh too, though in the meantime some necessary question of the play be then to be consider'd (Ham. III.ii.38-43). The implication is not only that the fool must not add lines or stage business (as editors have usually glossed it) but also that he must not exaggerate voice, expression, and gesture in attempting to make his audience laugh. In the body's language he must aim at the ridiculous, not the burlesque. Close in time to Hamlet, Twelfth Night offers a practical exposition of bad acting in a clown: Feste's reading of Malvolio's letter. When Feste "delivers the madman" (V.i.291), the phrase connotes theatrical delivery: he acts out Malvolio's "mad" passions in his voice. To Olivia's objection, the clown replies, "And your ladyship will have it as it ought to be, you must allow vox" (V.i.294-6). Employing the idea that acting expresses character to disguise his real aim, the audience's laughter at the caricature of Malvolio, Feste is a bad actor by Hamlet's standards, one who gives a false imitation and thereby exploits his audience. Olivia, a "judicious," not a "barren spectator," remains unmoved by Feste's burlesque, and demands a delivery allowing her a reasoned assessment of Malvolio. We have only to imagine Sir Toby's response to see what the result of a bad actor and a bad audience would be: "some necessary question of the play" would indeed be lost in the laughter, for Malvolio would be left in the dark closet, and there would be less justice in the play's ending.

In Thomas Heywood' An Apology For Actors we may see the final stage in the moral defense of acting. Defending the drama along traditional lines in Books II and III, for moral content, in Book I Heywood creates a new defense, one based on the power of the aesthetic means of acting to reach a moral end. Hercules, he claims, was moved by the life of his father Jupiter, "Which being personated with liuely and well-spirited action, wrought such impression on his noble thoughts, that in meere emulation of his fathers valor . . . he perform'd his twelue labours."[20] By the substitution of emulating virtue for moving passion in the audience, Heywood directly answers the Puritans' objection to acting.

Modeling his defense not on rhetorical theory, but on Sidney's Defense of Poesie, Heywood argues that acting surpasses both oratory and painting, just as Sidney had argued that poetry surpasses both philosophy and history. Since neither oratory, "a shadow receiued by the eare," nor painting, "a forme seene by the eye," can "shew action, passion [or] motion . . . to mooue the spirits of the beholder to admiration," Heywood concludes that only acting realizes the full potential for the body's language:

> What English blood seeing the person of any
> bold English man presented and doth not
> hugge his fame, and hunnye at his valor, . . .
> as if the Personator were the man Personated,
> so bewitching a thing is liuely and well
> spirited action, that it hath power to new
> mold the harts of the spectators and fashion
> them to the shape of any noble and notable
> attempt.[21]

In Heywood's idea of "personation," the actor identifies with the character he plays, and, by the power of his delivery, spectators identify with his personation. Moving the audience to admiration, the actor's imitation becomes a way of releasing the power within spectators to reshape themselves. For Thomas Heywood, acting might provide a Henry V to make other Henry V's.[22]

Heywood does not require a discerning audience for acting to achieve this effect. Attributing the civility of the ancient Greeks partly to acting, he infers that then, as now, "Action was the neerest way to plant vnderstanding in the hearts of the ignorant."[23] Not at all vulgar, acting is the noblest universal art because it moves even the ignorant to ethical and political government.

Shakespeare's last reference to acting, in The Tempest, shares with Heywood's treatise the claim of a

171

reforming power for the art. Communicating through music and actions alone, the spirits move the King to wonder: "I cannot too much muse/ Such shapes, such gesture, and such sound expressing/ (Although they want the use of tongue) a kind/ Of excellent dumb discourse" (III.iii.36-9). The universality of gesture in Prospero's pageant appeals even across the barriers between alien peoples, and Gonzalo is also moved to admire the "people of the island,/ Who though . . . of monstrous shape, yet" possess "manners . . . more gentle" than those of "Our human generation" (III.iii. 30-4). The acting has immediate emotional effect, for the men respond with acceptance to the "gentle actions" (l. 20), and then with fear to the violent ones, when Ariel "like a harpy, claps his wings . . . and . . . the banquet vanishes (ll. 52-3). But the actors arouse emotions only to a moral end, and Ariel begins his sermon: "You are three men of sin" (l. 53); you must reform through "heart's sorrow,/ And a clear life ensuing" (ll. 81-2). Prospero praises his spirits for the "good life" (l. 86) of their performance, moving the audience to "heart's sorrow." Heywood had almost said that acting can make men good against their wills, but in The Tempest, the actors cannot provide the "clear life ensuing": Alonso is moved to repentance, Gonzalo to pity, but Antonio and Sebastian only to fear and anger. Shakespeare's vision suggests that acting has a force equal to that which Sidney found in poetry: like the poet's, an actor's creation opens the way to re-creation in the audience, "if they will learn aright why and how that maker made him."[24]

Soon Heywood's idea of the moral power of personation became a commonplace. In 1616, even the Puritan Thomas Gainsford admits that in ancient times (though not in modern ones) through "gesture and personated action" the actor "was euer the life of dead poesie, . . . so that vice was made odious, [and] vertue set on a throne of immitation."[25] He is refuting the claims for the modern actor by the writer of one of Overbury's characters: "By his action hee fortifies morall precepts with example; for what wee see him personate, wee thinke truly done before vs: a man of a deep thoght might apprehend, the Ghosts of our ancient Heroes walk't againe."[26]

Surprisingly, the further development of the theory of personation works against the trend toward relatively realistic acting. "To see as I haue seene," crows

Heywood, "Hercules in his owne shape . . . pashing the Lion, squeezing the Dragon, [and] dragging Cerberus in Chaynes, . . . Oh these were sights to make an Alexander!"[27] But they are not sights to sustain realistic acting. While actors are claiming to make the ghosts of heroes walk again, they are also devising a new standard for their art. In The Tempest Prospero judges even the violent actions of Ariel's harpy by artistic style: "a grace it had, devouring" (III.iii.84). The requirement of "grace" represents a qualification of the earlier goal of life-like character.

The ideal of grace originates with classical rhetoricians, who required an orator to be temperate in gesture, selecting only important words for emphasis, and implying the deeper emotion that may not be shown with dignity in public.[28] Moreover, grace becomes a distinctively Renaissance ideal. Castiglione's Sir Frederick demands that the courtier employ "gestures . . . tempred with a manerly countenance and with a mouing of the eyes that may giue a grace and accorde with the wordes, and . . . signifie . . . the intent and affection of the speaker."[29] Shakespeare's Hamlet urges that the players "use all gently," aiming at "a temperance that may give [passion] smoothness," suiting "the action to the word, the word to the action" (Ham. III. ii.4-18).

But it is Heywood who adapts this rhetorical ideal to the special ends of acting: the actor seeks "a gratious and a bewitching kinds of action," fitting "his phrases to his action, and his action to his phrase," his purpose being "to qualifie euery thing according to the nature of the person personated."[30] Heywood combines what might seem opposed qualities to modern actors: convincing portrayal of character, and idealized symbolic gesture. In the Jacobean theater, this combination becomes a new standard: in the preface to The Devil's Law-Case, Webster judges, "A great part of the grace of this . . . lay in Action; yet can no Action ever be gracious, where the decency of the Language, and Ingenious structure of the Scaene, arrive not to make up a perfect Harmony."[31] In the sixteenth century, actors defend their art by arguing that they deliver passion through voice, expression, and gesture, and so teach its viciousness. In the seventeenth century, they add other defenses: first, that they imitate nature, portraying men as they are, and then, that they embody men as they should be in graceful delivery, and so remake their audience in heroic shapes.

    Whether Shakespeare helped to formulate these ideas, or merely took up others' interpretations, I do not know; both, I suspect. What is clear is that acting theory changed radically during Shakespeare's career, and Shakespeare's conception of acting along with it. In fact, this general development corresponds remarkably to Shakespeare's changing dramatization of emotion and character. In the plays of the 1590's, voice and gesture are often used for immediate effect, and with the aim of arousing emotion in the audience: and so we have the plucking of roses in the Temple Garden scene of 1 Henry VI (II.iv) or the throwing of gages before first one king, and then another in Richard II (I.i, and IV.i). In the middle plays and tragedies, we see a more realistic handling of voice and gesture; rather than passion, the kneeling in Othello expresses character: the courtesy of Cassio, welcoming Desdemona to Cyprus (II.i.84), the hypocrisy of Iago, vowing revenge (III.iii.460-3), and the submissiveness of Desdemona when she begs to know the cause of Othello's rage (IV.ii.31). The later tragedies and romances reveal increasingly effective use of voice and action as symbol: Edgar in King Lear embarks on an odyssey of voices, refashioning his father as well as himself in nobler shape; and Ariel's singing and acting force on many of the ship-wrecked men in The Tempest journeys of self-discovery. From the early histories to the late romances, it is as if Shakespeare's stage practice developed in the way that English Renaissance ideas on the actor's art developed: from the expression of the life and force of human passions, to the communication of men's power to remake themselves.

NOTES

All references to the classics will be to the Loeb Library editions and translations (Cambridge, Mass.: Harvard Univ. Press) and will be noted in short form.

[1] This and all references to Shakespeare's works will be to The Riverside Shakespeare, ed. G. Blakemore Evans (Boston: Houghton Mifflin Company, 1974).

[2] Those who argue that Elizabethan acting was formal or idealized in style on the basis of rhetorical influence are Bertram L. Joseph, Elizabethan Acting (London: Oxford Univ. Press, 1951); Alfred Harbage, Theatre for Shakespeare (Toronto: Univ. of Toronto Press, 1955), pp. 92-118; and Lise-Lone Marker, "Nature and Decorum in the Theory of Elizabethan Acting," The Elizabethan Theatre II, ed. David Galloway (n.p.: The MacMillan Co. of Canada, 1970), pp. 87-107. The main spokesman for a naturalistic style is Marvin Rosenberg, "Elizabethan Actors," PMLA, 69 (1954), 915-27. What both schools share, however, is the assumption that Elizabethan acting and theory did not change from the opening of Burbage's theater in 1576, to the closing of the theaters in 1642; this assumption is improbable if we consider that in the same length of time, sixty years, acting style and theory have varied remarkably in films. I would agree with Daniel Selzer, "The Actors and Staging," in A New Companion to Shakespeare Studies, ed. Kenneth Muir and S. Schoenbaum (Cambridge: Cambridge Univ. Press, 1971), pp. 35-54, that the Elizabethan acting style must have been a fairly "large" or formal one, but one that changed over the period with the playwright's changing techniques of characterization; Selzer, however, does not treat the concomitant change in acting theory.

[3] Sir Thomas Overbury, et al., His Wife with . . . New Newes, and diuers more Characters (London, 1616), sig. M2^r.

[4] Sir Thomas Heywood, An Apology for Actors (London, 1612), sig. B3^v; and Overbury, Characters, sig. M2^v.

[5] Richard Edwards, The excellent Comedie of . . . Damon and Pithias (London, 1571), sig. Aii^r.

[6] The Faerie Queene, III.xii.4, in Poetical Works, ed. J.C. Smith and E. de Selincourt (London: Oxford Univ. Press, 1912).

[7] For rhetorical delivery defined as conveying and moving the passions through voice and gesture, see Cicero, De Oratore, III.lvii.216, and III.lix.221; Quintilian, XI.iii.2-14; Thomas Wilson, The Arte of Rhetorique (London, 1553) sig. Ggii^v; and Thomas Wright, The Passions of the Minde (London, 1604), sig. M8^v. For the universality of communicating through gesture, see Quintilian, IX.ii.65-7, and XI.iii.87; Wilson, Rhetorique, sig. Ggii^v; and Abraham Fraunce, The Arcadian Rhetorike (London, 1588), sig. I7^v. For the appeal of rhetorical delivery to the vulgar, see Cicero, De Oratore, III.lix. 223; and Shakespeare, Cor. III.ii.76-7.

[8] Pierce Penilesse His Supplication to the Divell, in The Works of Thomas Nashe, ed. Ronald B. McKerrow (1904; rpt. London: Sidgwick & Jackson, 1910), I, 212.

[9] "Prologue," to If This Be Not a Good Play, the Devil Is In It, in The Dramatic Works of Thomas Dekker, ed. Fredson Bowers, III (Cambridge: Cambridge Univ. Press, 1958), 122. When Shakespeare speaks of "action," or delivery in Lucrece, he sounds very much like the celebrators of passionate acting: "To see sad sights moves more than hear them told,/ For then the eye interprets to the ear/ The heavy motion that it doth behold" (ll. 1324-6).

[10] Quintilian, XI.iii.61-2.

[11] See The Arte of Rhetorique, sig. Ti^v, where Wilson warns that an orator will persuade only if "from his harte" he "fetche his complaintes"; and Wright, Passions, sigs. M7^v-M8^r.

[12] See Andrew Gurr, "Elizabethan Action," SP, 63 (1966), 144-56; his thesis, that Elizabethans thought the orator delivers "real" and the player "feigned" passions, is disproved by Dekker's prologue and Elizabethan rhetoricians; in these cases, both player and orator are supposed to deliver fictional, true emotions.

[13] Examples of such Puritan attacks are Stephen Gosson, The Schoole of Abuse (London, 1579), and Philip Stubbes, The Anatomie of Abuses (London, 1583). See

Elbert Thompson's analysis of their arguments in The Controversy Between the Puritans and the Stage (New York: Henry Holt and Co., 1903). Examples of such defenses are Thomas Lodge, A Defence of Poetry, Music, and Stage Plaies (London, 1579), and Sir Philip Sidney, The Defense of Poesy (London, 1595).

[14] John Greene, A Refutation of the Apology for Actors (London, 1615), sig. H4r.

[15] Henry Chettle, Kind-Heart's Dream, ed. E.F. Rimbault, in The Percy Society Early English Poetry, Ballads, and Popular Literature (London, 1841), V, 35-8.

[16] Euery Man out of his Humour, in Ben Jonson, ed. C.H. Herford, and Percy and Evelyn Simpson, III (Oxford: Clarendon Press, 1927), 423.

[17] The Plays of John Marston, ed. H. Harvey Wood, I (Edinburgh: Oliver & Boyd, 1934), 7-8.

[18] The Complete Works of John Webster, ed. F.L. Lucas (London: Chatto & Windus, 1927), I, 192; and "Dedication" to The Tragedy of Caesar and Pompey, in The Plays and Poems of George Chapman, ed. Thomas Marc Parrott (London: George Routledge & Sons, 1910), I, 341.

[19] See Arthur Clark, Thomas Heywood (Oxford: Basil Blackwell, 1931), pp. 70-9, for Heywood's borrowings from previous defenses and condemnations of plays.

[20] Heywood, Apology, sig. B3r. Heywood's Apology for Actors was not published until 1612, but Sir Edmund Chambers argues that it may have been written as early as 1607; see The Elizabethan Stage (Oxford: Clarendon Press, 1923), IV, 250.

[21] Heywood, Apology, sigs. B3v-B4r.

[22] Heywood mentions the acting of Henry V, sig. B4r. The phrasing of my sentence, however, is Sir Philip Sidney's, in The Defense of Poesy, ed. Lewis Soens (Lincoln: Univ. of Nebraska Press, 1970), p. 10: the poet's "Idea" works "substantially . . . to bestow a Cyrus upon the world to make many Cyruses. . . ."

[23] Heywood, Apology, sig. C3r.

[24] Sidney, Defense, p. 10.

[25] T.G. [Thomas Gainsford], <u>The Rich Cabinet</u> (London, 1616), sig Q4^r.

[26] Overbury, <u>Characters</u>, sig. M2^v.

[27] Heywood, <u>Apology</u>, sig. B4^r.

[28] See Cicero, <u>De Oratore</u>, III.xxvi.101-2; and Quintilian, XI.iii.88-91, and XI.iii.181-4.

[29] Baldassare Castiglione, <u>The Courtier</u>, tr. Thomas Hoby (1561; London, 1588), sig. E8^r.

[30] Heywood, <u>Apology</u>, sig. C4^r.

[31] <u>The Complete Works of John Webster</u>, II, 236. In his dedication to <u>Caesar and Pompey</u>, Chapman similarly says that his style may add to "elocution some assistance to the acceptation and grace of it," in <u>The Plays and Poems</u>, I, 341.

PART THREE

SHAKESPEARE AND ARTISTIC THEORY

The essays presented here all ask implicitly or explicitly the question, in Michael Platt's words, "What did Shakespeare think of his own art?" And further, how does his sense of the nature of art and the artist manifest itself in his work? Thus, these essays follow a less well charted course than do some of those earlier in this volume. Iconography, stage history, and genre are established issues; a critical tradition at least gives the critic a familiar plank to walk, though he may dive into strange waters. But Shakespeare's theory of art, his notion of imitation, even his attitude to drama demand fresh definitions, partly because Renaissance views of these subjects are so complicated.

Art in one sense could be <u>ars</u> or <u>techne</u>, the skill of the craftsman, whether physician, writer, gardener, or sculptor. It was also the medium in which the artist worked. More narrowly, art was the codified body of rules which could be taught in the classroom, but which related problematically to the achieved craft. At its broadest, art was a timeless comprehensive ideal. It surpassed the efforts of the individual artist, but in anticipating or containing his achievement, it gave his creation permanent validity. This definition allowed Sidney and Puttenham to compare the poet's creation to God's. And it lies behind Polixenes' symbolic defense of gillyvors in <u>The Winter's Tale</u>: "Nature is made better by no mean/ But Nature makes that mean." The artist accomplishes nothing that "great creating Nature" has not already made possible; "the art itself is Nature" (IV.iv.89-97).

The obvious parallels between individual arts led Renaissance theorists to tiresome arguments over the relative merits of poetry, painting and music. But the same parallels could also encourage a sense of rich analogy. Mary E. Hazard's discussion of "living art," with its background in rhetorical <u>enargeia</u> and its contemporary connection to pictorial vividness, gives us a theoretical link between <u>pictura</u>, <u>poesis</u>, and the audience, which was expected to complete the circuit by seeing with the mind's eye. A different set of analogies is suggested by Michael Platt in his consideration of Shakespeare's images of princely control and natural tempest: he shows the Platonic and iconographic basis for comparing the ruler and navigator, and significantly, the magician and dramatist. Here Platt joins Richard Snyder and J.S. Lawry in focusing directly on Shakespeare's preeminent interest in the implications of drama. Snyder's modern concern with "metadrama" and role-playing and Lawry's historical interest in "homeopathic imitation" overlap more than once. Together they show the degree to which Shakespeare meditated on and even questioned the assumptions of his own art and its relation to the world of colliding and contradictory experiences. All four of the essays suggest the possibilities of exploring further the implications of aesthetic thought in the Renaissance.

HSL

SHAKESPEARE'S "LIVING ART": A LIVE ISSUE FROM LOVE'S LABOUR'S LOST

Mary E. Hazard

> Our court shall be a little academe,
> Still and contemplative in living art.
> (I.i.13-14)[1]

Shakespeare's use of the phrase "living art" in the opening speech of Love's Labour's Lost presents an ambiguity which can significantly enlarge our reading of both the phrase and the play itself if only we can recover some of the Renaissance associations with the term. Modern editors tend to read the phrase as signifying the "art" of living according to ethics. For example, in a footnote citation of the reading supplied earlier by J.S. Reid (1922), "ars vivendi," the modern Arden edition would substitute "vital learning." Neither interpretation incorporates the aesthetic sense which I find suggestively used by Rosalie Colie in the title for her book Shakespeare's "Living Art" and also assumed by William Carroll in his book-length study of Love's Labour's Lost.[2] Both of these valuable studies imply a shift in the emphasis of the phrase from the participle to the noun, from the sense of "the art of living" to, rather, "the living quality of art," a shift of emphasis from ethics to aesthetics. Useful as their studies are in all other respects, neither Colie nor Carroll explicitly defines, explains, or illustrates the phrase as I should like to do.

The sense of the term "living art" assumed by Colie and Carroll has a linguistic history which it is helpful to recall. Renaissance literature is rich in pertinent uses of the word "living" (and "lively" as an interchangeable synonym) which signifies an honorific aesthetic quality in a work of art.[3] In Sir Thomas Hoby's translation of Baldassare Castiglione's Book of the Courtier, Count Lewis defines writing as "a manner of speech, that remaineth still after a man hath spoken, or (as it were), an image, or rather the life of the wordes."[4] Alberti speaks of how "the face of a man who is already dead certainly lives a long life through painting."[5] Leonardo distinguishes between likeness and liveliness in painting; likeness is mere physical similitude which creates an image "twice dead"; liveliness captures the life of the mind of the subject.[6]

The artists and writers of the Renaissance may have transmitted this aesthetic concept, but its origins lie in the rhetorical theory which was so important to the Renaissance. One of the most important sources is Quintilian's definition of <u>enargeia</u>, which establishes an important point. <u>Enargeia</u> is the "great gift to be able to set forth the facts on which we are speaking clearly and vividly. . . . displayed in their living truth to the eyes of the mind" (VIII.iii.61-62).[7] This intellectual or spiritual quality distinguishes honorific uses of "living" from the literal biological sense. It is the kind of "true lively knowledge" which Sidney describes as the end of poetry and which Spenser plays upon six times over in the Proem to Book Three of the <u>Faerie Queen</u>, where he discusses the problems of trying to portray in "living art" the virtues of his Queen.[8]

It is no coincidence that I have cited artists among those who have used the concept of living art, and no coincidence that all of the sources represented thus far allude to the visual arts in their discussions. Each of these writers identifies living art as an appeal to the mind which simulates the vividness of visual art in the medium of words. Implicit in this definition is the important role of the viewer or reader in completing the work of art through his recognition of the artist's appeal to the mind. Renaissance writers would add that the work of art had been completely effective only if the reader or viewer had also been moved by instruction and delight.

Liveliness does not necessarily connote representational verisimilitude. It is a quality of energy which is essentially mental, although that energy flows through the circuit of the senses, often charged by the sense of sight. Hence even the "speaking picture" praised by Sidney and by countless other Renaissance writers as a mode of liveliness in literature need not refer to the verbal construction of a literal picture. A picture may be simply evoked through allusion to an already familiar pictorial image, or the "picture" may be more on the order of a scheme or a diagram or an apothegm. In short, as Stephen Orgel reminds us, the speaking picture is a rhetorical mode and it may not involve a picture at all.[9] More essential to the Renaissance appropriation of the phrase from Horace[10] is the moral end of the speaking picture. Sidney puts it succinctly:

> Poesy therefore is an art of imitation, for so Aristotle termeth it in the word μίμησις--that is to say, a representing, counterfeiting, or figuring forth--to speak metaphorically, a speaking picture--with this end, to teach and delight. (25)

I am concerned with the larger issue of Shakespeare's concept of living art rather than his use of the speaking picture in particular, but as we shall see, these essential qualities of the speaking picture also characterize the living art of Shakespeare's drama: the figuring forth or embodying of an idea in order to teach and to delight. It should be remarked that the moral point may be embodied in appeal to any of the senses, including, most importantly, the engagement of kinesthetic responses. Kinesthetic appeal is, of course, a particular resource of rhythm in prose and poetry. To this resource, drama adds the dimension of action and motion through time. Thus, whatever the legitimacy of the interpretation of "speaking picture" as a reference to an isolated static image in poetry or prose fiction, it is the nature of drama to activate a more sustained response. The audience must look at not only the details in the dramatic picture, but also, to speak metaphorically, at its frame. The viewer must consider the provenance of the picture and its status as a pendant or a part of a series. In addition, he must weigh the qualifications and especially the veracity of the cicerone as well as the painter. That a character's actions may belie his words, that a later speech or action may qualify an earlier one, that a more enlightened character may even simultaneously through words or actions on stage correct the errors of another, that the play constitutes a larger vision than that of its separate speeches, characters, or actions--these are the special resources of drama. I should like to consider Shakespeare's use of these resources in Love's Labour's Lost by concentrating upon a small number of passages wherein characters allude to pictorial commonplaces in art and literature. Although some of these passages are pictorially organized, not all of them are pictorially descriptive. In each of these passages, there is an important disjunction between the character's ad hoc allusion to an image and the traditional significance of the evoked image. I suggest that in <u>Love's Labour's Lost</u>, the audience recreates the living quality of Shakespeare's art by perceiving that disjunction and by recognizing its portent.

Shakespeare's use of the visual arts does not necessarily entail specific reference to putative sources. First, Shakespeare does not simply quote sources: often he evokes rather than recreates a pictorial commonplace. The omission of an expected iconographic association from a well-known allusion or commonplace, the absence of an example from a conventional series or system, is often the most significant point to be noted. By indirection we have to find directions out. Second, it is in the nature of a commonplace that its origins are obscure--they were likely obscure even to Shakespeare. It is sufficient to know that the pictorial commonplace existed and that Shakespeare alludes to it as a commonplace in order to study the more fruitful question of how he embodies or figures forth--rather than "contains" --his variations upon it. Shakespeare's pictorial language does not simply illustrate, nor does it only corroborate, his verbal language. Shakespeare's pictorial allusion may also adumbrate verbal thematic development, or even render verbal exposition unnecessary. I shall briefly discuss how three visual arts illuminate <u>Love's Labour's Lost</u>: the triumph, the emblem, and <u>pictorial exempla</u>. I select these three because they demand our attention in the play and because each is represented by surviving illustrations which have not previously been used together in order to deepen our understanding of the play or of what Shakespeare might have meant by "living art." Most importantly, these examples can serve to demonstrate Shakespeare's own living art.

I have taken for my opening text Navarre's famous lines about his projected academe. It is necessary now to recall that those lines occur midway in the speech which opens the play and to quote the first lines in order to begin discussion of Shakespeare's use of the triumph. Navarre addresses the three courtiers who have sworn to live with him as fellow-contemplatives during a three-year retreat;

> Let fame, that all hunt after in their lives,
> Live register'd upon our brazen tombs,
> And then grace us in the disgrace of death;

> When, spite of cormorant devouring Time,
> Th' endeavour of this present breath may buy
> That honour which shall bate his scythe's
>   keen edge,
> And make us heirs of all eternity.
> Therefore, brave conquerors--for so you are,
> That war against your own affections
> And the huge army of the world's desires--
> Our late edict shall strongly stand in force:
> Navarre shall be the wonder of the world;
> Our court shall be a little academe,
> Still and contemplative in living art.
>   (I.i.1-14)

Within the first seven lines of the play, the King has named the subjects of four of Petrarch's six triumphs in his poetic <u>Trionfi</u>. The poem had been translated into English by Henry Parker, Lord Morley, and published sometime between 1553 and 1556. However, I am not concerned to establish that Shakespeare necessarily knew the poem, because its iconography was commonplace in literature and the other arts, especially the decorative arts.[11]

    In Petrarch's poem, each of the six processions pictures a triumphant personification who advances with a number of supporters, many of them examples famous in history, myth, or literature. After the initial triumph of love, each successive personification triumphs over its predecessor, so that Chastity triumphs over Love, Death triumphs over Chastity, Fame triumphs over Death, Time triumphs over Fame, and Eternity triumphs over Time. The triumphs were a favorite subject for Renaissance tapestries, and many superb specimens are extant, including some now at Hampton Court which had been purchased by Cardinal Wolsey in 1523. The "Triumph of Death" personifies Death as the three Fates. In one part of the scene, two Fates attack Chastity while Cupid rides as a bound captive and Venus lies on the ground below. In another part a chariot holds the three Fates with the captive Chastity below. On the tapestry of the "Triumph of Fame over Death," Death or Atropos falls from one chariot while Fame rides triumphant in another, surrounded by famous heroes from antiquity like Pompey and Hercules, who also figure as examples in <u>Love's Labour's Lost</u>. A miniature illustration from a sixteenth-century French manuscript in the Bibliothèque Nationale conjoins the triumphs of Death and of Fame in a clearer image which conveys some of the morbidity

Shakespeare assigns to "cormorant devouring Time." In the French image Death, with its bowels exposed and its écorché corpse entwined with a snake, stands propped by its scythe on top of the defeated body of Chastity while Fame towers in triumph overhead. The last of the triumphs named by Navarre, and the last also in Petrarch's series, is the "Triumph of Eternity," one of the less popular subjects among the decorative arts, typically represented by an image of the Godhead.

Navarre alludes by name to fame, to death, to time, and to eternity. He omits the names of the first two in Petrarch's series, the "Triumph of Love," followed by the "Triumph of Chastity over Love." Rather he implies that the courtiers will triumph over both love and chastity (ll.8-10). Highly significant to the theme of the play is Navarre's implied banishment of even chaste love--precisely that omission which indicates the inadequacy of the academy as an exemplary model. It will be the assault of love which will loosen the resolve of the academicians, and the foolishness of the academy will be rewarded by a year of penance and chastity. Ironically, the two triumphs missing here will triumph in the last. Already, proleptically, within the first speech of the play, academe figures forth in living art as the negative inversion of the kind of model which Navarre blindly envisions in his opening speech. But that the latter end of his academy forgets its beginning is the theme of the play, and the charm of Navarre's opening lines is their unreflective self-revelation. This is the first instance within the drama of what this speech both names and ironically embodies as "living art." Shakespeare's allusion to pictorial tradition here serves without verbal exposition to adumbrate the later development of the play's theme. This chiaroscuro is most dramatically effective for those in the audience who recall the Petrarchan pictures as a complete series. The art of Shakespeare's device lives in the mind of the audience which sees the truth more completely than does Navarre.

Just as the omissions from the allusion to Petrarchan triumphal iconography are significant as a critique of Navarre's conception of the ideal academy, so too does Maria's later allusion to an emblematic commonplace serve as the text for a critique of the ideal courtier depicted in the emblem. In the second act, Maria describes Longaville, whom she once saw at a wedding:

"A man of sovereign parts he is esteem'd,/ Well fitted in arts, glorious in arms" (II.i.44-45). At this point in the speech, Longaville would seem to be the ideal Renaissance courtier. Maria's description fits, for example, the model courtier of William Segar's Booke of Honor and Armes.[12] Pictorial representations of the topic were also popular, most notably in the emblem from Alciatus reproduced by Geoffrey Whitney in his Choice of Emblemes in 1586.[13] Entitled "Marte et arte," the picture represents the figures of a scholar and a soldier, the combination which, the accompanying verses explain, is essential for success. It is important that the audience recall the commonplace picture of the model man in order to recognize the seriousness of the reservation which follows in the second half of Maria's speech:

> The only soil of his fair virtue's gloss,
> If virtue's gloss will stain with any soil,
> Is a sharp wit match'd with too blunt a will;
> Whose edge hath power to cut, whose will
>   still wills
> It should none spare that come within his
>   power.
>
> (II.i.47-51)

It is particularly appropriate that a female character should note the absence of the kind of love called charity in a model Renaissance soldier/scholar. In this respect, Maria serves us well as a keenly observant cicerone as she comments on the faults of the picture of the perfect courtier.

    The particular interest of Maria's reservation is that it could apply as well to the model as it does to Longaville, whose shortcomings we have in any case already observed in his quibbles and his enthusiasm for Navarre's overly ambitious project. Maria's speech points toward a recognition of limitation and inadequacy in the implicit assumptions of a cultural ideal as well as a specific dramatic character, but she does not--and properly so--generalize as we in the audience must do if we are to grasp the living truth which this passage embodies. It is not that all Renaissance men disregarded the place of love in the life of the soldier/scholar. Castiglione, of course, devotes a whole book of the Courtier to the subject, and Sidney, Spenser, and Shakespeare himself are always sensitive to the claims of the heart; but when reduced to the cliché of commonplace and to the simplification of pictorial image--two of the most popular Renaissance media--the ideal of the soldier/scholar does neglect the whole human dimension of love. Knowing the significance of Shakespeare's allusion to the ideal involves our knowing the commonplace in situ as it appears in some popular emblem books. So vulgarized, the concept neglects love whether it be construed as sexual attraction or as the virtue of charity, or as a combination of both. Herbert Ellis' reminder of the sexual connotations of "will" as sexual volition and "wit" as genitalia may be germane.[14] If so, both Shakespeare's pictorial allusion and his implicit pun work together as critique of an incomplete ideal. In any case, Maria's speech anticipates the lesson of love which academe has yet to learn through the living art of the ladies' responses to the courtiers' sterile wit as the play unfolds.[15]

    Significant misapplication plays a subtle and satirical part in the comic characters' use of exemplary figures, figures invoked, as Armado says, "that I may example my digression by some mighty precedent" (I.ii. 109). Shakespeare's use of example assumes a long tradition in the literary and pictorial arts, from Boccaccio's famous De Casibus Mulieribus and Petrarch's De Viris Illustribus to myriad tapestries and other decorative arts which picture the Nine Worthies and other heroic figures.[16] When Armado attempts to justify his earthly love for Jaquenetta by an appeal to historical exemplary precedent, he implores Moth to supply examples of great men who have been in love. Moth names two significant examples, Hercules and Samson. Moth offers no explanation for the nomination of Hercules, but he reminds Armado that Samson was "a man of good carriage, great carriage, for he carried the town-gates on his back like a porter; and he was in love" (I.ii. 66-68). The image which Moth has in mind is the familiar medieval and Renaissance picture of Samson bearing off the gates of Gaza, as he appears, for instance, in an illustration from the Biblia Pauperum.[17] Historically, Samson's action is associated with Jonah's emergence from the mouth of the whale and with Christ's emergence from the doors or the top of his tomb--sacred parallels suggested by the pattern of the act of emergence from a confining space. The conventional context for the type does not permit the secular interpretation implied by Moth, nor does the example of

Samson legitimately offer the comfort which Armado seeks
to infer from it. Ironically, Armado's self-serving
appeal to authority and Moth's compliant research both
exemplify Berowne's observation in the preceding scene:
"Small have continual plodders ever won,/ Save base
authority from others' books" (I.i.86-87). And there
does seem to be resonance of Berowne's "base authority"
in Armado's slavering homage to the "base" ground beneath Jaquenetta's "baser shoe," which is guided by her
"basest foot" (I.ii.156-59). Whatever the additional
pertinence of this verbal echo, the ironic effectiveness
of Shakespeare's art depends upon our recollection of
the sacredness of the traditional iconography misappro-
priated in this scene.

    The scene ends with Armado seeking to comfort him-
self regarding some of the more troubling aspects of
love:

> Love is a familiar; Love is a devil: there is
> no evil angel but Love. Yet was Samson so
> tempted, and he had an excellent strength;
> yet was Solomon so seduced, and he had a very
> good wit. Cupid's butt-shaft is too hard for
> Hercules' club, and therefore too much odds
> for a Spaniard's rapier.   (I.ii.162-67)

When Shakespeare's audience heard Armado's allusion to
Love as a devil, they would likely have conjured up any
one of many popular images--or perhaps a combination of
several of these--which associate love, women, and the
devil. Cupid himself, for example, was sometimes pictured with the clawed feet which were a more usual
attribute of the devil. Love is so pictured in the
"Triumph of Love" as it appears on the tapestry from
the Kunsthistorisches Museum in Vienna.[18] Closer to
home, illustrations in books current in England similarly
associated women, love, and the devil. The woodcut
labelled "Superbia," or "Pride," in Pynson's 1509
edition of Alexander Barclay's translation of Sebastian
Brant's _Shyp of Folys_ shows a woman gazing at her
reflection in a mirror while a devil lurks behind her.[19]
A similar woodcut in the _Book of the Knight of the Tower_
by Geoffrey La Tour-Landry even more bluntly pictures
the association between women and the devil in a scato-
logical image of a woman consulting her mirror, which
reflects the indecently exposed rear of the claw-footed
devil standing behind her.[20] Closest to Shakespeare's

own day, Stephen Batman's Christall Glass adapts the image to even more pointedly didactic purpose by featuring a skull beneath the woman's foot.[21] I do not mean to suggest that Armado's rationalizations should be read in a ponderously moralistic fashion, but much of the comedy does depend upon our awareness of Armado's ponderousness weighing the scales in his favor.

    The concatenation of Samson-Solomon-Hercules would also call to the Renaissance mind's eye a series with rather more foreboding implications than Armado wishes to extrapolate. Samson-as-lover evokes, even today, the story of Delilah's emasculation of the hero, as in the representation of the disarmed giant lying in the lassitude of love in the well-known painting by Mantegna in the National Gallery in London.[22] Modern audiences may miss the intended point about Solomon. For earlier audiences, his foolishness was proverbial. Chaucer alludes to the topic in three of the Canterbury Tales.[23] Popular imagery pictured Solomon's act of idolatry provoked by a woman, as described in 1 Kings 11, and as portrayed by Georg Pencz.[24] The type seems to have been often reproduced by northern artists during the sixteenth century--sometimes as one in a series of images of wise men made fools by women, such as "Virgil in a Basket" or "Phyllis Astride Aristotle."

    As for Armado's last example, Hercules-as-lover, it too is one of the type of wise men made fools. Some combination of three images might be implied in Shakespeare's allusion. Perhaps the most famous is the picture of Hercules at the crossroads where he must choose between Virtue and Pleasure, or as it came to be read, Virtue and Vice. Another image of Hercules familiar during the Renaissance was that of the hero disguised as a woman, doing women's work in the service of Omphale. Hercules appears in this guise, for example, in Henry Peacham's Minerva Britanna as a cautionary emblem for having made an unwise choice.[25] Another available image of Hercules undone by love was the story of how his death was caused by the poisoned shirt sent him by Deinara, as in a horrific image of Hercules in flames which appears in the Florentine Picture-Chronicle.[26] Well might Armado regard his passion as a form of surrender when he ends the first act with the series of commands: "Adieu, valour! rust, rapier . . . . Devise, wit; write, pen." Wise man he is not, but fool for love he certainly is, and Armado fits the type better than he knows, as the Renaissance audience would see. His rationalizations are facile; his surrender is an abject perversion of the historically moral intention of exempla to arm one against temptation. This intention is explicit, as it is, for instance, on the title page of Whitney's Emblemes, where "by the office of the eie, and the eare, the minde maye reape dooble delighte throughe holsome preceptes, shadowed with pleasant deuises: both fit for the vertuous, to their incoraging: and for the wicked, for their admonishing and amendment." Through his silly misapplication of example, Armado paradoxically becomes a new example of an old type, the miles gloriosus.

Not yet does Armado realize that service by the plough rather than the pen will redeem him and his love. It is not until the end of the fourth act that Berowne articulates at last the living dimension of art which has been missing from the art of academe:

>Never durst poet touch a pen to write
>Until his ink were temper'd with Love's sighs;
>O! then his lines would ravish savage ears,
>And plant in tyrants mild humility.
>From women's eyes this doctrine I derive:
>They sparkle still the right Promethean fire;
>They are the books, the arts, the academes,
>That show, contain, and nourish all the world;
>Else none at all in aught proves excellent.
>   (IV.iii.342-50)

The courtiers at this point agree to forswear their vow of abstinence from womanly company, but although they recognize the need for love, they have not yet learned how to signify feeling through living art. They disguise themselves as Muscovites and compose conventional, interchangeable sonnets which their ladies mock, under the masks of mistaken identity. Only through the lesson of love as it is lived during the spontaneous exchange which follows the masquing do the courtiers begin to experience the liveliness of love.

The first step is to abjure the use of excessive artificiality, disguise, "taffeta phrases, silken terms precise," "maggot ostentation," in favor of "russet yeas and honest kersey noes" (V.ii.406ff.). Berowne diagnoses the cause of the academe's ineffectual wooing and their sterile art: "The ladies did change favours, and then

we,/ Following the signs, woo'd but the sign of she"
(V.ii.468-69). The lovers have formerly created life-
less sonnets as courtly reflexes to attractive signs.
Addressed not so much to their ladies as to the conventional idea of Lady, the sonnets appropriately elicit
scornful laughter rather than delight, to apply Sidney's
distinction.[27] Indeed, the scene enacts Sidney's
discourse on inept and precious sonneteers in the <u>Defence</u>
wherein he observes, "if I were a mistress, [they] would
never persuade me that they were in love: so coldly they
apply fiery speeches, as men that had rather read lovers'
writings . . . than that in truth they feel those passions, which easily (as I think) may be bewrayed by
that same forcibleness or <u>energia</u> (as the Greeks call
it) of the writer."[28] Boyet objects to the ladies' plot
to reject the suit of the courtiers. The Princess makes
clear in her answer that the rejection is a therapeutic
effort to shock the lovers into a more feeling, a more
lively response:

> <u>Boyet</u>. Why that contempt will kill the
>   speaker's heart,
>   And quite divorce his memory from his part.
>
> <u>Prin</u>. Therefore I do it; and I make no doubt
>   The rest will ne'er come in, if he be out.
>   (V.ii.149-52)

Berowne's last long speech in the play reveals
that the courtiers have indeed been properly chastened,
not only by the ladies' rejection, but also by the pall
which Marcade has cast upon the whole party with his
news of the death of the father of the Princess, the
King of France. Berowne immediately attends to the
issue that the courtiers have abused language and he
resolves to speak more directly:

> Honest plain words best pierce the ear of
>   grief;
> And by these badges understand the king.
> For your fair sakes have we neglected time,
> Play'd foul play with our oaths.
>   (V.ii.745-48)

The rest of this speech, however, attempts to rational-
ize the courtiers' foolish behavior, which the Princess
then more plainly labels "as bombast and as lining to
the time" (V.ii.773). The ladies' prescriptions at last

awaken the courtiers to the nature of their malady: the
courtiers used words unfeelingly and thoughtlessly, more
careful for their own wit than for the heart of the
other. Rosaline's diagnosis, the last and the longest
of the three ladies' speeches on the subject, is precise
on the art of language. She had often heard of Berowne
before she saw him, "the world's large tongue/ Proclaims
you for a man replete with mocks" (V.ii.834-35). If
Berowne is to win her, he must reform by his language
as he has sinned by it. For a year, he is to

> Visit the speechless sick, and still converse
> With groaning wretches; and your task shall be
> With all the fierce endeavour of your wit
> To enforce the pained impotent to smile.
> (V.ii.843-46)

Berowne objects, "Mirth cannot move a soul in agony."
Rosaline's response goes to the heart of the matter,
the essential sympathy between speaker and audience:

> A jest's prosperity lies in the ear
> Of him that hears it, never in the tongue
> Of him that makes it. (V.ii.835-55)

    Living art consists in that silver chord of harmony
which unites artist and audience. The life of the work
is revivified with each new viewing, each new reading,
each new performance. The work of living art may be
highly finished, but it is never complete. By that
aesthetic criterion, a play may offer provisional
closure, but not a completed action, as Berowne implies:

> <u>Ber</u>. Our wooing doth not end like an old play;
> Jack hath not Jill: these ladies' courtesy
> Might well have made our sport a comedy.
>
> <u>King</u>. Come, sir, it wants a twelvemonth and
> and a day,
> And then 'twill end.
>
> <u>Ber</u>. That's too long for a play.
> (V.ii.866-70)

<u>Love's Labour's Lost</u> does not end with this comment,
however. Rather, the last action is the performance of
the <u>débat</u> between Spring and Winter, the "Song of the

Owl and the Cuckoo." It is fitting that the play should end on this note. The song is a model of living art which incorporates both the harsh realities of live and the delightful consolation of artful form[29] for audiences which are in harmony--both on stage and off. <u>Love's Labour's Lost</u> ends, as it began, with the enactment of a text on living art.

NOTES

[1] *Love's Labour's Lost*, ed. Richard Davis, rev. edn. (1951; rpt. London: Methuen, 1968). All subsequent references will be to this Arden edn. of the play.

[2] Rosalie L. Colie, *Shakespeare's "Living Art"* (Princeton: Princeton Univ. Press, 1974); William C. Carroll, *The Great Feast of Language in "Love's Labour's Lost"* (Princeton: Princeton Univ. Press, 1976).

[3] I have treated this concept at greater length in "The Anatomy of 'Liveliness' as a Concept in Renaissance Aesthetics," *Journal of Aesthetics and Art Criticism*, 33 (Summer, 1975), 407-18.

[4] Baldassare Castiglione, *The Book of the Courtier*, trans. Sir Thomas Hoby (1561), in *Three Renaissance Classics*, ed. Burton A. Milligan (New York: Scribner, 1953), p. 291.

[5] Leon Battista Alberti, *On Painting*, trans. John R. Spencer, rev. edn. (New Haven: Yale Univ. Press, 1966), p. 63.

[6] Leonardo Da Vinci, *Leonardo Da Vinci On Painting: A Lost Book ("Libro A")*, ed. Carlo Pedretti (Berkeley: Univ. of California Press, 1964), p. 46.

[7] Quintilian, *Institutio Oratoria*, trans. H.E. Butler, III, Loeb Classical Library (London: Heinemann, 1922). See n. 28 below.

[8] Sir Philip Sidney, *Sidney: A Defence of Poetry*, ed. J.A. Van Dorsten (London: Oxford Univ. Press, 1966), p. 32. Subsequent references will be to this edn. of the *Defence*. Edmund Spenser, *The Complete Poetical Works of Spenser*, ed. R.E. Neil Dodge (Boston and New York: Houghton Mifflin, 1908), p. 325.

[9] Stephen Orgel, "Affecting the Metaphysics," in *Twentieth-Century Literature in Retrospect*, ed. Reuben A. Brower, Harvard English Studies, 2 (Cambridge, Mass.: Harvard Univ. Press, 1971), p. 236.

[10] On the history of the idea, see Rensselaer W. Lee, *"Ut Pictura Poesis": The Humanistic Theory of*

Painting (New York: 1967), and Jean H. Hagstrum, The Sister Arts: The Tradition of Literary Pictorialism and English Poetry from Dryden to Gray (Chicago: Univ. of Chicago Press, 1958).

[11] D.D. Carnicelli, ed., Lord Morley's "Tryumphes of Fraunces Petrarcke": The English Translation of the "Trionfi," (Cambridge, Mass.: Harvard Univ. Press, 1971), reproduces plates of some decorative uses, including the tapestries at Hampton Court and the French miniature illustration mentioned below. On p. 58, Carnicelli points out Shakespeare's use of the trionfi in LLL. A comprehensive source for reproductions of illustrations of Petrarch in the decorative arts is Prince D'Essling and Eugène Müntz, Pétrarque: ses études d'art, son influence sur les artistes . . . (Paris: Gazette des Beaux Arts, 1902).

[12] William Segar, The Booke of Honor and Armes London, 1590), Bk. V, Chap. 25, pp. 66-70.

[13] Geoffrey Whitney, A Choice of Emblemes, and Other Devices, For the most parte gathered out of sundrie writers, Englished and Moralized. And Divers Newly Devised, ed. Henry Green (1586; facs. rpt. London, 1866; rpt. New York: Blom, 1967), p. 47. On p. 245, Green indicates that Whitney's emblem comes from the Lyons 1551 edn. of Alciatus.

[14] Herbert A. Ellis, Shakespeare's Lusty Punning in "Love's Labour's Lost" with Contemporary Analogues (The Hague: Mouton, 1973), pp. 102-10.

[15] Richard Cody, The Landscape of the Mind: Pastoralism and Platonic Theory in Tasso's "Aminta" and Shakespeare's Early Comedies (Oxford: Clarendon Press, 1969), pp. 108-09, gives a similar reading, basing his argument, however, upon an ingenious analysis of Shakespeare's use of significant grouping of characters as a mode of expressing ambivalence. Cody also notes the pertinence of the Hercules in bivio topos (p. 108) which I have found relevant below.

[16] For a broader study of this topic, see my "Renaissance Aesthetic Values: 'Example,' for Example," The Art Quarterly, 11 (Winter, 1979), 1-36.

[17] Elizabeth Soltesz, ed., Biblia Pauperum ([Budapest]: Corvina Press, 1967), Pl. No. 29.

[18] Madeleine Jarry, World Tapestry from Its Origin to the Present (New York: Putnam, 1969), p. 127, color pl.

[19] Alexander Barclay, trans., The Shyp of Folys (1509; facs. rpt. New York: Da Capo, 1970), fol. CLXXXXV[v].

[20] Geoffrey La Tour-Landry, Der Ritter vom Turn (1493; facs. rpt. Munich: Koland, 1922), p. 14 reproduces the earthy woodcut from the Basel edn.

[21] Stephen Batman, A Christall Glass of Christian Reformation, wherin the Godly may beholde the coloured Abuses used in this our Present Tyme (London, 1569), sig. Hiiir.

[22] Andrew Martindale and Niny Garavaglia, The Complete Paintings of Mantegna (London: Weidenfeld and Nicolson, 1971), Pl. LVII, in color.

[23] In "The Knight's Tale," "The Tale of the Wife of Bath," and "The Merchant's Tale," as noted by D.W. Robertson, Jr., in A Preface to Chaucer: Studies in Medieval Perspectives (1962; rpt. Princeton: Princeton Univ. Press, 1970), pp. 323-24, 371.

[24] For many plates illustrating this and other topics on the relationship between the sexes, see Clifton C. Olds, Ralph G. Williams, and William R. Levin, Images of Love and Death in Late Medieval and Renaissance Art ([Ann Arbor]: Univ. of Michigan Museum of Art, 1976). Pl. XVII, fig. 53A reproduces Pencz's "Poet Vergil Suspended in a Basket"; fig. 41, Lucas van Leyden's variation on the theme. Pl. XVIII, fig. 53B shows Pencz's version of "Vergil's Revenge"; fig. 90, a late medieval aquamanile of "Phyllis Astride Aristotle" from the Lehman Collection at the Metropolitan Museum of Art.

[25] Henry Peacham, Minerva Britanna Or a Garden of Heroical Deuises, furnished, and adorned with Emblemes and Impresa's of sundry natures, Newly devised, moralized, and published (1612; facs. rpt. Leeds: Scolar, 1966), p. 95.

[26] *A Florentine Picture-Chronicle Being A Series of Ninety-Nine Drawings Representing Scenes and Personages of Ancient History Sacred and Profane by Maso Finiguerra*, ed. Sidney Colvin (1898; facs. rpt. New York: Blom, 1970), Pl. XLI. Colvin's attribution of the work to Finiguerra is rejected by more recent scholarship.

[27] In his discussion of comedy, Sidney maintains that delight and laughter are not inseparable. "Nay, rather in themselves they have, as it were, a kind of contrariety: for delight we scarecely do but in things that have a conveniency to ourselves or to the general nature; laughter almost ever cometh of things most disproportioned to ourselves and nature. Delight hath a joy in it, either permanent or present. Laughter hath only a scornful tickling." (*Defence*, p. 68.)

[28] Sidney, *Defence*, pp. 69-70. Note that Sidney here refers to "*energia*," which is to be distinguished, with some difficulty, from "*enargeia*," the homonymous term used by Quintilian above. Jean H. Hagstrum's explanation of the distinction is not only lucid and brief, but also pertinent to Renaissance aesthetics: "*Enargeia* implies the achievement in verbal discourse of a natural quality or of a pictorial quality that is highly natural. *Energeia* refers to the actualization of potency, the realization of capacity or capability, the achievement in art and rhetoric of the dynamic and purposive life of nature. Poetry possesses *energeia* when it has achieved its final form and produces its proper pleasure, when it has achieved its own independent being quite apart from its analogies with nature or another art, and when it operates as an autonomous form with an effectual working power of its own." (*The Sister Arts*, p. 12.) Renaissance artists and writers valued both qualities highly, sometimes confusing the two, but *energeia* is more essential to the liveliness of art.

[29] S.K. Heninger, Jr. analyzes the relevance of the emblematic tradition to the song in "The Pattern of *Love's Labour's Lost*," *Shakespeare Studies*, 7, (1974), 26-33.

DISCOVERING A "DRAMATURGY OF HUMAN RELATIONSHIPS" IN SHAKESPEAREAN METADRAMA: TROILUS AND CRESSIDA

Richard C. Snyder

In 1971 James L. Calderwood published Shakespearean Metadrama, a study of five plays. By the term "metadrama" he meant a "drama about drama," in the sense that many of Pirandello's plays are dramas about the art of drama. He went on to claim that, although Shakespeare's plays are never explicitly metadramas, as Pope's Essay on Criticism is explicitly a "metapoem" or poem explicitly about poetry, nevertheless Shakespeare's concern about drama in his plays is real.[1] It is not just the type of unconscious poetics or dramaturgy that any ingenious critic might extrapolate at will. For the "idea of the play" is there in Shakespeare's plays and "seems to have fascinated Shakespeare throughout his career," so that Calderwood and other metadramatic critics claimed that "Shakespeare's plays are not only about the various moral, social, political, and other thematic issues with which critics have so long and quite properly been busy but also about Shakespeare's plays" and that "dramatic art itself--its materials, its media of language and theatre, its generic forms and conventions, its relationship to truth and the social order--is a dominant Shakespearean theme, perhaps his most abiding subject."[2]

The notion that writers write mostly about the art of writing has been a hot one in critical circles for some years. Even before Calderwood, Anne Righter wrote Shakespeare and the Idea of the Play (1962);[3] and another type of metadramatic study was done by Lawrence Danson, who claimed in his 1972 Tragic Alphabet that "language itself becomes one of the overriding questions of the tragedies."[4] At the least, most readers would agree with Calderwood that Shakespeare's plays are a goldmine for the metadramatic critic, with their many surrogate dramatists such as Iago or Edmund who continually stage scenes, their recurrent metaphors about the theatre, and their explicit or implicit plays-within-the-play habitually employed by Shakespeare.

The great danger, however, as emphasized by William C. Carroll, is that metadramatic criticism could become just another form of thematic studies, an "idiosyncratic contamination" or theme "imported into a play because the critic has a special interest in it." Like "Macbeth and Mutability," we then get "Macbeth and Metadrama"--just another form of "critical narcissism" or "just another trick carried around by the critic to be applied to any text within reach" so that "the text will no longer be allowed to reveal itself to be metadramatic; rather, the metadramatician . . . will . . . inevitably . . . create such texts."[5] Carroll makes a good point: we should discover Shakespeare's metadrama, not invent it.

My own quarrel with Calderwood, however, is that he does not seem to realize how important Shakespearean metadrama is. He seems to see Shakespeare's interests (with regard to metadrama) as purely formalistic--solely concerned with the problems of theatre and art and artist and audience, as if these problems had no wider, more common significance. But I would prefer to think of metadrama--at least in Troilus and Cressida--not just as "drama about drama," but as drama about the strikingly theatrical process that underlies and governs both drama and our everyday existence. Part of Shakespeare's point seems to be that what we normally call "reality" is just as much an imaginative construct, and more particularly a "theatrical" construct, as any play. The conflict of artist and audience is really only the conflict of individual and society in disguise. That is why Shakespeare can and does slip so easily into theatrical terms to describe events that never occur on or near a stage. We might say that the fundamental problems which we have to put up with every day--while not identical to theatre in all respects--are informed by a process that underlies both: our need to see ourselves in a "role," to perform in a variety of roles, some major and some minor; our need to put up with audience expectation and audience demand; our need to counter dramatic stereotypes, or to create a theatrical "distance" between ourselves and others, or to overcome such barriers. In this sense, I rather agree less with Calderwood than with Lionel Abel who claims that "dramatic forms are related to and take their life from values which are important outside of the drama."[6]

If it is true that the conflict of the artist and his audience in Shakespeare is really the conflict of the individual and society in disguise, then that other major artistic conflict, between the artist and the objects or persons he depicts, is also our own struggle between our imagination and the world about us. And from all that Shakespeare portrayed in the good and bad of these artistic relationships, especially as a metaphor for our own struggles for honesty and acceptance, we can and ought to discover in his works an evolving "dramaturgy" or "aesthetics of human relationships."

Troilus and Cressida is an especially useful play in this regard since it continually employs the problems in the artist/audience situation as a metaphor for the breakdown of healthy relationships in society.

Anne Righter claims that a pessimism in "the temper of the age" at the turn of the century emerged in Shakespeare's later plays as a disillusionment with "the actor's and the dramatist's craft" and as growing consciousness of "the poverty of the resources of the stage." She notes that Shakespeare turned to "the exploration of resemblances between the world and the stage which were negative and curiously grim" and that Troilus and Cressida is "filled with theatrical imagery, all of it of a kind most unflattering to the stage." The main examples given are Patroclus and Thersites, two obvious interior dramatists, who do ridiculously inept impersonations of their own officers in Achilles' tent, including "the pageant of Ajax" (III.iii.270), while Ulysses complains in a long description of a smug actor that Patroclus "pageants us . . . like a strutting player" (I.iii.151-3).[7]

Other explicit references to the theatre in Troilus and Cressida seem to confirm the standard view of this play as cynical about both the theatre and human relationships in general. The play's preoccupation with drama and its distortion of reality are announced by the Prologue in the first line of the play ("In Troy there lies the scene") and in its rather apologetic announcement of itself as coming "not in confidence/ Of author's pen or actor's voice" to present only "what may be digested in a play" (I.i.29).[8] According to the preface, it is a play that was "never staled with the stage, never clapper-clawed with the palms of the vulgar . . . [nor] sullied with the smoky breath of the multitude." This was added later, of course, but it echoes an apparent refrain throughout the play itself about the tyranny and corruptive influence of audiences upon not only the artist but upon the performer that is in us all. Ulysses complains of the swell-headed Achilles "who broils in [the] loud applause" (I.iii.378) of his reputation and grows lazy in his tent. There he takes on the role of a corrupting audience himself, lolling heavily on his pressed bed" while "from his deep chest [he] laughs out a loud applause" for Patroclus's "fusty" imitations, commanding "Now play me Nestor" and "Now play me him . . . arming to answer in a night alarm" (161-70). Ulysses, becoming an interior dramatist himself, sets up his own play-within-a-play so that the Greek officers will pass by the "fat-already proud" Achilles "as if he were forgot," then casually informs the peeved Achilles in dramatic terms that "no man is lord of anything . . ./ Till he communicate his parts to others . . ./ [and] behold them formed in [their] applause" (III.iii.115-9). Meanwhile by a similarly directed scene, the "blockish" Ajax has been convinced that he is a hero in a great drama, struts up and down the camp, and "drinks up his applause" (II.iii.195). The "crafty dog-fox" (V.iv.9-11) Ulysses himself begins his famous speech on order and degree with fifteen lines of flattering "applause and approbation" for Agammemnon and Nestor, who are in turn quick to listen and approve (I.iii.55-70, 138-41.) It appears that we may exist only in the applause of others whose effect is nevertheless corruptive. But if audiences corrupt their performers, so actors corrupt their audiences in the oppressive role-playing we meet with in everyday life. This is the import of Cressida's complaint that she cannot reveal her heart to Troilus, when she tells him, "If I confess much, you will play the tyrant" (III.ii.112).

Turning from metadramatic expressions to the many metadramatic scenes in the play appears to reaffirm the theory of Shakespeare's disillusionment with both drama and people in general. What I have called a "metadramatic scene" would consist of a scene or part of a scene that constitutes a drama-within-the-drama, or a performer/audience situation dramatized for us within the play. We may think of three groups, from the most obvious to the most subtle: (1) actual planned "shows" or staged scenes with not only performers and an audience but a director pulling the strings; (2) a single impromptu performer with an audience; (3) "private affairs," i.e., various places or scenes in which there are no fixed performers or audiences but rather some sort of closed arena, tent, or love-lair that is cut off from the outside world and has its own designated roles and rules of decorum.

Perhaps the most memorable example of the first group of metadramatic scenes would be the cast of officers that Ulysses directs to pass by and ignore Achilles. We know that Achilles is used to being a withdrawn audience himself, since we have seen him refuse even to come out of his tent to meet with the delegation that arrived to implore him. But here, as he "stands in the entrance of his tent" (III.iii.38), the tables are turned--the audience is ignoring him: "What mean these fellows? Know they not Achilles?" (70). Fortune is not to blame, he reflects, for all his previous riches are still his, "save these men's looks." He is finally bothered enough to seek out Ulysses, who is nearby pretending to be reading a book, and who gives him a lecture on the integral role that the "applause" of others has in creating personal identity. The direct counterpart of this little show, of course, is the other arranged scene wherein the officers flatter the "dull, brainless" Ajax while mocking him behind their hands. Ajax then "drinks up his applause" and "goes up and down the field, asking for himself" (244). But an "applause" so conspired and artificial, so arbitrarily withheld or bestowed, and so based on political expediency and personal vainglory seems a particularly dismal image of both the stage and society. This makes the director Ulysses hardly better than Achilles directing the private burlesque routines performed by Patroclus or Thersites in his tent, where from his bed he shouts, "Excellent!" whether the performance is worthy or not (I.iii.168).

Pandarus, in his efforts to fit Troilus and Cressida together, is another disingenuous director. Since he must create an image of each that he believes will please the other, he tries to cast them both in the role of shy young lovers, despite their already tearful experience in love. In their rendezvous scene, Troilus is in a frenzy of audience anticipation ("I am giddy; expectation whirls me round," III.i.16) while Cressida "makes ready" behind an enclosure or curtain like a performer getting ready to go on stage. Here Pandarus, popping his head in and out of the curtain, prepares Troilus to see her as if he were a prologue trying to put the audience in the right frame of mind for the show:

> She's making her ready; she'll come straight;
> you must be witty now. She does so blush,
> and fetches her wind so short as if she were
> frayed with a spirit. I'll fetch her. It
> is the prettiest villain; she fetches her
> breath as short as a new-ta'en sparrow.
> (28-32)

Finally embracing, the lovers speak little while the verbose Pandarus continues to direct them in the role of shy lovers, like a director shouting acting instructions in the shooting of a silent film, lest they step out of character (37-50, 93). In scene two, Helen and Hecuba go to watch the battle from one of Troy's high towers as if they were going to be spectators in a play (I.ii.1-5). Then, in the parade of returning soldiers, Pandarus conducts himself like a noisy and nervous ring-master, identifying each of the military celebrities and trying to build up the suspense for Troilus' arrival:

> Mark him, note him. O brave Troilus! Look
> well upon him, niece. Look you how his
> sword is bloodied, and his helm more hacked
> than Hector's; and how he looks, and how he
> goes. O admirable youth! he never saw
> three-and-twenty.
> (219-23)

In the same scene, Pandarus is a teller of tall stories, winding out a fable--with considerable difficulty--about Troilus's witty encounter with the celebrated Helen, while Cressida puts on a performance of her own--what we now call "putting someone on." She ironically undercuts his every lie with the common sense of a wise fool or the gag-man in a vaudevillian comic-dialogue:

> Pandarus: But there was such laughing, and
> Helen so blushed, and Paris so
> chafed, and all the rest so laughed,
> that it passed.
>
> Cressida: So let it now, for it has been a
> great while going by.
> (I.ii.158-60)

We may think of Pandarus as a painter of persons as well as a director of them--at least in words. In the first scene of the play, Troilus indirectly reveals how Pandarus has created, image by image, the vision of

Cressida that haunts him, when he complains to him that
Pandarus, by describing Cressida's swan-like complexion
and softness, only plunges into his every "gash" of love
"the knife that made it" (I.i.52-60) and even

> Pour'st in the open ulcer of my heart
> Her eyes, her hair, her cheek, her gait,
>   her voice.
>
> (50-1)

It is the same method that image-maker Pandarus later
uses in trying to sell Cressida on Troilus: his youth
(I.ii.78), "his wit" (82), "his qualities" (84), "his
beauty" (86), "his complexion" (94) "his chin" (107),
his dimples (116), and "his smiling" which "becomes him
better than any man in all Phrygia" (117). As prologue,
director, ring-master, story-teller, and image-maker,
Pandarus is a con-artist for each of the lovers in turn;
and by having a pimp as the busiest interior dramatist
in the play, Shakespeare seems to make dire comment on
the misrepresentations of art or drama, as well as on
human love-relationships which require them.

This is no less true of the "assignation scene"
played out between the lustful Diomedes and the false
Cressida (V.ii). It is perhaps the most well-known
play-within-the-play here, since, with two sets of
eavesdroppers--Ulysses and Troilus spying on Diomedes
and Cressida, Thersites spying on them all--it is really
a play-within-a-play-within-a-play, which affords
Shakespeare an opportunity to dramatize diverse audience
reactions to the same situation. Cressida is the
dramatist as well as the performer here. Operating on
the principle she had observed for us that "men prize
the thing ungained more than it is" (I.ii.275), Cressida
repeatedly offers and withdraws the love-token to and
from Diomedes in a now-I-will-now-I-won't pattern that
is analagous to the illusory art of both the prostitute
and the dramatist in creating suspense for their cus-
tomers. By putting on her "act," she illustrates that
there are pressures on women to make their materials
seem more interesting than they are. Meanwhile, the
reactions of the three audiences to the human frailty
on display here amount to a satire on audience reaction
itself; for from the seething cynicism of Thersites and
the bland worldly acceptance of Ulysses to the untested
naivete and self-righteousness of Troilus, none of the
on-lookers appears to have the right mixture of both

human understanding and moral value necessary to comprehend the scene and its characters rightly. If the performer is a whore, the audience are voyeurs, who come only to have their expectations fulfilled and not to learn anything new.

A similar ambivalence infects the second type of metadramatic scene, in which a performer appears with an audience, but with no director. I have already mentioned how audience flattery is a standard opening rhetorical ploy in the winning war-council speech of Ulysses ("Thou great commander, nerves and bone of Greece . . . Venerable Nestor, hatched in silver," I.iii. 55-65). Similar encomiums accompany the appeals of the "ceremonious courtier" Aeneas ("the god in office, guiding men," 231), Troilus ("a king so great as our dread father," II.ii.26), and Pandarus's "complimental assault" on "sweet" Paris and his "honey-sweet queen":

> Fair be to you, my lord, and to all this fair company. Fair desires in all fair measure fairly guide them. Especially to you, fair queen, fair thoughts be your fair pillow.
> (III.i.42-44)

All these "fair words" (45) win their audiences, while Cassandra, who speaks the wisest words in the play ("It is the purpose that makes strong the vow;/ But vows to every purpose must not hold," V.iii.22-3) finds none. The performer who corrupts his audience is in turn corrupted by them, for the stimulus to perform well or truly evaporates with an audience already won over by flattery. Hence, Pandarus' ridiculous love-song, crooned for Paris and Helen, receives its empty applause.

The same danger lurks in the third type of metadramatic scene--the various closed tents, love lairs, or private arenas cut off from the larger world outside. The lazy, secretive, ingrown, and illusory relationships of Patroclus and Achilles, Paris and Helen, Troilus and Cressida create an arbitrary just-between-you-and-me type of world and are partnerships in escape rather than in living. Having lost Patroclus, Achilles re-establishes such a charade with his gang of followers who have just stabbed Hector in the back:

> On, Myrmidons, and cry you all amain,
> "Achilles hath the mighty Hector slain!
> (V.viii.14)

Thus far I have seemed to support the idea of
Shakespeare in Troilus and Cressida as a cynic about
both the theatre and human relationships in general.
But perhaps we assume too much if we conclude, with
Anne Righter, that Shakespeare was following "the temper
of his time." Least of all need we assume that because
Shakespeare chose during this period to deal with patho-
logical relationships in terms of flawed drama, his
overall view of human relationships, of art, or of the
imaginative process which underlies and governs them
both was pessimistic. It would be wiser for us to say
simply that the play illustrates a breakdown of the
healthy and organic author/audience relationship that
should exist both between lovers and in society at
large.

If this is true, then what is the healthy relationship between the artist and his audience upon which all
other relationships are based?

I believe the organic relationship between author
and object and between author and audience that Coleridge
described in his Shakespearean Criticism is the type of
organic relationship we find affirmed in Shakespeare's
plays--both for the artist and for ourselves. Here the
great dramatist, it is said, does not attempt to "impress" his imagination on the persons he depicts "as on
a piece of wet clay" but allows form to grow from them
naturally.[9] Here the same organic relationship exists
between artist and audience too, for the artist does
not spurn his audience and their "commonplace realities"
but regards them and their needs as an integral part of
his creative process, while the audience cultivates a
"willing suspension of disbelief" in the artist's
private imaginative construct, as a possible contribution
to their already shared public one.[10] Sigmund Freud
said that the artist "finds a way of return from [his]
world of phantasy back to reality, and men concede them
a justification as valuable reflections of actual
life."[11] It is in this willingness both to go out and
to "return," as the eye of the painter continually
leaves and returns from his canvass to his model or as
the eyes of the orator finally return to meet those of
his audience, that the healthy rhythm of life lies both
for the artist and for ourselves.

In fact, the two extremes and the final balance
which Coleridge describes seem to duplicate the three

stages of Shakespeare's maturing relationship to his audience (and to his society) in his early plays as Calderwood has seen them:

> Shakespeare [in A Midsummer Night's Dream] has come to acknowledge the audience's creative role in the collaborative enterprise of drama; it is no longer regarded as merely a corruptive appetite for sensations that must be catered to as in Titus Andronicus or disregarded as in Love's Labour's Lost.[12]

But in Troilus and Cressida we find author and audience neither open nor genuine with each other, but either pandering or withdrawn--"catering" or "disregarding." Troilus is the epitome of the withdrawn neo-artist; in the war council, in his love scenes with Cressida, in watching her vamp Diomedes, in his pitiless regard for defeated soldiers, he utterly ignores "commonplace realities," would rather impress his mind's image of Cressida upon her as "on a piece of wet clay" than see the real woman she is, even refuses to believe his very eyes in the scene with her flirting, as Thersites observes in astonishment, "Will 'a swagger himself out on's own eyes?" (V.ii.132). And to the end he is the character least interested to "find a way of return from his phantasy back to reality." He parallels Achilles, who lazes about in the little play-world of impersonations created by Patroclus in his tent; or Paris, who sings drunken ditties in his love-lair with Helen while the bloody external world that is their celebrity-worshipping audience goes by outside; or Ulysses, whose rigid and self-serving notions of order and degree are an impress of his selfish imagination on society at large, the way Troilus's fantasy is imposed on Cressida.

In contrast to Troilus, Cressida is one type of the pandering artist in the play: cautious and bawdy with Pandarus, innocent and open with Troilus, a flirt with the Greeks, she has no inner vision of herself, no single self to struggle for but is totally dependent on others for her identity and caters to each new audience with her bag of personalities as a purely commercial artist giving in to every new audience demand. Where Troilus will not believe his own eyes, she cannot believe anything else, concluding: "The error of our eyes directs our mind" (V.ii.106). Her obvious parallel is Pandarus, the pimp and pandering false-image maker for each of the lovers in turn. But Ajax belongs here too because, in contrast to Achilles, he falls right into the ridiculous role that everybody wants him to play; so does Patroclus, with his impersonations to order for Achilles; and Hector, who argues in the war council for giving in to practical demands, giving in to natural law, giving in to the laws of nations, and then finally gives in to not giving in after all as soon as he sees that his audience of more "spritely brethren" will not be swayed (II.ii.190).

The two war councils parallel Cressida and Troilus in this regard, which makes it fitting for Cressida to join the Greeks. The Greeks conclude for a pandering harmony with the supposed order and degree in Nature and commonplace realities, while the Trojans blindly defy the storms of Fortune for the sake of an inflexible "honor." Hence, the Trojans are aptly represented by Aeneas, who delivers a message to the Greek camp and is so enamoured of his own ceremonious and theatrical speech-making that he cannot find the audience he is supposed to address it to--Agamemnon, who is standing right in front of him (I.iii).

But our audiences, like our artists, may be withdrawn or pandering too: withdrawn like the audience of officers that Ulysses sets up to deliberately ignore Achilles, or pandering like the one he sets up to puff Ajax into feeling himself a great hero. Helen and Hecuba are a withdrawn audience as they go to the high tower of the city to view the battle from afar, where no stench of blood or gore need reach them, like people at a play or film who close their eyes during the rough parts. And, of course, the three audiences of Cressida--Pandarus, Troilus, and the Greek officers--all have their minds made up about her differently in advance, like the audience with no organic openness to its performer, with no "willing suspension of disbelief" for the person who walks onto the stage.

The title of the play has symbolic value if we realize its two mythically paired characters represent the often linked opposites of being too "disregarding" of commonplace externals or too "catering" to them. Calderwood described "the most recurrent and dominant issue in the early plays" as the conflict between the young artist's desire for poetic language and the audience's need for action, or "the interplay of language and action in drama" (p. 20, italics mine). Similarly, Cressida hints to Troilus that his poetic soul which regards more highly the "will" in love than "the act" or the "performance" (III.ii.74-8)--note the dramatic terms--may be too disregarding of the importance of externals:

> They that have the voice of lions and the act of hares--are they not monsters? (82-3)

But Troilus and Cressida are only the two main "metadramatic monsters" of many such in the play which Shakespeare has employed as foils for each other. I have already hinted at some of these foils: the sulking Achilles who "carries the stream of his dispose/ Without observance and respect of any" (II.iii.158), and the "altogether more tractable" Ajax (145); their helpmates, Patroclus, whose words cater to his audience, and Thersites, whose words assault each audience with the acerbic images of a vicious editorial cartoonist: "There's Ulysses and old Nestor, whose wit was mouldy ere your grandsires had nails on their toes, yoke you like draught-oxen and make you plough up the wars" (II.i.99-102). The elder Pandarus obsequiously singing at command of Paris and Helen is a picture of a pandering artist before a spoiled, withdrawn audience; Aeneas and Cassandra make an interesting contrast as interrupting messengers in the middle of each war council--one with almost too much politeness to communicate to his audience, the other with too little.

We understand the play much better if we note these contrasts and confrontations. Hector and Ulysses, for instance, advance identical arguments in their separate war-councils--respect for law and order. Both affirm to an inordinate degree the idea of personal identity based on public applause. Ulysses uses it to move Achilles, and Hector continually runs to the battlefield when he feels his name is in jeopardy. Hector respects the rules of the game: is affable at the truce, spares wounded enemies out of "fair play" (V.ii.41), spares Ajax because he is out of condition. It is all part of "fair play," and war is "good sport" (I.i.109) as Aeneas had said, so that Hector even "hunts" an enemy soldier like a "beast" for the "hide" of his fine armor (V.vi.30-1). And when Achilles catches him without his own armor on, he naively expects that the rules of the game will protect him. But Achilles, who, by contrast, "carries on the stream of his disposal/ Without observance and respect of any," murders him for personal revenge and not for the sport of it. For both the disregarding Achilles and the disregarding Troilus, "fair play" is "fool's play" (V.iii.42).

I have described specific metadramatic <u>words</u>, <u>scenes</u>, and <u>characters</u> in <u>Troilus</u> and <u>Cressida</u>. I will now treat what I believe to be some of its more specific metadramatic <u>themes</u>.

In Shakespeare's pathology of dramatic relationships the withdrawn or pandering artist and audience seem fundamental types; but more specific problems can be described. In <u>Troilus and Cressida</u>, I believe at least five such socio-dramatic neuroses arise. In naming them I have kept to my habit of mixing psychological, dramatic, and everyday terms (as Shakespeare does) to push my main point that drama is itself a psychology of everyday life.

(1) <u>Becoming a Victim of Dramatic Circumstance</u>. In the third chapter of Joyce's <u>A Portrait of the Artist as a Young Man</u>, Stephen Dedalus must play the part of a "farcical pedagogue" in the high school play. But Stephen's part is only emblematic of the other false roles which society thrusts upon him at this time. As the preconceived plot of a play determines the role of a character in it, often the preconceived structure and values of society determine in large part the personal identity of the individual, caught in a play or movie not of his own making. One theme of Shakespeare's play, then, is the difficulty of resisting roles which dramatic circumstances in society create for us and how quickly these roles change as dramatic circumstances alter. Daniel Seltzer is mistaken to suppose that the radical alternation of personality in the play is a result of an unfortunate nod on Shakespeare's part in the matter of character consistency;[13] rather, the play is itself centrally concerned with the radical alternation of personality as it is perceived and as it perceives itself under radically altered circumstances. As mentioned above, Ulysses stages scenes around the tents of Achilles and Ajax to subvert or puff their identities, and as director of both state and stage he is wary of the subversive threat to his own identity of

Patroclus's irreverent impersonations. The truce in the war reverses the relationships of the top enemy officers, frequently illustrated by such absurd comments as, "No man can love in such a sort/ The thing he means to kill more excellently" (IV.i.23-4). But Hector forgets and insults Menelaus by reminding him that he is a cuckold (IV.v.179). Though Cressida's reference to her "sweet" Diomedes (V.ii.7) scandalizes Troilus, he and Hector have just called their own enemies by the same name: sweet Menelaus (V.i.73) and sweet Ulysses (86). We know that hostages often grow to love their captors since they are so dependent on them for their lives, and Helen is the most famous victim of dramatic circumstance in this sense. We have already mentioned Cressida's unusual capacity for changing personalities with each new audience, a trait which she admits to having (her "kind of self" and her "unkind self," III.ii.140-2). Later Troilus is shocked: "This is, is not Cressid!" (V.ii.142). But the frequent arbitrariness of roles in both love and war had been underlined by Troilus and Aeneas when they spoke of them as "sport" (I.i.109-11).

(2) Becoming a Victim of Audience Expectation or Audience Demand. The expectations of an audience often determine what they see on the stage whether it is really there or not. Moreover, the expectations of an audience often pressure a performer to slip into a role he would not have chosen otherwise. So it is in life. In a roomful of persons who expect us to act like a dolt, we will appear stupid whether we are or not; and it often occurs that after sufficient time in such circumstances we actually begin to play the role our life-audience expects of us--since it amounts to a choice between that and virtual non-existence. Cressida's role as a pandering artist who slips from one identity to another is more understandable in connection with the biased expectations of her several audiences. Pandarus, for instance, has carved out the refined Cressida in Troilus' brain image-by-image well before the actress arrives to play the part:

> [Thou] Pour'st in the open ulcer of my heart
> Her eyes, her hair, her cheek, her gait,
> her voice.   (I.i.50-51)

Ulysses, our other busy interior dramatist, later accuses her of being a "daughter of the game" for receiving kisses from the generals, but actually set up that little scenario himself with her part in it ("'Twere better she were kissed in general," IV.v.21), then manufactured limb-for-limb her role with the Greeks as Pandarus had done with Troilus:

> There's language in her eye, her cheek, her lip,
> May, her foot speaks.   (IV.v.55-6)

As I described earlier, Troilus before his first meeting with Cressida is in a frenzy of narcissistic audience expectation ("I am giddy; expectation whirls me round," III.ii.16), while Pandarus, as prologue and director of the scene, pops his head in and out of the curtains and Cressida gets ready backstage. Although we have already seen Cressida as a witty and experienced woman of the world, she now appears as a sweet and pure young maiden because that is what her audience expects. In the end Cressida succumbs to the expectations of her audiences, both inside and outside the play, as well as to their frequent low expectations about women. Troilus's "weaker than a woman's tear" (I.i.9) becomes Cressida's "Ah, poor our sex!" (V.ii.105).

(3) <u>Trying to Create a "Theatrical Distance" in Love from the Lover</u>. The need to create a theatrical distance from the audience is a well-known principle of dramaturgy that is reflected in <u>Hamlet</u>. Hamlet wants the actors to be more "real" in their speeches and not "mouth it" or "tear a passion to tatters." And this metadramatic concern in <u>Hamlet</u> contributes to the core conflict of the play: performed emotion is often more in demand than real emotion. Since audiences wish to be entertained, the playwright must create a certain distance from reality--however much truth may be his aim. Surely there is some danger here in art as well as in life; it is as if we always preferred the distant copy of the thing to the thing itself. And one way that the need for theatrical distance in the drama translates into life is as the need to create a theatrical distance in love between oneself and the lover in order for love to thrive. We even use a theatrical term--"playing hard to get." As audiences demand the unreal, lovers want lies, and both Cressida and Troilus try by turns to create a theatrical distance between each other for love's sake. Cressida's soliloquy on men shows that she is aware of this psychology, for "Men prize the thing ungained more than it is" (I.ii.280).

Troilus, too, fears presenting himself directly but must use Pandarus to dramatize himself to Cressida.

(4) __Trying to Fulfill Theatrical Stereotypes to Create Sexual Appeal__. As sex appeal on stage or screen is determined by theatrical stereotypes, so in real life it is defined by figures in the spotlight of notoriety. The beauty of the actress waxes as actors swoon or fight for her. Likewise, it is not the face of "Miss America" alone but the "Pageant" of millions bowing down to one that makes her beauty. So Troilus says, "Fools, on both sides! Helen must needs be fair,/ When with your blood you daily paint her thus" (I.i.86-7), using the horrific theatrical image of "paint" (or make-up used by actors and women) drawn from the blood of soldiers fighting for Helen. For the same reason, Pandarus, haunted by the preeminence of name-value in this play, tries to make a Helen out of Cressida in scene one with Troilus and a Hector out of Troilus in scene two with Cressida. Theatrical stereotypes contribute to distance in love: we would rather love each other through movie idols than experience the real thing. Cressida is resigned to distance as a necessary evil in love (III.i.112); but Troilus, like Truffaut's __The Man Who Loved Women__, seems to desire only "Th' imaginary relish" (17) and fears the real woman as "Death" (20).

(5) __Language, Art, and Love as Acts of Violence__. The play is filled with words empty of reality like Pandarus's "fair words" or the "words, words, mere words" of Cressida's letter. They may seem harmless enough, and Troilus claims that "In all Cupid's pageant there is presented no monster" (III.ii.69). But Cressida answers that those are "monsters" who have "the voice of lions and the act of hares"; empty words can irreparably distort the image of ourselves and others. "No more words, Thersites, please!" (II.i.108). Thersites has threatened to take apart Ajax with his sharp tongue. "I will begin at thy heel, and tell what thou art by inches, thou thing of no bowels, thou!" In the same way the fantasy world of words created by Pandarus has dismembered Cressida and wounded Troilus: "Her eyes, her hair, her cheek, her gait . . . every gash [of] love . . . [and] the knife that made it." Both art and love have this tendency to harm, distort, and devour their objects or audiences, to lack sufficient respect for their otherness. Hence, the frequent, disquieting food

images for love and art--"what may be digested in a play," "the spice and salt that season a man" (I.ii.242), "love's thrice-repurèd nectar" (III.ii.20), the grinding, the bolting, the leavening, the kneading, the baking, etc. (I.i.13-24)--seem to describe a love that would "kill those pretty eyes" (IV.ii.4) in pursuit of its "imaginary relish." Yet prostitutes in effect invite violence because it is their business to pander to even the darkest sexual fantasies, which, under conditions of more genuine response, might never have surfaced. Pandarus sins not because he is an interior dramatist but because he is a mendacious one, not because--like the friar in Romeo and Juliet--he brings forbidden lovers together, but because he keeps them apart by creating illusions of themselves for each other, like a madame in a bawdy house richly furnished with costumes, props, and period bedrooms. Hence, his syphilis at the end: a penalty not for lovers but for those who pursue every illusion of desire. His song for Paris and Helen ("Love, love, nothing but love, still love still more!/ The shaft . . . tickles the sore," III.i.107-10) shows the top-forty-hits monotony and violence of both art and love withdrawn from the "commonplace realities" of the larger world, with only an imaginary or pandering audience.

NOTES

[1] James L. Calderwood, *Shakespearean Metadrama* (Minneapolis: Univ. of Minnesota Press, 1971), p. 8.

[2] Ibid., p. 5.

[3] Anne Righter, *Shakespeare and the Idea of the Play* (London: Chatto & Windus, 1962).

[4] Louis Marder, "Shakespearean Hyperactivity, Metadramatic Criticism, and Shakespeare Scholarship," *The Shakespeare Newsletter*, 27 (Nov. 1977), 36.

[5] Quoted by Marder, 36.

[6] Lionel Abel, *Metatheatre: A New View of Dramatic Form* (New York: Hill and Wang, 1963), p. viii.

[7] Righter, pp. 172-183.

[8] All references to *Troilus and Cressida* shall be made to Virgil K. Whitaker's edition of the play in *William Shakespeare: The Complete Works*, ed. Alfred Harbage (Baltimore: Penguin, 1969).

[9] See his "Mechanic and Organic Form" and "Poetry Is Ideal" in David Perkins, ed., *English Romantic Writers* (San Francisco: Harcourt, 1967), pp. 500-501

[10] See his "The Character of Hamlet" and "Stage Illusion" in Perkins, pp. 496-499.

[11] "The Relation of the Poet to Day-Dreaming," quoted in Harold P. Simonson, *Strategies in Criticism* (New York: Holt, 1971), p. 61.

[12] Calderwood, p. 136.

[13] Daniel Seltzer, "Introduction," in Daniel Seltzer, ed., *The History of Troilus and Cressida* (New York: Signet, 1963), pp. xxii-xl.

IMITATIONS AND CREATION IN <u>MEASURE FOR MEASURE</u>

J.S. Lawry

When Duke Vincentio introduces the words of the title directly within the play, they follow an outcry attributed to law itself: "An Angelo for Claudio, death for death!" (V.i.409).[1] Putting aside for the moment the implication of Christian redemption possible within the formula "death for death," in this immediate context the words "measure for measure" seem to validate the popular notion that they signify an eye for an eye or, at the least, an opposite reaction to a given action. However, in the fuller context also supplied by the Duke, the title formula appears alongside three other such equations, within one couplet:

> Haste still pays haste, and leisure answers leisure;
> Like doth quit like, and <u>Measure</u> still <u>for</u> <u>Measure</u>.
> (V.i.410-411)

Also putting aside all consideration of the exigencies or opportunities of rhyme, it is obvious that within this fuller context the title formula must accept a range of meaning far greater than that of "death for death." The increased range in turn leads the title into far greater relevance for the full play. If haste "still" matches haste as such, it however is answered with a great opposite, leisure; the two individual sets have generated a single, and larger, new one. Not quite so ready an expansion appears in the succeeding verse. If "like doth quit like," each like thing or action must be so inseparably one with its kind that no opposition can occur, or else seeming opposites must be seen as one, by virtue of an action in common. Furthermore, the verb "quits" in this set introduces an ambiguity not present in the earlier sets: "quits" can suggest "acquits" as well as "gets even with." Finally, if "measure for measure" for the first time intimates process or movement (if only that of exchange), this nearly verbless formula also maintains that measure is, unmovingly, "still for" measure. Unlike "haste" with "leisure," then, "like" and "measure" appear to offer no new, greater set. However, if the earlier combination can be taken to be a precedent, "measure" may be supposed to receive some of the absoluteness present in like with like, and "like" in turn may receive some of the intimation of process in "measure . . . for measure."[2] Then the final "doubled" set may suggest not only opposition or retribution but also reconciliation and conversion, such as that possible in "death for death." Quite outside the play, if "like" Christ "quits" Adam, then a measure of grace balances--is "still for"--a measure of law.

In other couplets, Duke Vincentio all but justifies such an interpretation of the title. In closing Act III, he predicts a dramatic (and perhaps a distantly theological) use of "craft against vice." By its means, "disguise shall by th' disguised/ Pay with falsehood false exacting" (III.ii.277, 280-281). He assures Isabella, conversely, that to the love he has "in doing good a remedy presents itself" (III.i.198-199). In these passages, like does not so much quit like as dramatically rehearse a vicious act in order to convert it into a true good. Such a dramatic cure is taken to be none the worse for being a homeopathic imitation of the disease.[3] If such a version of the reversal and catharsis usual in tragedy seems much more pessimistic than that in Hamlet, under which virtue must beg leave of vice to do it good, it also is free from Hamlet's self-pity. It suggests as well a more reformable imitation of humanity than that offered by either Hamlet or his players. In Measure for Measure, then, a measure of grace or law is somewhat darkly imposed upon the measure of license which it had dramatically imitated. But what else would have been possible to a Duke of dark corners, whom even a slanderer suggests will "have dark deeds darkly answer'd" (III.ii.177)? Vienna must look in a dark mirror before it can see "face to face."

The words "measure for measure" thus may intimate 1) opposition, as in action and reaction, but also 2) equivalence or even identity, as in like with like, or 3) a process in which the relationship of two things or events comes to be revealed or validated. If, in the first meaning, a "measure" of vice is answered with a "measure" of either punishment or mercy, the first "measure" is opposed by the second. On the other hand, if, in the second meaning, an open and public "measure" of vice is paired with a private and concealed measure of that same vice, or if an Isabella asks the cold Angelo to put himself in her brother's warm place and

Angelo takes her exactly at her word, then the one "measure" has proved to be equivalent or even identical with the other. Finally, if, in the third implication, a measure in law generates a measure in lawlessness, or conversely if a measure of lawlessness brings about a measure in law, then not only has a process of changing or conversion replaced the implied stasis of a mere exchange, but also the power of the one measure to generate the other has been revealed. Although something of such a radial effect is familiar to us in the verbal paradox, it is relatively unfamiliar as the system of meaning for a full-length play. That is part of the "problem" in Measure for Measure.

Much of the play is a scrupulous and fluent interpretation of the play's title, considered within its full context. At one point, the play vigorously rehearses those very words: Isabella and the Duke exchange compliments upon "leisure," and with Escalus the Duke moves in one speech from "sinister measure" to "good leisure" (III.i.153,157; III.ii.242-247).

In its turn, the title of this discussion is an oblique interpretation of the title of the play. It suggests that the art of Measure for Measure is in part an art of imitations within the play: specifically, of two early opposed imitations of man, which produce the need for a homeopathic drama. The internal drama is a third kind of imitation, at once reflective but also corrective. The appearance of art in the play thus goes far toward identifying the art of the play.

I

Ever since the Greeks, we have thought of art--especially, dramatic art--as involving imitation. That imitation often is realized in, or develops, a significant action. And ever since the appearance of the idea of God as artist, or of the artist as creator, we have thought of art as creation. In Measure for Measure, the two notions join. The quality or idea of mankind is imitated by means of specific kinds of material creation. The Duke intimates that process of imitation and creation when he speaks to Escalus of the "art and practice" of government (I.i.12). It is as if the general idea or art gave rise to the specific act and practice. As it happens, however, the Duke specifies neither the one other, and it remains for the play as a whole to explore their definition.

Measure for Measure accordingly works with three internal arts of imitation, which produce three corresponding practices of creation. In the first, which seems public and fatal, both Angelo and Claudio are effectively formed anew under the law, as imitations of natural man in a fallen world. In the second, which seems private and voluntary, Isabella and the Duke elect imitations of religious man, if not quite of Christ or God. Although such rival imitations seem rigidly opposite, they always lean together toward identity. Angelo would become the sinner Claudio had been; Isabella and the Duke shift from being a purely religious "sister" and "brother" to Claudio into sharing a familial or fleshly relationship with him. Despite such inclination from opposition into identity, the conditions that produced the two imitations remain essentially static. Thus most of Vienna belatedly agrees that a permissive government is a breeder of license: which is almost to say that mercy generates sin. Angelo and Claudio alike will urge the reverse formula on Isabella, claiming that her sin would constitute a charity. And even the uninvolved counsellor Escalus manages to conflate judge and criminal by recommending, "Let us be keen, and rather cut a little,/ Than fall, and bruise to death" (II.i.5-6). Seemingly divergent or opposite lines thus lash back to form a circle. Shakespeare then introduces a third kind of imitation, and its accompanying embodiment in practice. Its creation is not of another kind of man, but of a mirror for men. Both literally and figuratively, this dramatic creation is a plot, but it effects recognition, revelation, and affirmation. To do so, it reflects earlier internal "plots," such as the betrothals of both Claudio and Angelo; they would have prevented the present difficulties. In the present, the imitative plot is homeopathic. Its imitated vice may recall or initiate a virtue. By such means, the promise of conversion always present in the title may inform the future. In its practice of drama, Measure for Measure thus offers a manifold imitation of the idea of drama.

The first two imitations and creations of men will now be considered in somewhat more detail, in order that the third imitation, and the third creation that begins in dirty tricks but concludes in recreation, may be better seen and valued. Like the Duke and Isabella, it has received an often hostile modern reception.[4] Perhaps its function is the best argument for its process and form.

II

When the "Duke of dark corners" proposes to vacate his public office, he tells his counsellor Escalus that both of them know the art and practice of governing. If so, none of the other characters do, nor does the uninformed audience. Even Escalus, to say nothing of the Angelo who now must discharge the practice, must wonder about the unspecified "strength and nature" of the transmitted power (I.i.79). The play thus begins with no clear idea of law or license in governor or subject. Instead of providing his deputies with an imitation of the idea of law (or the Governor), the Duke in effect creates a material likeness of the lawgiver. Angelo is created in the material image of the Duke, in explicit imagery if not quite in fact. The Duke wonders what "figure of us" Angelo will bear (I.i.16); accordingly, Angelo wishes that his mettle might be tested before "so great a figure/ Be stamp'd upon [him]" (I.i. 48-50). The word "mettle" seems to invite the pun.[5] Angelo will return to the image of his minting, and of minting as creation, in speaking to Isabella of a lecher that can "coin heaven's image/ In stamps that are forbid" (II.iv.45-46). When his own crime is completed, he continues (in a peculiar conflation of himself with Claudio and Julietta), "This deed unshapes me quite, makes me unpregnant" (IV.iv.20). Although the Duke's election of Angelo at times suggests the making of man in a divine image, the actual creation in Vienna is metallic. It shows more of "Pygmalion's images newly made" (III.ii.45), or the king's "stamped face" in John Donne, than of earthly dust and divine breath. From such a creation, mechanical law and retribution are far more likely than flexibility and mercy. Such an imitation has not shown man what he *is*, but only what, given authority, he may <u>do</u>. As art and practice, such imitation and creation <u>are</u> those of political man within a materialistic city. They readily give into the measuring of bodily punishments for bodily crimes.

Although Claudio would seem to be the opposite of Angelo, much the same general imitation and creation occurs for him. He is "born" as sinner the instant law replaces license. It makes little difference that Claudio is on the wrong side and Angelo is on the right side of the law. At the instant when Claudio's lust is minted with "characters too gross" (I.ii.155) in the pregnancy of his mistress, nothing from the past (which had included a betrothal within law, and sexual pleasure that was not "fornication" because it was not "published") is relevant. The almost identical materialistic definition and minting of Claudio and Angelo is an early proof that between such seeming opposites "like quits like," justifying an early contention that only a "pair of shears" differentiates the list from the velvet in a garment (I.ii.27). The creation of men under such an imitation is rigid and fixed, however. Angelo becomes the rigor of the law, and Claudio the danger of an attractive lawlessness.

Any suggested alterations upon these two creations, so like in their seeming unlikeness, tend to compound the difficulty. As Pompey Bum says to Mistress Overdone, "Though you change your place, you need not change your trade" (I.ii.107-108). It is true, of course, that Isabella briefly envisions a different kind of creation, telling Angelo that a God-like pity might instead "breathe within [his] lips,/ Like man new made" (II.ii. 78-79); such a creation would approximate that of a New Testament regeneration. However, Vienna chooses to remain fixed within the fatal embrace of the Old Testament predications of law and flesh. When Claudio argues that Isabella's proposed adultery would be no sin if it saved his life, Isabella accordingly demands, "Wilt thou be made a man out of my vice?" (III.i.137). For men so created, no alteration would obtain, even if Angelo did extend mercy or if Isabella consented to a saving sin. A Claudio would not have been "born again" in the New Testament meaning, nor even forgiven. He would only have been not-punished.

<u>Measure for Measure</u> opens, then, upon these two men created as imitations of political man. The Duke had supplied nothing more. From seemingly opposite temperaments in nature and opposite practices before the law, Claudio and Angelo become as one "figure" for public mankind.

III

In contrast to Angelo and Claudio, those two unlikes who are nevertheless like in their creations as men newly minted, Isabella and the Duke always are seen as being like. Such unlikeness as appears between them comes about mainly from the Duke's knowing all of his homeopathic plot, whereas Isabella knows only half. The basic likenesses between them incidentally suggest a mutual defence against a generally hostile, or unconvinced, modern press.

The imitation of man chosen by the Duke and Isabella is a direct reaction to that of men such as Claudio and Angelo. The Duke and Isabella will not imitate so much worldly man in a fallen world as the Creator who removes himself from it. Their retirement from the world and its relationships, whether those of the family within nature or of the State within law, is voluntary and heartfelt. Far from being "stamped" into a new public being, they would retire to an original being. Accordingly, they seek out the all-but-silent cloister and the dark corners of anonymity. They would alter the world's fleshly definition of "brother" and "sister" into a purely spiritual meaning. In this sense, each acts to "unmint" the image of man offered by nature and office, in favor of a creation in God's image.

However, because they are Christians, each reserves some qualifying, and paradoxical, relations with the world: largely because they always wish to serve that world. Although the Duke assumes the habit of a friar in order to see still more of "prince and people" (I.iii. 45), whereas Isabella would take orders in order to see neither, each advocates charity toward men. Both then are forced to admit that their mercy probably encourages exactly that license which they deplore, and which they themselves have avoided. Similarly, each recommends a law-abiding society, but then has to admit that the law may take men's lives. Thus, despite their voluntary imitation of the Creator or of his image in man, they remain suspended between Old and New Testament intimations of deity: of God as offended <u>Deus absconditus</u>, or as incarnate redeemer.

In their own way, the Duke and Isabella continue the terrible irreconcilable likenesses of Claudio and Angelo. In neither the one creation nor the other are law and love reconciled; they are only tensely parted, yet tensely paired. Like cannot yet acquit like. Indeed, opposed "likes" in the first half of the play cannot even apprehend the likeness within their seeming differences. The creation of a dark dramatic mirror that darkly imitates mankind will bring them into that saving recognition. It also will reconcile law and license within love, and suggest a related definition of governance.

IV

Before *Measure for Measure* removes into the Duke's homeopathic imitations of vice that serve to generate (or regenerate) virtue, it insistently explores the need for such a darkly illuminating device. As has often been noted, Vienna so widely repeats the disastrous twisting of law and license that all the underplots of the play openly imitate the principal action. Thus Elbow complains that all the people "use their abuses in common houses," and comically converts malefactors into "notorious benefactors" (II.i.42-43, 50). Thus Escalus can demand, "Which is the wiser here; Justice or Iniquity?" (II.i.172). And thus Barnardine resolutely refuses both the law that would kill him and a penitence that might, in a religious sense, save him. Even when a Julietta sincerely repents and moves from sense-gratifying nature to sense-defying spirit (thus altering from an imitation of Claudio to an imitation of Isabella), she does nothing that can either relieve Claudio or challenge Angelo. For her, as for Mariana in her secret consummation of marriage with Angelo; for Pompey Bum, in his conversion from pimp to hangman; and for Lucio, is his comically misapplied acting as the Duke or Isabella, like remains frozen with like. If the sides are opposite, the coin is single. Despairingly, Escalus therefore will complain, "Mercy is not itself, that oft looks so;/ Pardon is still the nurse of second woe/ . . . There is no remedy" (II.i.283-285). The Duke will echo him: "When vice makes mercy, mercy's so extended/ That for the fault's love is th' offender friended" (IV.ii.112-113). So far, the Duke seems justified in looking not to a cure but to a conclusion of mankind, as if with Timon of Athens: "There is so great a fever on goodness, that the dissolution of it must cure it" (III.ii.222-223).

Alternatives of any sort other than a homeopathic cure also are causes for despair rather than hope. Thus, in rapid sequence, the Duke hopes to reconcile mercy (or license) with judgment (or law) by "minting" Angelo, but must wonder if power will not merely release a tyrant. Similarly, when Claudio correctly suspects that license is a bait laid to make the taker mad, he might be speaking for the Duke, but lets fear of death obscure that awareness. In her turn, Isabella shifts from being a "sister" inflexible to sin and the world into being virtually a seducer of Angelo, egged on by Lucio; at the least, she becomes more a Portia than a nun, far removed from vows of silence and of modesty before man. Angelo therefore is not entirely wrong in holding that her argument can cause a lecherous "sense [to breed] with it," and asking, "Is this her fault, or mine?/ The tempter or the tempted?" (II.ii.142, 162-163). Vienna thus threatens to remain fixed in the settings into which the play had opened: a jail, and a brothel.

Finally, the somewhat desperate impulse to separate art from practice, imitation from creation, or doer from deed accomplishes nothing. The resultant attempt to strike between the horns of a dilemma posed by the rival pulls of law and license yields sophistry, not redemption. When Isabella asks that the fault of Claudio be punished but not the man, and when Escalus holds that in like circumstances Angelo the judge could have been Claudio the criminal, Angelo properly scoffs at their arguments. And the Duke merely restates the same problem by wondering if "tyranny be in [the] place,/ Or in his eminence that fills it up" (I.ii.163-164). Such gestures do nothing to untangle the intimate knot joining permissiveness and crime. In particular, they offer nothing to a Mariana waiting at the grange or a Julietta with her unborn child. Julietta would suffer from careless license if Claudio lives, or harsh punishment at second hand, if he is executed.

Vienna plainly needs conversion in each man, not convertibility of vice and virtue among men. In the second half of Measure for Measure, it is provided. A quite different act and practice, or imitation and creation, produces regeneration rather than mere repetition. It comes about when all the preceding oppositions--human and divine, sisterly and brotherly--are carried well beyond any merely local or legal convertibility. They are led into the double plotting suggested of the Duke by Lucio: "His [givings]-out were of an infinite distance/ From his true-meant design" (I.iv.54-55). In the concealed design of the Duke, truth will displace all deceits. It will bring about large-scale dramatic alterations: <u>anagnorisis</u>, <u>peripeteia</u>. It is wholly fitting that the ultimate imitation in the play should be that of drama. It is moved by the Duke's several plots-within-the-plot. It achieves some of the unparadoxical pairings initially associated with Isabella: "Peace and prosperity," "gentle and fair," "fewness and truth" (I.iv.15, 24, 39).

    Lest it seem that such a resolution is like that in comedy, tragedy, or romance, however, it should be acknowledged that the plots used by the Duke and Isabella are open to as many objections as have been made to their characters. In this play's bed-trick and head-trick, we are far removed from the internal plot of <u>Hamlet</u> and the character of Helena in <u>All's Well That Ends Well</u>. Here, fire directly fights fire. Lechery and mortality are dramatically imitated by the two people who had wished to flee them utterly. In the process, "disguise . . . by th' disguised/ Pays with falsehood false exacting." In the fallen world of this play, men can be altered only by motives real and present within that world. Only an imitation of the crime can make the criminal "judge/ Of [his] own cause" (V.i.166-167). After a penitential recognition, the offense may then pardon itself (V.i.534).

    The "makers" in the play's final imitation--the Duke and Isabella--are divinely intending, but humanly charitable. They replace the preceding "plots" of Claudio and Angelo, both of whom would have had Isabella, not Mariana, secretly meet with Angelo. Their plot (in both senses of the word) will cause Angelo with his secretly-replaced Mariana to believe that he is a lecherous Claudio. Actually, however he plays exactly the original <u>Angelo</u> who had offered her an honest love within the promise of marriage. But that was also the "part" of the original Claudio, with Julietta. The reversal and recognition experienced by Angelo then can apply for Claudio and Julietta. It may conversely offer a model for a "like" punishment of Lucio, and a like exaltation of the Duke and Isabella in their own love. Those ends emerge when Isabella and the Duke become surrogate creators, dramaturges, and universalizing brother and sister. They effect a profound union of biology and community, of sensual urge and mutual ("legal") contract in love. The results accomplish an early charge, or prayer, of the Duke: "Mortality and mercy in Vienna/ Live in they tongue and heart" (I.i. 43-44).

The Duke intimates such an end from such a design midway in Measure for Measure. In doing so, he not only recapitulates much of the action, but also speaks for mankind, in speaking of Isabella:

> The hand that hath made you fair hath made you good; the goodness that is cheap in beauty makes beauty brief in goodness; but grace, being the soul of your complexion, shall keep the body of it ever fair. . . . How will you do to content this substitute [Angelo], and to save your brother? (III.i.180-188)

The Duke also assures her, "The doubleness of the benefit defends the deceit from reproof." Isabella responds, "The image of it gives me content already" (III.i.257-259). By means of duplicity, then, duplicity will be transformed into double benefit. By imitation of disease, a "remedy presents itself."

Once the homeopathic internal plots have begun their work, we become aware that the impulse for such a recreation has not come from the Duke alone, and not merely in the present. Indeed, the present, which commands the first half of the play, has shown man in a massive aberration. In contrast, the past had recorded apparently unforced and unmercenary contracts that united love and law, for Angelo and Mariana as well as for Claudio and Julietta. By means of the Duke's plot, the modern deviations from such contracts are corrected, and the original conditions reestablished. Included in the correction, although with little if any rebuke, is that of the implied withdrawal from the world and the flesh by the Duke and Isabella. Such a withdrawal seems to have implied a withdrawal as well from the Word that was made flesh and defined as Love. In a fine expansion of the title formula, the Duke accordingly holds that in a wife such as Isabella, a husband may instead find a "worth worth [his]" (V.i.497).

In a far more distant recovery, the Duke's plot permits the return--even in Vienna--of something like a creation of man in the originating image of God. Because the Duke is a dramaturge, Escalus may truly say,

"The Duke [is] in us" (V.i.295). Because Lucio's impertinence leads the Duke to resume his office, Lucio similarly is "the first knave that e'er mad'st a Duke" (V.i.356). And with a double meaning, Angelo can now be "moulded out of faults" (V.i.439; italics added) rather than minted in possible public vice.

Finally, in the lesser lovers' once-abandoned but now recovered union of love and law, we at last perceive that "art and practice" of government so long left undefined. As the past imitations by Claudio and Angelo of love with law evidently had preceded their "minted" imitations of nature and retribution, so now, with the help of an internal drama, those original imitations can strike between the horns of the play's dilemma.

In the play's dramatic imitation of drama, Shakespeare has at once resolved the knotty questions of the play and also supplied a mirror to the art of his play. Using most of the elements of drama stipulated by Aristotle, but concentrating principally upon idea and argument, Shakespeare has reconciled private will with human and divine law. He has tried the tension between love and law within the fundamental human acts: marriage, childbirth, death. The play ultimately accepts as one the initially combative, yet suspiciously convertible, imitations of man that had necessitated the Duke's plot. Combining those imitations and the Duke's responsive dramatic imitation into one action, Shakespeare conducts a witty, moral, dramatic, and extremely various exploration of the words of his title, which are so multiply-meant: Measure for Measure.[6]

NOTES

[1] Quotations are taken from *The Riverside Shakespeare*, ed. G.B. Evans *et al.* (Boston: Houghton Mifflin, 1974).

[2] Among others who have considered the title, David L. Stevenson, in "Design and Structure in *Measure for Measure*: A New Approach," *ELH*, 23 (1956), 256-278, notes that "measure" may suggest "moderation in human affairs."

[3] The present study obviously does not agree with Marco Mincoff, "*Measure for Measure*: A Question of Approach," *ShakS*, 2 (1966), 149, that "Vincentio is an excrescence who ruins the play."

[4] Two surveys of the criticism of *Measure for Measure* may be recommended: Jonathan R. Price, "*Measure for Measure* and the Critics: Towards a New Approach," *SQ*, 20 (1969), 179-204; and Rosalind Miles, *The Problem of Measure for Measure: A Historical Investigation* (London: Vision, 1976).

[5] Cf. R.J. Kaufmann, "Bond Slaves and Counterfeits: Shakespeare's *Measure for Measure*," *ShakS*, 3 (1967), 89-90; and Darryl J. Gless, *Measure for Measure, the Law, and the Convent* (Princeton: Princeton Univ. Press, 1979), pp. 29-30.

[6] The design of the Duke is emphasized by Harold Wilson, "Action and Symbol in *Measure for Measure* and *The Tempest*," *SQ*, 4 (1953), 380. That of Shakespeare is emphasized by Elizabeth Marie Pope, "The Renaissance Background of *Measure for Measure*," *ShS*, 2 (1949), 66-67.

SHAKESPEARE'S APOLOGY FOR POETIC WISDOM

Michael Platt

What does Shakespeare think of his own art? How does he understand dramatic poetry? What does he conceive to be its aim, its effects, its means, and its advantages? Since Shakespeare wrote no Confessions, no Discourse of the Method, no Ecce Homo, and spoke to no Boswell, his thoughts on his own art can only be found, if at all, in his poetic works.

In what follows I shall examine the beginning of The Tempest. To understand the relation between the tempest that prevails in the first scene, the Boatswain's art that fails to command it, and the art that not only commands but creates such a tempest, I shall refer to an icon, placed in the inner court of the Palazzo Rucellai, meant to represent the relation of fortuna (or tempestas) to art and chance that Plato's Athenian Stranger teaches his interlocuters in the Laws (709a-712a). But let us begin. The curtain is going up.

All is tempest; a boatswain struggles to control his ship and keep it from running aground on Prospero's isle. He exercises the art of seamanship in order to save his life and the lives of those who accompany him. He is the rope of their destiny. Destiny depends upon the outcome of the struggle between the tempest and the art of seamanship. In a storm the ruler of the ship is not the ruler of society; only the man who knows about ships and storms rules. And so the boatswain sends below all those anxious nobles ("remember whom thou hast aboard") who cannot command the winds.

> if you can command these elements to silence, and work the peace of the present, we will not hand a rope more; use your authority. If you cannot, give thanks you have liv'd so long, and make yourself ready in your cabin for the mischance of the hour, if it so hap.
> (I.i.20-24)[1]

If The Tempest is crucial to the understanding of all of Shakespeare's works, so this tempest is crucial to the understanding of The Tempest.[2] For the tempest, as many have noted, is the central metaphor for the great suffering to which his greatest works expose his greatest men. Here this tempest, as the second scene reveals, is the work of one of the characters. The second scene discloses to us a wise ruler who can and does command the tempest. What others suffer from, Prospero commands.

In order to understand this strange scene, we must seek aid from a consideration of the storm scenes in Lear and also from an image fashioned by Renaissance iconographers who, scrutinizing some passages in Plato's Laws, found an image of the harmony of chance, art, and god.

None of the noble or regal passengers aboard the ship in The Tempest can command the winds. To command the winds is the noble, dreadful and disastrous ambition of Lear. His education begins at the point of his greatest folly.

> Blow, winds, and crack your cheeks. Rage, blow
> You cataracts and hurricanoes, spout
> Till you have drenched your steeples, drowned
>   the cocks.
> You sulph'rous and thought-executing fires,
> Vaunt-couriers of oak-cleaving thunderbolts,
> Singe my white head. And thou, all-shaking
>   thunder,
> Strike flat the thick rotundity o' the world,
> Crack Nature's moulds, all germains spill at
>   once,
> That makes ingrateful man.   (III.ii.1-9)

Does Lear command the winds? To his commands there is no conspicuous answer. The winds do blow, the rains do fall; but they were already in motion before he commanded them. Moreover, his commands far outstrip mere wind and rain. Grasping at the winds, Lear touches a thread which, if tugged, would unravel all creation. The winds he would command gust and swirl into a full tempest which, trumpet-tongued, summons an apocalypse which will drown those familiar markers of old earth--cocks of weathervanes. We see a white-haired Noah calling for a second deluge, but this deluge differs from the first in that all "germains" will spill and no ark (or bark) will float upon the waters. Commands which lack power are wishes only; so are Lear's. Lear's commands aspire to divine powers; to command the rains of the deluge and the winds of the Apocalypse is divine. Lear's wish to

make out of something, nothing (ex aliquo nihil fit), is
the divine power of a creator god. Tacitly acknowledging that he does not possess this power, Lear recognizes
that when it rains he cannot know whose will the winds
obey. Perhaps it is the will of his daughters that
commands the winds to pelt his old infirm head.

> Rumble thy bellyful. Spit, fire. Spout, rain.
> Nor rain, wind, thunder, fire are my daughters.
> I tax not you, you elements, with unkindness.
> I never gave you kingdom, called you children;
> You owe me no subscription. Then let fall
> Your horrible pleasure. Here I stand your
>   slave,
> A poor, infirm, weak, and despised old man.
> But yet I call you servile ministers,
> That will with two pernicious daughters join
> Your high-engendered battles 'gainst a head
> So old and white as this. O, ho! 'tis foul.
>   (III.ii.14-24)

But this is not the end of Lear or the tempest he walks
in. Two scenes later, the same winds still pelting the
same heath, Lear in the company of his Fool and his
companion Caius (Kent) comes upon a shelter. It is the
little things which are revealing; a courteous gesture
signifies a soul-change in Lear.

> KENT   Good my lord, enter here.
> LEAR   Prithee go in thyself; seek thine own
>   ease.   (III.iv.22-23)

Lest we slight the importance of his courtesy, we are
made to understand that this is a sacrifice for Lear.

> This tempest will not give me leave to ponder
> On things would hurt me more, but I'll go in.
>   (III.iv.24-25)

Outside in the tempest, Lear would be protected from
thought; for the sake of his companions, his former
subjects, he goes in. Again he urges another to go
before him.

> [To the Fool] In, boy; go first. You house-
>   less poverty--
> Nay, get thee in. I'll pray, and then I'll
>   sleep.
>   Exit [Fool].
>   (III.iv.26-27)

The rain continues to fall, the storm to pelt, the wind to blow; Lear remains for a moment in the tempest's command--not as before, to magnify his power by identification, but to fix in prayer what he has been taught by the thunder. Command has been replaced by prayer.

> Poor naked wretches, wheresoe'er you are,
> That bide the pelting of this pitiless storm,
> How shall your houseless heads and unfed sides,
> Your looped and windowed raggedness, defend you
> From seasons such as these? O, I have ta'en
> Too little care of this! Take physic, pomp;
> Expose thyself to feel what wretches feel,
> That thou mayst shake the superflux to them,
> And show the heavens more just.
> (III.iv.28-36)

In this prayer, Lear gives testimony to the discovery of a duty that is at once a king's highest and a man's highest; failing to command the winds or to employ the tempest for justice, he comes to see that justice does not come from the heavens; the winds are not only uncommanded by men, they are indifferent to the chief concerns of men; neither comfort nor justice give place to human agents who can provide distributive justice. Misfortunes like the rain fall indifferently; the duty of a king and of any man in a storm is identical: to provide shelter. Lear is a great king; not great in power, but great in his heeding the duty of a king to come between his subjects and the tempest. Lear has to learn this; he does not know it in Act One.[3]

It is a measure of the wholly different order of rulership exercised by Prospero that he can command the winds; unlike Lear, he has a bark to ride out the tempest and the deluge. Through Ariel he attains divine powers. Like Lear, Prospero seems to have neglected rulership, and by that neglect allowed the wicked to prosper. But to him is granted an auspicious exemption from the mortal penalties of that neglect. To him is granted a power which seems in Lear a blasphemy to usurp, the power to command the tempest itself. Perhaps the reason why Lear does not command the winds and Prospero does has something to do with the differing aims to which they would put such divine power. Lear would employ the tempest in all-terminating revenge. Prospero would employ the tempest to teach the teachable to be just to themselves and to others; but for the unteachable (Caliban and Antonio) he would not invoke a second deluge; to the unteachable he offers rule and forgiveness; unteachable Caliban he will rule; the unteachable Antonio he will forgive.

In the man who can control the tempest and direct the fortunes of a ship tossed in the sea, we recognize extraordinary powers and extraordinary art. But our recognition can be more precise than this if we avail ourselves of one of the achievements of the Renaissance, which aimed to make visible in icons and symbols the most subtle and philosophic discriminations. It has not, I believe, been remarked that the first scene of The Tempest, together with the revelation given us in the second scene, treat a theme common in Renaissance iconography. In this iconographic emblem we see a vessel; on that ship stands the figure of a woman too large to be human; this woman, marked by a shock of hair, appears to be blowing into the puffed sails of the vessel. Simultaneously, she also holds the sails and, hence, directs the course of the ship. To trace the ultimate source of this icon would take us to a passage in Book IV of Plato's Laws (709a-712a), a passage for which we are fortunate to have the commentary of the Renaissance Neoplatonist Marsilio Ficino who selected this theme for a coat of arms for the Rucellai family in Florence. This figure of the nautical Fortuna appears in the inner court of the Palazzo Rucellai. Ficino points to the following Platonic passage to explain the union of chance, fortune, and God which the emblem signifies.[4]

> Anyone who sees all this [the vicissitudes of weather, pestilence, war, and poverty] naturally rushes to the conclusion . . . that in human affairs chance (τύχη) is almost everything. And this may be said of the risks of the sailor, and the pilot, and the physician, and the general, and may seem to be well said; and yet there is another thing which may be said with equal truth of all of them . . . that God (θεός) governs all things and that chance and occasion (τύχη καὶ καιρός) work with him in the government of human affairs. There is, however, a third and tamer view, that skill (τέχνη) should also participate; for I should say that on the occasion of a storm (καιρῷ χειμῶνος) there must surely be a

> great advantage in having the aid of the pilot's skill.[5]

About this passage Ficino's commentary reads:

> [When God] moves the sea by a storm and the storm rocks the ship, God also moves the ship through the mind of the pilot, that is, by the exercise of his skill which is continuously dependent on God. When the ship is therefore directed by skill to a certain harbor, and is also carried there by the storm, then skill is in perfect agreement with chance (tunc ars simul cum fortuna consentit).[6]

In Ficino's interpretation, the emphasis falls upon God; while this emphasis seems justified by the passage we have quoted from the Laws, if we continue our reading in the Laws we find that the emphasis in Plato falls upon the political art to which he has compared the art of navigation. Moreover, it is exactly in this political emphasis that the first scene of The Tempest resembles what Plato has to say.

For after Plato's Athenian Stranger compares the relation of chance, art and God to the situation of a pilot in a storm, he proceeds to say that we should see this in regard to politics. It is exactly the storm, or the worst political situation, that calls for the greatest pilot, or the man who has political knowledge, and it is exactly this man who would welcome a storm in which to exercise his art. Such a storm, the Athenian stranger announces to the astonishment of his interlocutor, would be found in a young tyrant.

> "Give me a state which is governed by a tyrant, and let the tyrant be young and have a good memory; let him be quick at learning, and of a courageous and noble nature; . . . for there neither is nor ever will be a better or speedier way of establishing a polity than by a tyranny."
>
> "By what possible arguments, Stranger, can any man persuade himself of such a doctrine? . . . You would assume, as you say, a tyrant who was young . . .?"
>
> "Yes; and you must add fortunate; and his good fortune must be that he is the

contemporary of a great legislator, and that some happy chance brings them together. When this has been accomplished, God has done all that he ever does for a state which he desires to be eminently prosperous. . . . But I suppose you have never seen a city which is under a tyranny?"

"No, and I cannot say that I have any great desire to see one."

"And yet, where there is a tyranny, you might certainly see that of which I am now speaking. . . . You might see how, without trouble and in no very long period of time, the tyrant, if he wishes, can change the manner of a state . . . he himself indicating by his example the lines of conduct, praising and rewarding some actions and reproving others, and degrading those who disobey. . . . Let no one, my friends, persuade us that there is any quicker and easier way in which states change their laws. . . . The real difficulty is of another sort . . . but when once it is surmounted, ten thousand or rather all blessings follow."

"Of what are you speaking?"

"The difficulty is to find the divine love of temperate and just institutions existing in any powerful forms of government. . . . And this may be said of power in general: When the supreme power in man is combined with the greatest wisdom and temperance, then the best laws and the best constitution come into being; but in no other way. And let what I have been saying be regarded as a kind of sacred legend or oracle, and let this be our proof that, in one point of view, there may be a difficulty for a city to have good laws, but that there is another point of view in which nothing can be easier or sooner effected, granting our supposition."[7]

The words of Plato's Athenian Stranger help us to understand certain details in the first scene of The Tempest. The condition of the crew in that scene is peculiar. The ruler of the ship is not the captain, for he lives below; the ruler is not the pilot whom Plato speaks of; it is the boatswain, the man in charge of the sails.

The meaning of these things is made clear by the appearance of Prospero in the subsequent scene. There is no pilot in the first scene because the pilot is Ariel. That pilot is, furthermore, in the command of another captain, Prospero. Right away we notice that he is much more powerful than Plato's wise legislator. Ultimately it is Prospero who, in his single self (including his power over Ariel), unites skill and god in his rule of fortune. The Platonic image of the ship in the storm coordinates with the storm in Lear; both show us that he who controls the tempest (or fortuna) is like unto a god. Prospero's recounting to Miranda of his trials in the scene subsequent to the tempest (I.ii.23 ff.) is suffused with a mingling of fortune, skill, and providence. He speaks of Miranda's smile as "infused with a fortitude from heaven" (I.ii.154). His whole account resembles the scene of tempest she has just witnessed. As once before he and his daughter were brought ashore "By providence divine" (I.ii.159), so he will bring the sufferers she has suffered with ashore by his power which resembles and replaces divine providence.

And what of Fortuna: does Prospero's art absorb the role of Fortuna? Edgar Wind makes the interesting remark that, "the word fortuna was used in his [Ficino's] day as a synonym of tempestas in signifying storm" (p. 491). However, in The Tempest, while Prospero can control the winds, Fortuna is still an independent power who, it is true, appears to do Prospero's bidding: "bountiful Fortune (Now, my dear lady) hath mine enemies/ Brought to this shore" (I.ii.179-80). It is hard to tell whether his words, "Now, my dear lady," mean that Fortuna happens to be in accord with his wishes or whether she is now in his service as well. Even though Prospero has appropriated divine powers, he is not a god, for his powers are not omnipotent or forever.[8]

Moreover, the Platonic discussion of the political understanding of the image sheds light upon the whole of The Tempest. According to their virtue or their vice, the men in The Tempest who suffer from the tempest incline to think Prospero a tyrant; the more they near the condition of the brutish Caliban the more they incline to consider Prospero an unjust tyrant who means them no good; but the more they near the virtuous condition of Miranda and Ferdinand the more they view him and the burdens he puts upon them (e.g., hauling wood) as trials to exercise their courage and moderation and to prove their virtue.

But the special appositeness of the Platonic passage adheres to Prospero himself.[9] Some of the most decisive features of Prospero's art emerge in contrast to the passage in Plato's Laws. As A.W. Falconer has made clear, the boatswain in Shakespeare does the best that he can (even risking an unusual maneuver) to avoid running aground on Prospero's island.[10] In Plato's image this would spell failure, the triumph of chance over skill with or without the aid of god. In Plato's image the best would be to weather out the storm, but in Shakespeare's image the boatswain's failure is desirable. Prospero wants the shipwreck Plato's pilot (legislator) tries to avoid by his art. Prospero wants to ground this ship on his island. His art requires that the scope of ordering human techne (e.g., legislation) be exhausted first. To reach Prospero's island, you must first shipwreck.[11] Shakespeare's alteration of the Platonic image underscores the more prominent place suffering plays in his understanding of the path to wisdom.

Hence, while Plato's art (the art of his Athenian Stranger) pits itself against fortune (or chance), the art of Prospero merely triggers chance in a timely and beneficial way. The natural shocks that flesh is heir to are not cancelled; they are employed by Prospero. Prospero's art aims to speed up and concentrate a natural education. In an important respect this aim differs from that of Plato's Athenian Stranger; his art is the art of legislation; he appears in a book significantly entitled Laws. His aim appears to be a durable regime which will preserve the best things through the best laws. By contrast Prospero's art is both more powerful and less enduring. Its magic aims at a swift transformation of the individual soul; hence, one of the first effects of the shipwreck is to separate the voyagers into individuals and small groups; deprived of the support of society, their natures will appear more readily and their treatment can progress more swiftly. A brief stay in the state of nature will lead to the civil state.

Prospero has neither the time nor the desire to rule through the ordinary effects of legislation; laws

affect the heart profoundly, as anyone who has lived in
different regimes can attest, but such effects are slow
and indirect; they reach the heart through policing
conduct. Prospero wants to reach the heart and soul of
his pupils more immediately. Hence, his rule is without law; it aspires to a justice and goodness above
mere positive human law. He delivers no decalogue and
leaves his polity with no foundation in law, no founding
constitution. Hence, his regime does approach that
happy, lawless natural utopia which Gonzalo (taking a
leaf from Montaigne's essay on cannibals) sketches (II.
i.143 ff),[12] not seeing how much men would have to be
educated, and educated by suffering, before they could
be set free.

To rule without law and only through enchantment
requires great power. By controlling the winds Prospero
acquires this power; with it he does not need a young
tyrant with a good memory. It is as if Shakespeare had
said to Plato's Athenian Stranger, "We do not need to
search for a tyrant and educate him. We can use an ever-
present tyrant (the tempest) to educate others. Let him
do his worst; let every man fear for the worst; with the
fear and suffering imposed by this tyrant we will be able
to go deeper than legislation; we can affect conduct by
going directly to its source in the heart. We will make
this natural tyrant (fear of violent death at the hands
of nature) serve us. With the tyrant's power and agility
my Prospero is able to seize the chance and the occasion
(τύχη καὶ καιρός) and to found a brief republic, a
republic which lasts for about two hours."

This brief republic is, of course, the stage. In
Prospero Shakespeare has portrayed the dramatist. The
enchantment he casts on the souls of those who venture
in the vicinity of his isle is the enchantment of poetry.
But since <u>The Tempest</u> as a whole is itself poetic, it
must raise poetry to a visible power. Hence, it is
masque, spectacle, music and event, rather than verses,
that in this play make poetry a visible power.[13] Only
when the poets and the rulers, runs Shakespeare's
answer to Plato's banishment of the poets, coincide,
will the just and happy state be realized; until then,
it will have a local habitation in the individual soul
of the beholder who is ruled and guided by the poetic
art of a wise man.[14] By suffering with those they see
suffer, by loving with those they see love, the readers
or beholders of the drama will be ruled and educated by

the poetic wise man. Of course, outside the magic isle of the Globe stage, we and Prospero know that the enchantment may wear off. Human powers, even when they imitate godly ones, are never omnipotent.

There is a final difference between the wise man according to Plato and the wise man according to Shakespeare. According to Plato, wisdom is far above human things, and so the philosopher or wise man would have to be compelled to attend to human things; he would have, for example, to be compelled to rule, for ruling would require him to leave the sunlit realm and descend to a dark cave.[15] Not so Prospero. As a young man he was such a Platonic philosopher; "my library/ Was dukedom large enough" (I.ii.109-110). However, unlike Plato, Shakespeare does not suggest that this student of the "liberal arts" was wise. It is only when he is put in a bark with his daughter on the windy seas that he begins to wax wise. To become wise this bookish man had to learn to care for his daughter. Without her he would have despaired, for he tells us that it was her smiles that pulled him through. It is through caring for her that he comes to rule his isle, and so rules those who wash up on its shores that he can leave it and return to his mainland dukedom. Prospero began as a Platonic philosopher, all wrapt in "secret studies." He only begins to become Shakespeare's wise man when he cares for the good that lies in human things in the person of his smiling daughter and later chooses to bring out that same good in others through poetic rule. Such is Shakespeare's final point in his apology for poetry and his challenge to ancient philosophy's denigration of human things. His poetry, he suggests, teaches us to find the good in human things. Only by caring for it as Prospero does do we grow wise.

NOTES

[1] All references to Shakespeare will be to the *Pelican Shakespeare*, ed. Alfred Harbage (Baltimore: Penguin, 1969).

[2] Other examples of Prospero's art are the disappearing banquet (III.iii), the masque of Ceres (IV.i), the temptation of Antonio (II.i), and the punishment of Caliban (IV.1). While obviously examples of teaching, none of these is as revealing or remarkable as the first episode. G.W. Knight writes, "*The Tempest*, patterned of storm and music, is thus an interpretation of Shakespeare's world." *The Crown of Life* (London: Methuen, 1947), p. 204.

[3] Lear presents some unpleasant truths we shall have to live with. Since only the powerless know whether they are loved for themselves and without suspicion, the man who wishes to know if he is loved must shed power; but in doing so he sheds all power to protect his beloved. To fail to protect one's beloved is not to love one's beloved. The desire, then, to know if one is loved is so far from acting out of love that it is its antithesis. Nor is Cordelia's desire to make Lear know that she does love him apart from power the same as an act moved by love. For to make another person know that he is loved is not necessarily an act of love, though it may be.

[4] Throughout this part of the argument, I am indebted to Edgar Wind, "Platonic Tyranny and the Renaissance Fortuna: On Ficino's Reading of *Laws* IV, 709A-712A," *De Artibus Opuscula XL: Essays in Honor of Erwin Panofsky*, ed. Millard Meiss (New York: New York Univ. Press, 1961), I, 491-496 (hereafter cited as Wind). See also the accompanying figure of the Rucellai coat of arms. My quotations from Plato are taken from Wind, who related this fortuna image both to Machiavelli and to Shakespeare's Sonnet 94, but not to *The Tempest*. The spread of this image is shown in *A Corpus of Italian Medals of the Renaissance Before Cellini*, ed. G.F. Hill, s.v. "Fortuna". Such images were widely diffused in the emblem books (e.g., Ripa) and books of iconographic explanation (e.g., Cartari). See note 7 in Wind, p. 492.

[5] Wind, p. 491.

[6] Wind, p. 492.

[7] Wind, pp. 492-3.

[8] Other Shakespearean employments of this image are found in Coriolanus (IV.i.6-8) and in Nestor's speech in Troilus and Cressida (I.iii.34 ff.). See also Plato's Republic (488b-489c).

[9] On the relation of Platonic philosophy to Shakespeare, Prospero and The Tempest, see Howard B. White, Copp'd Hills Towards Heaven: Shakespeare and the Classical Polity, International Archives of the History of Ideas, vol. 32 (The Hague: Martinus Nijhoff, 1970) (hereafter cited as White). See especially Chapters One, Six, Seven, and Eight.

[10] Shakespeare and the Sea (New York: Frederick Ungar Pub. Co., 1964), pp. 35-40. Falconer's commentary on Tempest (I.i) supersedes and corrects that offered in the Arden Tempest, ed. Frank Kermode (London: Methuen, 1966), pp. 3-9. Prof. Kermode acknowledged as much when I brought it to his attention in 1972.

[11] In his Literature and the Image of Man (Boston: Beacon Press, 1957), pp. 221-229, Leo Lowenthal offers a reading of this scene which parallels my own. He is especially sensitive to the corrupt and intemperate behavior of the nobles aboard ship (i.e., Antonio). However, his emphasis upon the virtue of the skilled laborers seems excessive. He slants The Tempest in the direction of The New Atlantis or Robinson Crusoe; without denying the virtue of the boatswain and his crew, I would deny that the play advances a brave new industrial man, for the skill of these mariners is insufficient, and must be, if Prospero is to ground them on his island.

[12] See the remarks of Middleton Murry on Shakespeare's selection from Montaigne, Shakespeare (1936; rpt. London: Jonathan Cape, 1965), p. 397 ff. (hereafter cited as Murry).

[13] Cf. Knight, p. 224, and Murry, p. 393.

[14] On the relation of Shakespeare and Plato, see White and D.G. James, The Dream of Learning (Oxford:

Clarendon Press, 1951), p. 57 ff.

15 <u>Republic</u>, 514a-517b.

NOTES ON CONTRIBUTORS

H. R. COURSEN is Chairman of the English Department, Bowdoin College, Maine. His most recent book on Shakespeare is The Leasing Out of England: Shakespeare's Second Henriad, University Press of America, 1982. His eighth book of poetry, Winter Dreams, appeared in 1982.

CLIFFORD DAVIDSON is Professor of English and Executive Editor of the Early Drama, Art, and Music project sponsored by the Medieval Institute at Western Michigan University. He has published widely on Shakespeare and other Renaissance subjects as well as on medieval drama. His next book will be From Creation to Doom: A Study of the York Cycle, to be published soon by AMS Press. He is also a co-editor of Comparative Drama.

JANE L. DONAWERTH is Associate Professor at the University of Maryland, College Park, where she has been teaching in the Department of English since 1974. Her book on ideas about language in Shakespeare's plays, Shakespeare and the Sixteenth-Century Study of Language, will be published by the University of Illinois Press in 1983.

MARY E. HAZARD is an Associate Professor of English at Drexel University. She has published several articles on Renaissance aesthetics, has completed the manuscript of a book on the interrelationships of the arts during the Renaissance, and is currently working on a book about non-verbal communication in Elizabethan England.

BERNICE W. KLIMAN teaches at Nassau Community College in Garden City, New York. Her most recent article, on Isabella in Measure for Measure, will be published in Shakespeare Studies XV. A participant in an NEH Summer Institute at the Folger Library, she is working on a study of Hamlet and media performances. With Professor Kenneth S. Rothwell from the University of Vermont, she is the co-founder and co-editor of the Shakespeare on Film Newsletter.

J. S. LAWRY is a Professor in the English Department of Purdue University. Well known for his articles on Elizabethan and Seventeenth-Century Literature, he has published two books, Sidney's Two Arcadias: Pattern and Proceeding and The Shadow of Heaven: Matter and Stance in Milton's Poetry.

PATRICIA K. MESZAROS is Associate Professor of English and Associate Vice Chancellor for Academic Affairs at the University of Maryland Baltimore County. She has published a number of articles on Shakespeare and on modern authors and is currently working on a book about The Changeling.

ELLEN J. O'BRIEN is Assistant Professor and Chairperson of the English Department at Guilford College in Greensboro, North Carolina. Her essay is an outgrowth of research begun during an NEH summer Seminar for College Teachers, "Shakespeare: Poet and Playwright," under the direction of Marvin Rosenberg. She has also presented papers on Shakespeare pedagogy and American literature and is working toward a book on Melville and Shakespeare.

MICHAEL PLATT is Associate Professor in English and in the Philosophic Institute at the University of Dallas (Irving). He has treated Shakespeare in four articles and a book, Rome and Romans According to Shakespeare. He has completed a manuscript entitled "Shakespeare's English Prince" and is at present writing a book about Nietzsche's Zarathustra while on a Humboldt Fellowship at the University of Heidelberg.

CATHERINE M. SHAW teaches at McGill and Concordia Universities in Montréal, Québec, Canada. The author of numerous articles on Shakespeare and his contemporaries, Professor Shaw has also written two books, "Some Vanity of Mine Art": The Masque in English Renaissance Drama and Richard Brome. In addition she has published a critical edition of The Old Law by Middleton and Rowley and is at present working on The Obstinate Lady by Ashton Cokayne.

RICHARD SNYDER teaches and is a doctoral student at Ohio State University in Columbus, where his major field of concentration is American literature. He has also read a paper on "Brecht's Social Gestus and Shakespeare's 'Talking Pictures'" at the 1982 Ohio Shakespeare Conference, "Shakespeare and the Common Man" (hosted by Cleveland State University).

ELIZABETH TRUAX is an Associate Professor of English at Chapman College, Orange, California. An essay, "Lucrece! What has your Conceited Painter Wrought?" appears in Shakespeare: Contemporary Literary Approaches. She is at present at the Huntington Library on an NEH Fellowship, writing a book on Shakespeare, metamorphosis, and

Renaissance iconography.

PETER B. YOUNG is Associate Professor of Theatre Arts and Scene Designer at the University of West Florida in Pensacola, Florida. In addition to numerous design credits, he spent four seasons as the Technical Director for the Oregon Shakespearean Festival in Ashland. The essay in this volume was developed while he was participating in an NEH Summer Seminar for College Teachers held in Stratford-upon-Avon, England, in 1980.

SUSAN WILLIS is Associate Professor of English at Auburn University at Montgomery. She has published essays on Shakespeare in production, on modern poetry, and on fantasy.

LOIS ZIEGELMAN teaches at Framingham State College in Massachusetts. In addition to this essay, she has articles forthcoming in Modern Language Studies and in Hartford Studies in Literature.

CECILE WILLIAMSON CARY and HENRY S. LIMOUZE, editors of this collection, are both Associate Professors of English at Wright State University (Dayton, Ohio). Professor Cary, who chaired the 1981 Ohio Shakespeare Conference, has published articles on Emily Dickinson and George Eliot as well as on Shakespeare, Heywood, Greene and Jonson. Professor Limouze has published on Milton.